AMERICAN WINGS IRANIAN ROOTS

Kristin Orloff

ISBN: 978-0-9975838-2-3

"There are only two things we can give to our children—

One is roots
And the other is wings…"

~Anonymous

This book is dedicated to Nimtaj

And to every mother
who raised a warrior.

Table of Contents

Introduction ix
Prologue xi
Chapter One: Spring 2004, California 3
Chapter Two: March 8, 1971, Kermanshah, Iran 7
Chapter Three: July 1975 21
Chapter Four : Laguna Niguel: 2008 36
Chapter Five: Kermanshah: Spring 1976 38
Chapter Six: Spring 1976 51
Chapter Seven: 2008 61
Chapter Eight: Spring 1976 63
Chapter Nine: January 1978 78
Chapter Ten: Laguna Niguel, 2009 93
Chapter Eleven: March 1978 95
Chapter Twelve: January 1979 116
Chapter Thirteen : 2009 133
Chapter Fourteen : Spring 1980 135
Chapter Fifteen: Spring 1981 152
Chapter Sixteen: Irvine, 2010 163
Picture Section 165
Chapter Seventeen: March 1982 169
Chapter Eighteen: July 1982 179
Chapter Nineteen: 2010 190
Chapter Twenty: August 1982 195
Chapter Twenty-One: August 12, 1982 209
Chapter Twenty-Two: Laguna Niguel, 2010 226

Chapter Twenty-Three: Kermanshah, 1983 228
Chapter Twenty-Four: Spring 1983 238
Chapter Twenty-Five 250
Chapter Twenty-Six: Summer 1983 252
Chapter Twenty-Seven: December 1983 267
Chapter Twenty-Eight: Laguna Niguel, 2010 284
Chapter Twenty-Nine 287
Epilogue 297
Abedi Family Tree 299
Discussion Questions 301
Glossary 305
Time Line: Events Relevant to the Islamic Revolution in Iran 309

Introduction

It is with great humility I offer to you the story of Reza, his family and many Iranians. When I started writing Reza's narrative, it quickly became my own journey and one that I could not complete alone. More times than I care to count, I considered giving up. Only through the support of family, friends and colleagues did I unlock those shackles of doubt. This is not to say I didn't fail; I did many times.

I ask Iranian readers for their tolerance of my cultural missteps. With an attempt to reflect the beauty, elegance and rich history of this society, I poured myself into countless hours of research and interviews. But I am still writing about a country I have not visited. Yet. In the end, I hope I have created an accurate account of one man's experience and, through him, a platform for discussion.

I want to acknowledge the use of my "writer's license" in the story. First, the Iranian calendar differs from ours by 621 years. For instance, 1981 in America was 1360 in Iran. I chose to use Western dates, even when discussed in dialogue by Iranians, to further an understanding of sociopolitical events to the Westerners, in particular student readers.

Secondly, although most of the dialogue would be in Farsi, I have used English while incorporating a few Farsi words. When Reza travels outside of Iran, he communicates through Farsi, broken English and even Spanish. However, I continue to use English dialogue to maintain the story's flow.

Finally in a few instances, I have compressed time.

Beyond the words you are about to read, I cannot say enough about Reza and his endless patience with me. Neither of us had a clue about the time, energy and finances required to publish a book. The genuine trust and respect shown to me by Reza and his family will forever touch my heart.

In the end, each key I tapped was inspired by the story of one man. A man of passion and sorrow, of sacrifice and will. One whose loyalty to his loved ones exceeded his instinct for self-preservation. A man who defeated the demons he wrestled.

Prologue

Genesis 32:22-32

So Jacob was left alone, and a man wrestled with him until daybreak. When the man saw that he could not overpower him, he touched the socket of Jacob's hip so that his hip was wrenched as he wrestled with the man. Then the man said, "Let me go, for it is daybreak."

But Jacob replied, "I will not let you go unless you bless me."

The man asked him, "What is your name?"

"Jacob," he answered.

Then the man said, "Your name will no longer be Jacob, but Israel, because you have struggled with God and with men and have overcome."

Reza would not know this story. He would live it.

Part I

Chapter One

Spring 2004
California

"The first time I hit a baseball I ran to third base."

"Third base?" I ask. "Why'd you run to third base?"

Munching sunflower seeds and watching our sons play Little League, Reza and I sit in our lawn chairs on a sunny Saturday afternoon. Since we teach at the same high school, we have been chatting casually about colleagues and other mundane topics.

"No one told me," he says between spits, "to run to first."

"You must have been little."

"Not really," he answers. "I was in college."

He offers me another helping from the torn corner of his plastic bag. I put out my hand and study his face. With his kind, dark eyes and a model-perfect smile, he pours the silver seeds into my palm.

I raise my eyebrows. "No baseball in Iran?"

"No baseball in Iran," he says with a laugh. "Soccer, gymnastics and wrestling."

I recall Reza sharing his World Military Wrestling Champion gold medal at a student assembly. Although he is short, his toned body pulses with the strength of an elite athlete.

"Watch me coach," he says. "Wrestling tournament's next week. Come see a real man's game."

Just as I'm about to defend all American sports, a dad from another team comes to me with a newspaper article in his hand. "Are you Kristin Orloff?" he asks.

"Yes, I am." I glance at the article. "Is that the article I wrote about 'fun' in little league?"

"It is." He hands it to me. "Could you sign it?"

"Be glad to."

I hear Reza clear his throat. "You liked it that much?"

The dad nods. "It gave me a completely new perspective."

He walks away and I turn to Reza, planning my defense of America's favorite pastime. But before I can begin, he looks to his feet and rubs his hands together. Like a little boy.

"Hey, ah, Kristin," he says, using a soft tone I hadn't heard before. "Maybe one day you could write my story."

"Yeah, maybe," I say.

• • •

The following week I enter our high school gym to watch our wrestling team. The bleachers are packed with screaming students and cheering parents. I am grateful to squeeze in next to a colleague.

"What do I need to know?" I ask as I pull open a package of red vines. "I promised Reza I'd come watch him coach."

He laughs at my ignorance. "A match is three periods of two minutes each. But if you pin a guy, it's over."

"That doesn't sound too bad," I say, tugging on the stale vine with my teeth. "Most sports take hours."

"You're wrong," he says. "Wrestling demands more strength, speed, discipline and . . ." He searches for a word. "Just guts than any sport."

"Looks like they're just rolling around."

"Don't let Reza hear you say that," he says. "He credits wrestling with saving his life."

I watch Reza pace about the match, his compact build moving with large gestures to match his exploding voice.

"Was Reza's life in danger?" I ask, trying to remember if Reza had mentioned anything like that during our conversations.

My colleague looks into the faces of those sitting around us. He leans into me. "You know about Reza, right?"

"Know?" I ask, my mind flying back to his words at the Little League game. *Maybe someday you can write my story.*

"He was an assassin for the Shah during the revolution. He had to escape without paperwork so no one knows his real age."

"Seriously?" The red vine snaps in mid-bite.

"Had to kill a man with his bare hands." His fists mimic twisting a rope. "Snapped his neck like a turkey bone."

"He told you this?"

"I've heard things."

A voice bounces across the gym announcing Reza's son as the next competitor. The crowd bursts into wild cheers as his son jogs into the center circle.

It is a grueling match. At times, Reza crawls around the perimeter to shout his guttural commands. His son struggles with his opponent. Again and again, their bodies slam to the mat.

"Pin him!" I say, not really knowing any other term to use.

The two wrestlers snarl as their limbs twist in positions that seem to rip them from the sockets. Reza continues his verbal barrage, his flying spit matching the sweat pouring from the young athletes. As I watch him, I wonder what he endured to come here, to live this moment, to coach his son in an American high school gym.

The referee raises his son's hand in victory. Reza pumps his fist.

After all the matches are over and the fans begin to clunk down the bleachers, I approach Reza.

"That was pretty exciting," I say.

With a grin, he embraces me. "Thanks for coming."

"Your son did well."

Reza nods. A few parents come to shake his hand, and various wrestlers pepper him with questions about tomorrow's practice or if he knows where they've left their shoes. His humble and patient manner intrigues me. I remember the words, "snapped his neck like a turkey bone." I look at Reza's hands. I wonder.

"Remember when we talked about writing your story?"

"Of course," he says.

"Still up for it?"

He places his hand on my shoulder. "Can you come over tomorrow?"

I walk to the parking lot with a bit of a bounce in my step. This is going to be exciting. An assassin for the Shah. I'm a little nervous about taking on my first book project, but I have published several articles. How hard could a book be?

• • •

The next night, I leave Reza's house with my spiral notebook, three hours of videotape and no idea how I am going to write his story. Do I begin with the night he tried to escape? How am I going to keep his ten siblings straight? Should I include the vignettes that might jeopardize our safety?

• • •

The cursor at the top of the blank page mocks me. I scan my notes again. Consult my writing books. Watch another section of tape. All right, then, I'll just begin with the first experience he shared with me. I'm sure it will flow from there.

Chapter Two

March 8, 1971
Kermanshah, Iran

"Muhammad Ali's going to pulverize Frasier tonight," Reza said. The eight-year-old struck with two lightning left hooks to knock out his imaginary opponent. Across the frayed wrestling tarp in the crowded gym, his calloused feet chopped and danced. "Everyone thinks Muhammad Ali will be our champion," Reza said and then raised his voice to secure his father's attention. "That's what all the kids at school are saying."

"Kids at school don't always think," Abbas replied as he rubbed his whiskers and brought his gaze just above his son. Reza watched his father ponder the puzzle of wrestling mats with struggling athletes sweating through workouts. With a sigh Abbas mumbled, "They just repeat what they're told."

Finishing a flurry of uppercuts, Reza rolled his head and shook his arms. *I think Muhammad Ali is going to destroy that Joe Frasier. How can anybody named Joe even be a fighter? Let alone a ghahreman*[1].

He rose on his toes and resumed his silhouette match. Streams of sun struggled through the dirty windows that edged the ceiling and painted a matrix of light on Reza's slender body. He swaggered to the gym's echo of grunts and thuds. Uppercut, uppercut, jab, jab. *I could beat that Joe. I'd give him some up top, then come down low and—*

"Reza! You think you're a boxer now?" Abbas said. "You're

1 Champion

not." His thick index finger pointed to the mat. "Finish your workouts." He paused, folded his arms and suppressed a smile. "Or you'll miss the fight."

"What do you mean miss the fight? How can I watch the fight? Farid's TV is broken. Did *amou*[2] fix it?"

Abbas pounded his fist into his palm. "Sit-ups!"

"But what about—" he started to ask.

Abbas answered with a stare.

Reza lay flat on his back. "How many?"

"You ask me how many?" Abbas barked. "How can I know?"

On the mats, dotted in puddles of sweat and stained with drops of blood, the young warrior trained. Reza stopped at seventy-seven, when he could no longer lift his head. He flipped onto his stomach and arched his back. Sweat blurred the figure of Abbas walking toward the wrestlers practicing one-on-one drills. Reza stood, waited for the burn of vomit to leave his throat and jogged after his father. A smile graced his face. He loved live drills.

Reza saw a few wrestlers edge over to climb the ropes that dangled from metal beams. He watched them go and shook his head. *Go climb your ropes. Cowards.*

A ten-year-old wrestler, Kaveh, disengaged himself from his current opponent and began to swing his arms and crack his neck. He glared at Reza and walked toward an empty mat.

"You've got three kilos on Reza," Abbas said as he pointed to Kaveh's thicker frame.

Reza hustled to catch up to his father. "I can take him, *Baba*[3]!" He shot a fierce look at Kaveh, who already stood in the center circle.

"Then do it," Abbas said. He took his place at the side of the mat.

Stepping into the center, Reza brushed back the thick locks of black hair and licked the sweat from his bare upper lip.

Setting his legs diagonally, Kaveh bent his torso at the hip and brushed his hands through the air like a praying mantis. His eyes locked on Reza and Reza returned the stare.

Reza grabbed Kaveh around the waist and tried to drive him into the mat. But Kaveh's legs stayed anchored. He reached around Reza, pulled up on his torso and then landed on Reza with crushing weight. Takedown for Kaveh.

---

2 Uncle

3 Father or dad

Staggering to his feet, Reza went to regroup when Abbas pulled him aside. "Your body is weaker, so you'll lose every time when you try to wrestle on strength alone."

"What? How am I supposed to—?"

"Instinct is your fiercest weapon," Abbas said as he held Reza's shoulders and gave them a tug with each word. "Each movement, each twitch, each flicker must feed into a warrior."

"*Chashm*[4], Baba," Reza said. He returned to the mat, eyes darted across Kaveh's face and body. *Twitches and flickers? Why does Baba always use these riddles?* Kaveh's right foot anchored into the mat, but his left couldn't find a solid place. Reza noticed. He shot his body to that leg, lifted Kaveh a few inches and then slammed him to the mat.

"That's it. Feel his weakness," Abbas said. "Find it." He circled the two wrestlers, his expert eye seeking weakness, possibilities.

Kaveh shot a double leg and drove his head into Reza's gut, but Reza sprawled and reached for Kaveh's ankles.

"Grab his shins!" Abbas commanded. "His shins!"

The young limbs bent around each other like vine tendrils slick with fresh rain. The muscles struggled to seize a hold before being ripped into a new position and struggled to grasp again. Reza's legs seemed to operate separately from his arms as they wrapped around Kaveh's head and drove it to the burlap surface. Abbas slapped his hand on the mat to indicate the end of the period. Reza released his victim. Two more practice periods yielded similar results.

Kaveh wiped blood from his split lip. "Come on, Reza!" Kaveh said. "It's just a drill."

"Exactly," Reza responded. "That's why you're only bleeding. Let's go. Stand up." *Coward.* Reza took a quick lap around the mat, shaking his arms and rolling his head before he returned to the center.

"Step up," Reza said.

"No way," Kaveh replied. "You find someone else." He walked around several entangled wrestlers before leaning against the scuffed wall to pinch close his bloody nose.

Reza looked to Abbas, who waved to let him go. Then Abbas pointed to the area where the strongest wrestlers worked out.

The intense lines sketched into Abbas's face masked his gen-

4 Yes I will

tle eyes. A slight man of perfect proportions, he carried every movement with balance and purpose. Thick eyebrows drew attention away from a thinning hairline, and his smile, although rare, could set everything right with the world.

"That was better," Abbas said. "Work to read your opponent's thoughts, know his next move." Abbas placed two hardened hands on the tops of Reza's shoulders and steered him toward the older wrestlers.

"*Chashm,*" Reza said. Then he scrunched up his face and looked to the ceiling. "I can do that sometimes, Baba. But today, I keep thinking about the American fighters."

"Perhaps," Abbas said, with the slightest catch in his rough tone, "Farid will come to our house to see the fight."

"Our house? Come to our house to see the fight? Does that mean we have a TV?" Reza raised up on his tiptoes and looked directly at his father. "Really?"

"Yes, a TV," Abbas said. "But first you have a match. Focus!"

Reza took a huge breath, stepped into the center and faced his next foe, an older and larger boy. In seconds, the boy smashed Reza's face into the mat, where blood trickled from his nose and formed a tiny puddle directly in front of his eye. *He caught me in the reversal.*

"Reza!" Abbas said. "You should've seen that coming. Get up. Do it again."

Shaking his arms and hopping from side to side to realign his muscles, Reza glared at the wrestler, who was nearly twice his size. "Let's go!" Reza said. He did not wipe away the blood.

His opponent rolled his head around his thick neck. "Ready to be pinned again, Abedi? Where do you want to bleed from this time?"

Reza responded by stepping into the center of the mat and glancing at the clock. The next thing he saw up close: a puddle of his own blood.

Abbas yanked Reza up by his arm. "You cannot hesitate." He grabbed Reza's shoulders and pulled Reza toward him. Their faces reflected the mirrored image of the other. Abbas raised a finger and pointed. "When you stop, you quit, you die."

Reza nodded and walked back to the center. *No one's going to die, Baba. I just want to see the fight. See American warriors. See a—*

"Abedi, let's go!" The opponent called out.

"Focus!" Abbas yelled. "Know him."

Three more live drills produced improved results for Reza.

"Better," Abbas said. "Now, go get your sister."

Reza pulled on his faded jeans and T-shirt, bolted out of the gym and down the bumpy asphalt road. He scurried into the smaller gym and searched for Soraya among the boys and girls doing flips and twists.

Seeing a classmate complete a summersault, he remembered the few weeks he trained there. Like some young boys, Reza had started with gymnastics but spent most of his time tackling his teammates or jumping from the high bars. One afternoon when Abbas came to walk him home, Reza's gymnastics coach engaged Abbas in a serious conversation. Reza was not allowed to hear. That night, his mother hugged him with tears trickling down her cinnamon cheeks. "My son, my son. You are so young, just barely older than a baby." Reza had never seen his mother cry.

Abbas stood a few feet behind and spoke to her with a voice Reza feared. "Nimtaj, he has the strength, the instinct. You cannot keep him doing summersaults."

"Why not play soccer with Farid?" she asked Reza. Her gentle eyes glistened as she brushed thick curls from his forehead.

"Just kicking a ball and running after it is boring," Reza told her.

Then Abbas stepped forward and took Reza away from his mother. "It is done. He comes with me."

"He's only six, Haj' Abbas. Can't you wait until he is at least—?"

"He begins his training tomorrow."

Training for what? Reza had thought. Now, as he looked at the other boys doing their gymnastics, he smiled. Whatever he was training for, he liked it a lot more than these cartwheels and back flips.

He walked across the mats, looking for his sister. On the far side, he spotted Soraya completing a perfect dismount from the balance beam and jogged toward her. *She better be ready this time.*

"Baba got us a TV and he said it's time to go." Reza called.

Soraya slightly turned her head. Ten months his senior, she had the exquisite markings of a fawn and eyes that spoke before she did. Clipped in a perfect knot on top of her head, her silken black hair seemed to provide ballast as she jumped and spun. She faced him with pouted lips. "Baba didn't say that. You did.

And," she said as she hopped back on the beam, "I'm not finished."

"Do you always have to be impossible? Just this once, can you cooperate?"

Soraya's lean, muscular body completed several back flips before she landed again in a perfect dismount. "No."

"If we miss the fight because of you, I swear, I'll—"

Behind Reza, Soraya could see Abbas walking in their direction. Raising her voice, she continued. "It's not fair that we have to go home just because you want to see some stupid Americans fight. I have a competition next weekend and I have to practice."

This time she did not return to the beam. She waited for her father. Reza turned around, held up his arms and pointed to Soraya. "She's being impossible."

"Soraya," Abbas said, "we're going home now, but Reza'll escort you back here early tomorrow so you can get in the rest of your routine." She grinned at Reza and pranced off to put on her warm-ups. Reza didn't say a word.

She returned in her loose-fitting pants, long shirt and unclipped hair. It poured down her back like a piece of night, accenting the brilliance of her eyes and sculpted face. She paraded toward the door, when Abbas stopped her. "Soraya, where's your *roosari*[5]?"

Her shoulders dropped. "I left my headscarf at home, Baba."

"If you are not in *hejab*[6], you do not leave the house. Reza, why did you bring your sister here this morning with her hair uncovered?"

"I'm sorry, Baba." He shot his meanest look at his sister, who looked away. *She's impossible.*

"No more, Soraya. You're almost ten and you must cover every time you leave the house. Every time," Abbas said.

"*Chashm*, Baba."

Abbas brought his hand to his face, the coarse skin making a scratching sound against his uneven beard. He pointed to the door and the three headed into the fading sunlight for their walk home.

Bursting through the thick wooden door, Reza ran into the courtyard. "*Salam*[7], *Naneh*[8]," he said as he passed his mother lifting

5 Headscarf worn over a woman's hair
6 Islamic practice of dressing modestly
7 Hello
8 Mother or mom

the large silver handle to pump water from the fountain-well.

In case Abbas came home with a male friend, Nimtaj swiftly took the *chador*[9] tied around her waist, covered her hair and continued her task. "Must you run, run, run to that box?"

Reza stopped before he headed into the large hallway that served as the main room. Floor-to-ceiling glass, checkered in small metal panes, created a barrier separating the entry, fountain-well and kitchen from the main hallway, two bedrooms and large closet. His hand touched the knob. Through the glass, he could see his two younger sisters and his younger brother sitting on the floor staring at the blank screen. *Why isn't it on? Where's the fight?* Behind him, he heard his father's voice coming up the path to the house. Reza went to his mother and wrapped his hands next to hers on the handle.

"Sorry, Naneh," he said. He pumped the handle twice to produce a stream of grey water. "But isn't it exciting? We have a TV!"

She let go and dipped the corner of a cloth into the water. Taking the wet edge, she wiped away a bloodstain from his lip. He held still, but only for a moment.

"There," she said. "Now I can see your whole face."

"It's still my whole face, Naneh," Reza replied, "just with a drop of Kaveh's blood."

"Um-hum," she said as she grabbed both handles of the huge pot and carried it back to her kitchen.

"I promise. It wasn't mine." Reza followed her. "But, the TV! Isn't it exciting?"

She glanced into the main room. "Exciting? No more exciting than bringing in a huge rock to stare at, but it has kept Hassan and your sisters busy today."

"Have they seen anything? Did they see the American boxers?"

Behind them, Abbas and Soraya came into the home. "Oh, you and your American fighters." Soraya said.

Nimtaj dried her hands on the *chador*, now tied around her waist. "Why is your hair not covered?"

9 A loose fitting cape-like garment used to cover a woman's hair and body

"I forgot. I'm sorry," Soraya replied.

With his mother's attention on Soraya, Reza followed Abbas and joined his younger siblings in worship of the only furniture in the room. The TV.

Anxiety mounted as time neared for the fight to begin. Nimtaj calmed the brood while Abbas desperately tinkered with wires and knobs. Sitting on the faded Persian rug under the framed portrait of the *Shah*[10], the chunky TV looked more like a roadside oddity than furniture. This magical box not only looked out of place, it refused to work.

Reza lived the excitement of the much-anticipated Muhammad Ali vs. Joe Frazier boxing match. He heard stories about the two American boxers at school, stories he wanted to see unfold before his eyes. His classmates argued that the legendary wrestler Takhti could have defeated them both, and Reza's heart swelled with impatience to see for himself. But no matter how many times Abbas clicked the two knobs or bent the silver antennas, only grey and white static crackled behind the thick glass.

"It'll work," Abbas said. "The shopkeeper told me it's the best."

Reza's three younger siblings gathered on the rug, standing in an unnatural cluster rather than sitting in the usual circle assembled for family meals. The two little sisters, four-year old Farah and two-year-old Pari, stood curiously in front of the TV studying their reflection. "We go inside too?" they repeated.

Six-year-old Hassan sat on the floor and moved in a side-to-side symphony with Farah and Pari, trying to catch his reflection, too. Fuzzy lines, diagonal patterns and a lot of static greeted them.

The oldest brother, Amir, came into the room and headed directly for the TV. In his long, lanky stride he stepped on Hassan's hand and paused for only a brief moment. He glared down his pointed nose at Hassan, who stuffed his fingers in his mouth.

"It's the antenna. It has to be," Abbas said as he looked up. "Is it on the roof right? Did you follow the directions?"

"Directions? TVs don't have directions," Amir said. "You plug 'em in and turn 'em on. That's how they work. Ours must be a broken one." The kids gasped—broken meant forever in a family with little means to support so many.

"It's the antenna wires? I'll go on the roof, Baba. Let me fix it." Reza begged his father.

10 Title of King of Iran

"How can you know anything about these TVs?" Abbas answered without looking up. "You'll just fall and hurt yourself. Again. Amir, you go."

"No, no, he won't know what to do!" Deciding his father's silence implied permission, Reza ran through the kitchen, out the door and scurried up the ladder to the flat, brown roof.

He squinted in the setting sun across the multitude of one-story brick buildings, watching his neighbors bending their antennas and shouting to waiting families below. "Now?" they would ask. "Can you see anything now?"

As he worked to connect the antenna wires, Reza's mind reeled in fear. *We're going to miss it! No one can get it. These stupid TVs never work like they're supposed to. How can anyone see what is happening a world away, a world called America? Baba wasted his money.*

Voices called up. "Reza, start bending the antenna! *Zood bosh*[11]*!* Hurry!"

Reza bent this way and that, twisting the wires and calling down to the faces peering up at him. His younger brother and sisters darted in and out, calling to Baba, calling to Reza.

"More left. More right. Up. No, down. No, back the other way."

The older brothers, twenty-one year-old Amir and fifteen-year-old Mostafa, climbed the ladder to stand on the roof alongside Reza. While Mostafa smiled at other families struggling with their antennas, Amir moved in to Reza. "Of course you don't know what you're doing, but you came up here anyway! That's why Baba wanted to send me. Give me the wire and move." He reached around Reza.

"No, I can do it. I can do it! Don't push me. Stop it!"

Reza's foot slipped on the loose rocks at the edge of the roof. Mostafa grabbed his arm and pulled him back. Before Reza could speak, Amir blasted, "You know we can't take you to the hospital. Ahhg! And I've dropped the wire because of you."

"I'll get it," Reza said stepping back toward the roof's edge. The black wire dangled from the window. "I can reach it."

"No, you can't. You're too short. Ugh! If we miss Muhammad Ali crushin' Frazier—" Turning from Amir's anger, Reza planned his reach for the wire. Glancing at the ground below, he estimated the fall should he come up short.

11 Hurry

Desperate calls from below. "It's not coming in! Nothing! *Hichi*[12]*!* What happened? There's nothing now!" The family frantic. The cable dangling from the window. Reza lay on his stomach and hung over the edge. *I'll get it.* Stretching to grab the wire, he called to Mostafa, "Just hold my legs, I almost got it."

Mostafa looked over at his brother. "Reza, you'll fall," he replied. "Get up and we'll . . ."

Reza's fingertips barely touched the ends. "I almost got it, just one more . . ." As he reached, stretched, pushed himself over the edge, the sound of small rocks crunching beneath his rolling body became a roar.

"Reza! No!"

Tumbling, Reza swung his arms in a desperate circling motion as if trying to take flight. He flipped himself in a brief moment of balance and landed on the hardened clay ground, feet first, with a grunt. In a defeated heap, he held his ankle and tried not to cry.

Amir shook his head while Mostafa hurried toward the ladder. Hearing the thud, Abbas rushed outside, but Amir cornered his attention. "Naneh will help him," Amir said. "You have to reach the wire."

"Go ahead," Reza said while his large brown eyes blinked back tears. "I'm not hurt."

Nimtaj leaned out the open window. "Not again! Are you sure you're not hurt?"

"*Baleh*[13]," he nodded. "I'm fine."

Only Hassan ran out of the house in search of his brother. He followed the brick wall around the perimeter until he found Reza rocking and holding his foot.

"Rezz!" Hassan's small figure, wearing only a pair of torn shorts, sprinted to his brother.

"I'm okay. I'm fine." Reza reached to the bony shoulder for balance. "Just help me up."

"I'll get Naneh. You're hurt." Hassan turned to run back into the house.

Reza grabbed his arm. "No! Get over here! I'm fine. I'm all right." With strength from Hassan, Reza steadied himself.

Leaning at the end of the alley, Mostafa shook his head at his stubborn younger brother. An impressive few beard sprouts,

---

12 Nothing

13 Informal Yes, like "Ya"

twisting in the mountain breezes, gave Mostafa's face the look of a young wizard. Only a few years older than Reza, he stood almost a foot taller and carried the wisdom of a thousand generations. He calmly approached the two and ordered Reza to sit.

Hassan protested. "Pick 'em up! *Zood bosh*! He'll miss the big fight."

Mostafa leaned over Reza's swelling foot and moved it side to side. "You'll walk, but I'd give up flying for a while." He reached under Reza's arms. "Here, let's get you up."

A man's shadow crossed the figures. "He should get up alone. He acts before he thinks and he only thinks about himself," Amir said. His large frame and naturally dark features were emphasized in the shadows. Hassan ducked behind Mostafa.

Reza looked down in shame, but Mostafa had already hoisted him to his feet. He whispered, "Sometimes you'll fall," and brushed dirt from Reza's back. "But you always get up."

The three brothers came into the home, hardly noticed by the family engaged in the only piece of furniture in the room. Nimtaj and Reza's two oldest sisters, Rasha and Mehri, brought the *deeg*[14] of steaming herbs to Reza. With his sheepish grin, he stood to place his swollen ankle in the brew. Smelling the rising steam, Nimtaj patted Reza's head and went to her kitchen with Rasha and Mehri to prepare the evening's meal, showing no interest in this new distraction crackling in their home.

The throbbing pain was soon blotted out by the image of two enormous warriors smashing fists into swollen faces while throngs of Americans cheered. Reza gasped as Frazier absorbed a blow from Ali that would have killed an elephant and howled in amazement when Frazier got up.

"Look, Baba!" Hassan said. "He's like an ox. He could lift the whole house!"

Farah's pudgy face nodded in agreement. "Maybe two houses!" she added.

The commentator fumbled through the translation of boxing terms, his voice crackling in and out with both surreal emotion and poor reception. Reza watched Muhammad Ali and marveled at how someone so powerful could also be so quick. *These are Americans,* Reza thought, from a land that might as well have been the moon.

He strained to study the American faces in the crowd at Madi-

14 Large pot

son Square Garden, people whom he figured just wandered in off the street to take in a good fight. He pulled his swollen red leg from the *deeg* so he could get closer to the screen and hear the announcer.

Sitting next to his eight-year-old cousin, Farid, who had just scrambled in since his TV couldn't be fixed, Reza whispered, "Muhammad Ali's got this guy beat. He's just waiting for the right moment to knock him out." Farid nodded in agreement and continued to write in the notebook he always carried with him.

Reza scooted even closer to the screen and became lost in the moment. Muhammad Ali punished Frazier with endless bloody blows. Now entering the fifteenth and final round, both fighters staggered with exhaustion. Screaming fans melted away leaving two ancient warriors facing one another in their broken bodies. Reza reached to the screen and pretended to touch them.

But he drew his hand back as Frazier lashed out with a punishing left hook to Muhammad Ali's exposed jaw. Ali dissolved to the mat. His legs flopped in the air while his arms crashed to his side. The referee leaned over the pulverized mass. "1, 2 . . ."

And then, like a burst of black smoke from a smoldering inferno, Muhammad Ali rose.

Mostafa cheered and the others joined in. Reza hopped on his good leg and yelled, "Baba! Did you see that? He won't stay down! He won't stay down!"

"Ahh, Reza, it's what I always tell you: getting up is what it takes to be Champion." Abbas paused and shook his head. "But that one moment of hesitation cost him this victory."

"Baba's right. One mistake and he won't be the *ghahreman*. It's over," Amir confirmed.

Reza looked up at Abbas and he nodded in agreement.

"But he got up," Mostafa said. "He got up."

At the sound of the bell, the warriors staggered to their corners. The referee took the card from the judges. The crowd took a collective breath as the referee's voice echoed through the arena. "Joe Frazier is the new Heavyweight Champion of the world."

Reza looked down and rubbed his swollen ankle.

• • • • •

A few hours later, the chilly spring evening found Reza, Farid and Hassan lying on the rooftop under the sparkling, ancient sky. Without the summer heat, the boys brought wool blankets to keep them warm. Hassan ensured his blanket touched Reza's before he adjusted his pillow and settled in. Reza was absorbed in the vast wonderment of the decorated darkness above them.

Farid, born only a few months after Reza, had an insatiable curiosity and sharp mind for details. He reviewed the notes he took during the fight and concluded that Muhammad Ali really should have been the *ghahreman.*

"What do you know about boxing?" Reza asked. "It's nothing like soccer."

"What's there to know? You land a punch, you get a point." Farid pointed to a page in his notebook. "And Muhammad Ali had more."

"Maybe it's different in America," Reza answered. "I mean, can you believe they were so huge? And fearless. I wonder if all Americans are like that."

Farid and Reza first reasoned all Americans must be fearless, huge and strong like oxen. But, after a few minutes of silent pondering, Hassan shook his head and declared, "I saw skinny ones in the crowd."

Reza agreed. "Lots of skinny ones." Images of the mighty warriors were still crisp in his mind. Reza felt their desire, their sweat and their force. "So, it must be that the big Americans are bred to fight. They're strong, like Takhti, but can a boxer be a true *pahlavan*[15]?" He gazed off into the night sky.

Farid pulled the woven blanket closer to his chin to offset the evening's chill. "Maybe, if you want to be a champion in America, you get all the best foods and all the best training 'till you're huge." Farid laughed a little. "And then all the skinny ones stand around and cheer while you get beat like a goat with a club."

Reza pounded his fist into his hand, mimicking the action he had seen Abbas use many times when making a point. "But a goat can't fight back. It has no chance. It's just always a goat."

"I've seen goats run really fast," Hassan said. "And then they can't get beat."

"Cowards run," Reza said. "Warriors fight."

"But *pahlavan* fight with honor," Farid said. "Like Takhti."

Reza stood and walked to the edge of the roof. For several minutes, his small figure blended into the night. "I think I'd like

15 A hero who is equally strong in body, mind and soul. In Iran, it is usually associated with wrestlers.

to go to America," Reza said. "I'll find Muhammad Ali and tell him he really won and not to be disappointed. At least, he should be proud he got up."

Silence followed Reza's statement, so he figured they had fallen asleep. He returned to his bedding, adjusted his pillow and closed his eyes to remember his warriors exchanging blow after blow.

In the darkness, Farid's voice cut into Reza's dreams. "But it's too much money to get to America and we don't know how to get there." He paused as if waiting for a response from Reza. "And your family is here and you're Iranian. Iranians live in Iran."

Reza stared into the brilliant path of the Milky Way. "Iran is just one part of the whole world."

A world that for now lay buried somewhere behind a thick wall of black and white glass.

Chapter Three

July 1975

"The Americans," Reza said, "are inside that building." He smoothed his shirt against his developing adolescent physique in yet another attempt to wipe away the dirt stains. Strapping arms on his hips created a triangular shadow on the road that led to the iron gates of the Sherkat Naft oil refinery.

Next to the oil refinery, stood a high-class hotel. This hotel had amenities most citizens in Kermanshah had never even seen. Security guards always stood at the gated entrance. With the Americans inside, two more armed guards circled the complex in fatigues.

"And there's no way to go inside," Farid said, "even for you. Can you just drop it?" He wiped his thin neck with a soiled cloth. Moving closer to Reza, he crouched in the hot shade of the brick wall surrounding the complex and drew stick figures in the dirt.

"Don't you want to meet one, see what they're really like?" Reza said as he rubbed out the stick figures with his foot.

"Even if you could get in, what makes you think they want to meet you?" Farid tossed a smooth rock into the river churning alongside the back wall. "And even if the guards don't shoot you, Haj' Abbas will punish you and then you—"

"Ah, Farid," Reza said as his eyes continued to scan every crack and crevice. "Sometimes you just have to make things happen."

Farid stood and shook his head. "And get shot in the process? No thanks."

"Not even a little curious to find out what's in there?" Reza asked as he pulled at the thin shirt that stuck to his body.

"You'll see them tomorrow at the wrestling tournament. And you better be ready to compete. These guys are the best from regional teams all over America."

Looking sideways at his cousin, Reza flexed his biceps and patted his iron stomach. "I'm always ready to compete. There's no one who even—"

"Comes close, I know. Hassan tells me all the time. But these guys are the real takedown wrestlers, Reza. Don't get hung up on the fact they're Americans."

Reza dusted off his pants and ran his fingers through his sticky thicket of hair. He took Farid's rag to wipe his face. "I'm not hung up. Just curious."

Before them the hotel's metal and glass rose defiantly against the backdrop of the jagged Zagros Mountains. Between the mountains and the town stretched endless pastures. These fertile fields, harvested in spring and tanned by summer, rested for the winter rains. A summer resort for kings of centuries past, Kermanshah's surrounding mountains boasted eternal carvings of royalty and warriors. Cut from granite and smoothed by time, this windswept cradle of civilization reflected history itself.

Reza stood with the burn of the timeless sun against his back and squinted into the mountain's reflection in the windows. He interlaced his fingers and placed his hands on top of his head. *There's got to be a way to get in there.*

Farid turned to walk back to the city. After a few steps, he stopped. He waited. No footsteps followed him and he turned to his cousin. "You can't get inside. You don't have a plan."

"I could have a plan." Reza's grin softened his chiseled features. He walked around to the back of Sherkat Naft. *I could follow the river along the wall. There's got to be foothold somewhere, maybe a rock I could roll and then step on and—*

"Seriously, let's go home," Farid said, shaking his head. "There's nothing more for you here, except a bullet in your butt."

"You sound like Soraya," Reza answered, moving his eyes back to the windows. "Let's just go to the other side and get another look." To answer Farid's protest, he added, "You already know what's in Kermanshah."

Farid and Reza edged along the back wall next to the river. Wet rocks slipped out from under their feet and bounced before being swallowed by the rushing water. Farid winced at each kerplunk, but Reza's steady pace pushed forward.

On the far side, they hid behind an oilrig to study the guards from a safe distance. Farid sketched an outline of the building and drew arrows to indicate the patrolling patterns. Reza pointed to a truck parked next to the back corner of the wall. "We could climb on top of that and then jump over."

Farid only shook his head and showed the drawing to Reza. "Think about it. Even if you get over the wall, without getting shot, you can't get in without help from someone on the inside."

"Then I'll find someone."

"And," Farid continued, "You'll only have a few minutes before a guard turns the corner and then you're dead. I mean really dead."

"Oh, really dead. Well, that's different," Reza said as he bit pieces of nail from his swollen thumb. "Go home if you want to. I'm going to find a way in."

"Some things aren't worth the risk," Farid said. He reached around to tuck his notebook into his back pocket. "And what if *Savak*[1] arrests your Baba? You know their headquarters is right there." He pointed at a low brick building with no windows and only one door. "You don't want to end up in there." But when he looked up, Reza had already started toward the truck.

Reza quickly put one foot on the tire and hoisted himself into the back. He winced at his loud thud and sprawled flat on the burning truck bed. He listened. *No shots.* Lifting his head, he saw the guard lean against the wall to light a fresh cigarette. When the guard walked around the corner, Reza sprang from the truck bed, clung to the wall's rough edge and pulled himself over in a single motion. Landing in the familiar cloud of dust, he noted no pain from any part of his body and sprinted to a sculptured bush.

From behind the bush, Reza focused on the fourth-floor

1 Shah's secret police

window where he saw the most movement. One of the figures stopped and seemed to be looking back at Reza. Approaching the window, the figure waved. Tentatively, Reza returned the wave. The window popped open and a speckled face with toasty red hair pushed through and yelled, "Hi!"

Reza waved again but quickly pointed to where the guard would be turning the corner.

The red head followed Reza's pointing and nodded. When clear, the boys exchanged many hand gestures. The guard came back around and Reza retreated to the shade.

Once the guard turned the corner, Reza met the redheaded boy at an open window on the first floor. Just as the guard came back around, Red pulled Reza in and the window slammed shut.

They snuck down the hallway to the back elevator. The doors automatically opened, so the redhead stepped inside and turned to Reza. Having never seen a wall open, Reza stepped back and shook his head "no." The American became agitated and reached his arm to grab Reza and drag him in. Reza resisted, until he heard heavy boot steps sounding down the hall. He jumped in and the doors closed.

Seconds later, Reza stepped out onto the hallway of wall-to-wall carpet. The Americans had their doors propped open and sang along with the latest music beats.

"Hey, you guys check out who I found," said the redhead. "This dude was waving to me outside. I think he's one of the Iranians we're going to wrestle tomorrow."

Reza tilted his head and smiled.

The wrestlers greeted Reza with big smiles, warm handshakes and genuine curiosity. Reza flexed his biceps and pointed to his strong legs, flashing his signature grin. "Fifty-seven kilos," he said as he pointed to himself.

One American wrote numbers on a pad, trying to figure Reza's weight in pounds to determine whom he would wrestle tomorrow. "One kilo is 2.2 pounds," the American said. He continued to scribble his calculations and called out, "Jimmy!" They ran down the hall to get Reza's opponent.

Reza felt like the foreigner in his own country. The beds that didn't roll up, fancy lights, water that came from faucets and a shower in every bathroom. He found himself turning the shower on and off and running his arm through the warm water. *I have to try this.* He pulled off his shirt and proceeded to remove his shoes when his opponent came in and stared at him.

Reza turned and sized him up. *This guy's the best America's got for me?* His skin looked like fine tissue paper, his hair like corn silk and his pale blue eyes reminded Reza of the day Pari came home from the hospital. Although Reza knew this American must possess great strength and skill, he could not erase the image of his flesh tearing off like a peach skin.

Crouching down with his arms in a wrestling stance, Jimmy approached Reza and pretended to engage him in a match. Reza did the same and the two began to wrestle. Slowly at first, but their competitive nature soon had them slamming into walls and knocking over a chair before the Americans broke them up. Reza and Jimmy stood, faced each other and Reza extended his hand.

Smiling, Jimmy motioned for Reza to come to his room and offered Reza a shiny red can with a brown, sugary drink. Reza took a swallow then ran to the sink to spit it out, shaking his head, "no" and squishing his face. That's when Jimmy pointed to the mouthwash.

Reza took a huge drink and swallowed the mouthwash as Jimmy motioned to "spit it out!" Reza gagged into the sink, eyes watering, as the blue liquid oozed through his nostrils. *What is this stuff!? He's trying to poison me!* But, when his head cleared, he joined Jimmy in the laughter.

Seeing books sticking out of Jimmy's bag, Reza pointed to them. Shrugging, Jimmy pulled them out and plopped them on the bed. Reza ran his hand along the slick pages and brought them to his nose. They smelled smart, with tight English letters that looked so efficient. Pointing to words and pictures, Jimmy taught him the English names of the objects in the hotel room.

Reza pointed to the light on the nightstand. "Lamp," Jimmy said.

Jimmy pointed to himself, puffed out his chest and strutted through the room, "Champion," he said.

Doing the same and pointing to himself, Reza said, "*Ghahreman.*"

Jimmy made a one with his finger. "Victory," he said.

"*Piroozi*[2]" Reza said.

Trying to imitate the marching of the guards, Jimmy said, "Guards," and gave a puzzled look.

---

2 Victory

"Agh, *negahbon*[3]," Reza said, shaking his head.

Insistent pounding on the door interrupted their lesson.

Hushed voices. "Jimmy, hide him! Coach Jones is here. He's going to kick our ass!"

Reza and Jimmy exchanged looks of genuine fear, and although Reza didn't exactly understand the words, he understood Jimmy's face. The closet? Too obvious. Out the window? Too high. Under the bed? Hurry, under the bed.

As Reza wiggled under the bed, Coach Jones entered the room. "Is he in here?" he bellowed.

"Is who in where?" Jimmy replied.

Reza followed the stripped shoes and long white socks as they paced about the room.

"I'm not playing, Jimmy. If that Iranian kid is in here, we need to turn him over to the guards," Coach Jones said.

"Why? He's not doing anything," Jimmy replied.

Coach Jones' voice came out in a harsh whisper. "We're guests in Iran. We have to go by their rules, and the guards want to talk to him. Now, where is he?"

Jimmy hesitated, "What does talk to him mean, Coach? We're just wrestlers."

"It means, it means they will talk to him. And it means you have five minutes to figure out where he is and get him the hell out of here." He stood next to the bed; his shoes almost touching Reza's nose. "Five, son. Not six!"

The coach left the room. Reza scurried out and caught his reflection in the mirror; his skin was the color of tissue paper. Fists pounded on the door. "Quick, Jimmy, open up! We have a plan."

Jimmy pulled open the door and five wrestlers poured in, one holding an American warm-up suit. "Put this on him. We'll put him in the middle, say we're going to run stairs and get him out the back."

"That's not going to—" Jimmy started to say, but they pushed past him.

"Hurry, kid, put these on."

Reza stared, confused, as they motioned for him to step into the shiny red sweats. From down the hall, deep voices sounded with the pounding of the fists. Reza looked at the door. *They're coming for me.* Their pounding grew louder, echoing only a few

3 Guard

doors away. The boys froze. Reza reached over and grabbed the red sweats.

Within seconds, he wore the bright red, white and blue colors and tucked himself into the middle of the Americans. One, two, three. They opened the door. The *negahbons,* walking in perfect unison with their gun barrels pointing down, marched toward them. Reza ducked his head.

Thud, thud, thud. Keeping his eyes down, Reza saw only their black boots and the tips of their weapons. Icy stares burned into the top of his skull. *They must see me. This can't work. Breathe. Breathe. Breathe.* They crossed paths and the American wrestlers pushed Reza to the stairs. Coach Jones stood in front of the door, spotted Reza and raised his bushy eyebrows. The six wrestlers held one breath, and then Coach Jones opened the door and motioned for them to run down the stairs. At the bottom, Reza tore off his sweats, hugged his new American friends and peered out the door. As the *negahbons* turned the corner, Reza sprinted to a pile of empty oil drums against the wall, climbed over and ran home.

He arrived just in time for dinner, but breathless. Taking the minimal amount of food, he remained quiet during the family discussions. Quiet, but speaking through an illuminated face. Soraya noticed his grin, but didn't ask.

• • • • •

The next day, Reza entered the gym and stepped on the weigh-in scale. With a merciless clink, it tipped a full kilo over. "Sorry Reza," said the official. "You're heavy. A full kilo."

"There's no way!" Reza protested as he stepped on and off the scale several times and looked to the weights for a different result.

"You're disqualified," repeated the official. "Unless you can drop it in . . ." He looked at his clipboard and then to the clock. "Thirty minutes."

A hand pulled Reza's shoulder back as he tried to step back on the scale. "That's not going to help," Abbas said.

Reza dropped his chin and then turned slowly to face his father. "I think I had too much meat." He snapped his head to the clock. "But I can lose a kilo, Baba! I can. I'm going to run around the—"

"*Baleh,*" said Abbas. "You're going to lose the kilo, but you're doing it on the mats." He turned and waved to a coach who walked in their direction with a wrestler by his side. "This is Coach Alizad. We trained here together many years ago." Then Abbas reached his hand around a wrestler, about Reza's age, but thicker. "And this is Ardeshir."

Reza looked at the wrestler's large bare feet, stocky legs and solid middle. *He's like a puppy that hasn't grown into his paws.* When he went to read his eyes, Reza discovered Ardeshir continued to scan his body. *Why's he looking at me like that? Who is this guy?*

With impatience, Reza thrust his chin forward to draw Ardeshir's attention. Their stares locked as faces narrowed, fingers twitched and temples pulsed. Abbas smiled.

"Well, let's go," Reza said. But neither moved.

Stepping forward, Abbas placed a hand on each shoulder. "Reza has twenty-five minutes to sweat out one kilo."

With a final snarl, Reza turned and jogged to the back mats. He hopped from foot to foot, swung his arms and rolled his head. *Baba thinks this guy can take me. I'm all over him. He's just some overgrown—*

Slam! Reza found his face smashed into a warm pool of yesterday's sweat. *What the hell?* Ardeshir bounced up, hunched at the waist and began to circle Reza with outstretched arms. "What you got, Abedi," Ardeshir growled.

Setting his feet and scanning Ardeshir's body, Reza escaped from time itself. The thuds and grunts of the gym dissolved and only two wrestlers remained. Flesh and bone, muscle and tissue collided, ripped apart and collided again. Neither warrior would go down. Nor relinquish a hold. Nor quit. As one pushed harder, the other shoved back harder still.

Standing to the side, with a wry smile and clear eyes, Abbas watched. He watched and nodded, but he didn't say a word.

After ten grueling minutes, Coach Alizad turned to Abbas. "Time to stop?"

Abbas rocked back and forth on his heels. "Not yet."

"Reza's going to be wiped out for his match," Coach Alizad said. "I'm sure he's lost his kilo, probably two."

"Probably," Abbas replied.

Reza snapped Ardeshir's head down and knee tapped him to his back. Ardeshir quickly grabbed Reza's leg, but it was too late because Reza already had the takedown. Limbs uncoiled and both wrestlers stood in the center, their faces mirrored in blood.

"Let's go," Reza said.

Ardeshir took a large step forward, glared at the slight tremble in Reza's right thigh and rounded his arms. With dangerous precision, he shot the right leg and lifted Reza. The two slammed back onto the mat.

Abbas glanced at the clock. "To the scales," he said. Reza did not hear him. Reza took a single leg and dumped Ardeshir into the mat. Ardeshir jumped to his feet and kept his eyes locked on Reza's, their bodies still tense, their breathing still measured. "Reza, to the scales," Abbas repeated.

Both wrestlers let their arms fall and stood straight. Neither moved for a moment. Then Reza stuck out his hand. "Good match."

"You, too," Ardeshir said and shook hands with Reza.

"Two minutes. *Zood bosh*!" Abbas commanded.

Reza and Ardeshir jogged over the scales and Reza stepped on. He had lost almost two kilos. Reza looked at Ardeshir and smiled. "In sweat and in blood."

"Anytime," Ardeshir said. The two walked off together, chatting like old souls.

They found themselves next to the American wrestlers warming up. Reza worked to memorize each of Jimmy's foreign moves, but he wondered more about Jimmy's life in America. *I should ask him if he's seen Muhammad Ali.* Watching Jimmy go to his team bench, Reza envied the bright red, white and blue gym bag and his shiny new sweats.

"What's with you?" Ardeshir asked. "The Americans look too scary?"

On instinct, Reza curled his bicep. "I have no fear."

As Reza and Ardeshir surveyed their competition with confidence, Abbas seemed to recognize the smile of fools and waved his hand for them to come to him. Reza knew what was coming next.

Abbas placed his hand on Reza's shoulder. "So you've won already have you?"

Looking down Reza answered, "No sir."

Abbas then turned to Ardeshir. "And you? You're celebrating *piroozi* already?"

Ardeshir glanced sheepishly at Reza. "No sir," he said.

"Oh, I thought I saw two victory smiles, but now I know I see only foolish pride."

"*Baleh*, sir," they answered in unison.

Abbas waited until the boys brought their faces to meet his. Then he held up a single finger and leaned forward. "There is one way to be a *ghahreman*. Work!"

"Yes, sir."

His voice grew harsh. "There're many takedown wrestlers here. You will earn your *piroozi*. Ignore pain. Banish doubt. To be a true—"

Coach Alizad hustled to the trio. "Haj' Abbas, my apologies. Has Ardeshir—"

Abbas relaxed his stance and faced the coach. "No, Coach Alizad. I am reminding Ardeshir and my son," he emphasized, "there is work to be done." He turned back to the wrestlers. "Go. Go prepare. You have matches in two short hours."

Ardeshir and Reza jogged off to a corner of the mats and were soon entangled in their respective practice matches.

Abbas stood in the corner of the gym, his square chin resting in his rough hand. Coaches cautiously approached to speak a few words to Abbas. With two hands, they held Abbas's hand in theirs, and with a slight bow of the head greeted him with "Haj' Abbas," the title of honor given to those who had completed the journey to the Muslim holy city of Mecca. Abbas responded with either an approving nod or a solemn shake of the head, and often he would add a warm grin or reassuring pat on the back.

Abbas placed his hand on Coach Alizad's shoulder. "They're too good to be weakened by pride. We must watch them. They could be *ghahreman*. God willing."

"*Inshallah*[4], Haj' Abbas. With their muscles continuing to develop like this, they have a great future in wrestling. Do you see any other potential champions?" Coach Alizad asked.

Abbas rubbed his chin and surveyed the gym. Careful not to draw attention, he gave a slight nod in the direction of a thick boy with a shock of death-black hair and deep-set eyes. "He has no fear. He could be dangerous."

Coach Alizad followed Abbas's gaze. "I know him. His father

4 God willing

is a high-ranking officer in Shah's Rastakhiz party." He paused, looked around the gym and directly into Abbas's eyes. "I hear it is his father who ordered the shots to be fired at the demonstration remembering those who—died." Without comment from Abbas, he cautiously continued. "You know, after three days of the students protesting, something had to be done."

Abbas lifted an eyebrow. "Students had to be shot?"

Coach Alizad let out a slow breath. "You know I agree that's never an answer. I think Shah must have feared after three days," he lowered his voice, "that *he* would be in people's conversations again. I hear his cassette tapes were smuggled in and praised the protests as evidence the people are liberating Iran from Western imperialism. And he was exiled in, what, 1964?"

"1963," Abbas corrected him. "And yet, you say there are still protests? And shootings?" He smiled. "That's why I like it here. Life is as simple as one man taking down another." He slapped Ardeshir's coach on the back. "There's nothing complicated about that."

The Shah's picture hung at the entrance of the gym, looking more like a postage stamp than a portrait. Abbas glanced toward the portrait and let out a long, deep sigh. He then scanned the many qualifying matches until he found Ardeshir's. He walked around the edge of the gym.

Arriving at Ardeshir's match just as the second period began, he stood next to Reza and leaned over to his son. "The American wrestlers like to keep in motion and on their feet, forever changing directions, going one way and then the other, pawing, waiting for an opening, for a chance for a takedown."

Reza nodded. "I noticed they work with arms more, like they're monkeys."

"Monkeys? Perhaps. But see how the Iranian wrestlers push straight ahead with pure strength. We bore in low, forcing mistakes, seldom reaching, using our strong legs, our mighty bodies from our ancient bloodlines to finish off opponents by crushing them into the mats." He pounded his fist into his hand. "We breathe, we sweat, we bleed as warriors!"

Reza glanced around to see if anyone was watching them. *Why does Baba have to act like this is life and death?* "Yes Baba," he said. "Ardeshir is going to destroy this guy."

On the mat, Ardeshir studied his foe with clenched teeth and eyes piercing all possibilities of weakness. With a swift motion, Ardeshir shot the leg, drove his shoulder and lifted him into the air before landing on him with a thud, a takedown worth two points. Ardeshir took the lead.

"Be patient," Abbas called from the side.

Preferring the pin rather than just victory, Ardeshir entered the third and final period in such a state of intense concentration that Reza wondered if Ardeshir actually thought he might be losing.

The American's right leg shook for an instant. And in that instant, Ardeshir pounced. He shot the leg, took his victim to the mat and laid all his weight exactly across the body. The American's shoulder touched the mat. Ardeshir pressed the second one down for good measure, and the referee slapped the mat signaling victory.

The referee raised Ardeshir's arm while he flashed a pearly white grin into a camera. Reza couldn't help but smile.

"What are you smiling at?" Abbas asked.

"Well, he won."

Abbas slowly shook his head. "One match."

Reza felt a trap coming, but he couldn't put together what Abbas wanted him to think about Ardeshir.

"Never smile into the camera, Reza," Abbas said. He held up a single finger. "You're always one move away from *piroozi* or defeat. You want to be a takedown wrestler? You keep your head down when your hand is high."

"*Chashm,* sir."

Reza's match was next and he needed to defeat an Iranian in his weight class before he could advance to a round with the American champion. He found himself staring into the fearless face of the wrestler Abbas pointed out earlier. Reza's opponent seemed to have arms that extended beyond natural length and twice he almost chocked out Reza. Behind by two points going into the third round, Reza struggled to erase the sensation of not being able to breathe. His head swooned a bit and his eyes fought to bring the foe into focus.

"A takedown ties it!" Ardeshir yelled.

A circle of American wrestlers formed around the match. Soft English words, with long vowels and even tones, punctuated the harsh guttural commands of his Iranian friends. *Maybe they're cheering for me.*

The opponent managed to stay strong in the tripod position and grabbed Reza's wrist. Reza regrouped to shoot the leg and bring his back to the mat. An instant scan of the opponent's flesh pressing against him revealed a weakness. Entwining his leg around his opponent's, he re-shifted his weight, ounce by ounce, and forced the opponent's shoulder blade to touch the mat. *Piroozi* by a pin. Reza's hand raised, his head down.

"I thought he had you, Rez!" Hassan said as he scurried to meet his brother.

"He never had me. When'd you get here?" Reza looked around the crowded gym for Abbas. "Where's Baba?"

"Over there."

Hassan followed behind Reza as they made their way to Abbas. Seeing his son approach, Abbas walked a few steps away from a coach and embraced Reza in a hug. "That was a good move. I've seen you practice that."

"I wanted to save that for the Championship, but—"

Another coach approached. "Haj' Abbas," he said, reaching for Abbas's hand. "We have a contested match. Both coaches are claiming his wrestler has won. Can you please come and help settle this?"

"I will be right there," Abbas said. He turned to Reza. "Always bring everything you have to every match."

Reza nodded.

Abbas left with the coach just as Ardeshir came up from behind. The noise of the gym masked his approach. In a swift motion, he grabbed Hassan and flipped him in a circle. Reza didn't flinch.

"Hey, put me down!" Hassan protested.

"This is Ardeshir," Reza said. He turned to Ardeshir and pointed to Hassan. "And this is Hassan, my little brother."

"He looks just like you," Ardeshir said. "Did you hatch him?"

"Yeah, he came out of a big giant egg."

Ardeshir smiled and looked down at Hassan. "You a wrestler?"

"No," Hassan said. "Not yet. But one day, I'm going to—"

Ardeshir turned to Reza. "Any sisters?"

Before Reza could answer, Hassan jumped in front of him. "We have five sisters and two more brothers! Rasha's promised to be married, and Mehri's older than you, and Farah's kinda chubby and I bet she stays that way, and Pari's sick a lot, but everyone says Soraya's pretty. I hear Naneh talk about her sometimes when she comes back from the bathhouse, but Soraya bosses Reza around all the time and she—"

"So she bosses you around?" Ardeshir said, looking at Reza. "The pretty one bosses you around?"

"You're going to believe little rat?" he said as he smacked Hassan upside the head. "And why is that your worry? You should be thinking about your opponent."

Ardeshir looked across the gym floor teeming with furious matches. "We do face the Americans my friend," he said. "Do you have what it takes to be a *ghahreman* like me?"

"And more."

Ardeshir lifted Hassan onto his shoulders and walked through the gym in a not-so-subtle display of his strength.

Reza ran several laps around the gym, practiced specific moves on his teammates and talked through a few scenarios with Mostafa.

The first period of Reza's match began with both wrestlers standing in the neutral position. As expected, Jimmy began to move side to side, with his hands clawing the air. Reza locked into the blue eyes, trying to the think his thoughts, predict his next move. Jimmy lurched forward and slid his arm under Reza's in an underhook, trying to throw Reza off balance. Reza countered by cupping his hands around Jimmy's head and pumping it to the mat like a ball. At the end of the first period, the score was tied.

Jimmy stayed elusive, squirming out of holds and using his strength to keep him far from being pinned. Both wrestlers found a groove with precise counter-movements to each attack.

Less than a minute remained in the final period. Reza couldn't look to Abbas and only Mostafa's voice banged in his head: "Shoot the leg!" It was a risky move. If he made a bad shot to the leg, Jimmy would sprawl and easily take Reza down. Reza looked to the left leg, shot a nice single leg and cut the corner. Jimmy went straight down on his face. Reza quickly used his leg to turn Jimmy to his back. The official's face pressed against the mat looking, looking for the white flesh of Jimmy's shoulder to touch. Just one touch and he would be pinned. Reza pushed and pushed. He heard Jimmy's gargles and groans, his white face becoming pink, becoming red, becoming purple. Jimmy fought the pin until a trickle of blood oozed from his blue lips. Seeing the blood, Reza increased his weight. Jimmy's shoulder touched the mat. Pin.

The official raised Reza's hand in victory and Reza tried to catch Jimmy's eye, but Jimmy looked away. He did not wipe away his blood.

Mostafa was the first to shake his brother's hand as Hassan hugged Reza. Abbas broke into a rare smile and Ardeshir smacked Reza forcefully on the back. Reza thanked them and then went to the American bench.

Pulling his sweats out of his bag, Jimmy yanked them on one leg as Reza approached. Anger flashed across his face, but Reza's repeating the only English word he could remember, "Lamp, lamp, lamp," softened his glare.

He looked at Reza. "I didn't come all the way here to lose! You're the gharawhatever and I'm a—how do you say loser?"

Reza struggled with what to say next. Shaking his head no, Reza pointed to both himself and Jimmy. He pointed at the red sweats and to himself, trying to show he appreciated Jimmy and the Americans saving him from the guards. "*Pahlavan,*" he said.

"Okay, *pahlavan.* Fine. Go be a *pahlavan* somewhere else."

An American teammate approached. "Dude, don't be such a dick. *Pahlavan*'s in my translation dictionary. He's saying you're, like, from a bloodline of hard-core heroes who are strong, but also do, like, good deeds. It's the best compliment you can give."

"Why is saying that to me?" Jimmy said. "I lost."

The American teammate pointed to a guard. "It's more than a match."

"*Pahlavan,*" Reza repeated as he looked directly at Jimmy.

Jimmy stuck out his hand, which Reza shook with a firm grip and followed with a hug.

Chapter Four

Laguna Niguel, 2008

Reza gives the bundle of typed pages back to me and I'm surprised at how nervous I am. What if he hated it? What if I got everything wrong? But, with his signature smile, he says, "Exciting."

"But, you know how it ends, right?" I grin as I settle onto the kitchen stool and continue to review his comments.

He laughs and returns to his boiling rice as I flip through the pages noting many circled words and question marks.

"Why'd you circle kitchen table?"

Reza tilts the steaming pot into the sink and the rice tumbles into the strainer. "Because we never had one."

"Where'd you eat?"

The pot clinks back onto the stove. "On the floor." He proceeds to grab four plates, pile them with rice and then top the rice with chunky stew. The fresh, spicy aroma alerts his two sons and the four of us sit down for dinner—at his table.

Although I continue to question Reza extensively about every possible detail of his childhood, I know I grew up more than a world apart. How could be I so educated and yet so ignorant?

"So," I ask Reza between bites of an amazing meal, "what was it like to wrestle in Iran?"

"Like wrestling anywhere else."

"Come on, Reza. You forgot to mention the kitchen table. I just don't want to miss anymore huge details."

"It's the same," he says. "It's about desire. How close you're willing to . . ." He pauses as he finishes a mouthful. "To touch death."

Touch death?

Chapter Five

Kermanshah, Spring 1976

"Everyone's talking about Nationals, Baba. Even Ardeshir said Coach Alizad thinks I should go." Reza dropped himself from the rope, landed squarely on the mat and stretched his arms above his head. "Ardeshir's going. You think I can go, too? Right?"

Reza, at 13, stood almost to his father's full height of 168 centimeters[1]. Adolescence had begun to lay claim to Reza's features, chiseling his cheekbones and invading his chin with hair. His boyish grin still captured his face and added mystery to impish eyes.

Abbas looked directly at his son. "Ardeshir's going, is he? And Coach Alizad says you should go? I see."

"You think I should compete, don't you? I mean, I dominate in the matches here. I beat the American, I—" A glance from his father stopped his speech. Reza bit this thumbnail and looked away. *I'm the best, Baba, and you know it!*

A symphony of grunts reverberated through the sticky gym air to harmonize with the barking of coaches and the yelping of athletes. Reza's heart beat in its rhythm and breathed with its tempo. Gripping the dangling rope, he climbed in a perfect hand-over-hand cadence to the top and dropped back to the mat. He waited, trying not to stare at his father.

Abbas scanned the gym and looked back at this son. "Nationals? You think you're ready for Nationals?"

1 Five and a half feet tall

"I do."

"I have a tournament here that weekend, so only Mostafa can go with you."

"I can do it, Baba," Reza said, his eyes bright with promise. "I will come home to you a champion."

"And there's the issue of your weight." Abbas's voice did not match the excitement of Reza's. "There will be many difficult dinners and hard training ahead."

Reza slumped to contemplate the torn mat under his calloused feet. "I know."

"I have not yet decided," Abbas said.

"Okay, Baba." Reza glanced across the gym at Ardeshir, whose smile faded with his.

Abbas walked along the perimeter of the gym to join Coach Alizad, who also had followed the body language of the conversation. He shook his head before Abbas could even speak. "Your son's a gifted wrestler, Haj' Abbas," he said. "He's pinned everyone in Kermanshah. Everyone should see his talent."

"He's only 13. And still a bit short. He should wait, get stronger," Abbas answered.

"Get stronger? Than who? He's special, Haj' Abbas. Your kids are all good athletes, but Reza—" He slapped his friend on the back. "He has the eye of a tiger."

Abbas paused and then looked directly at his friend. "The eye of the tiger, perhaps, but he still has the mind of a raccoon."

They looked across the gym where Reza had pulled Ardeshir into a headlock and seemed to be biting on his ear.

Coach Alizad pulled a dirty cloth from his pocket and wiped his weathered face. "You know, I bring Ardeshir here on the weekends to train, not for the scenery of the three-hour drive," he said with a smile. "I bring him here to Kermanshah to compete on these bloodied, brutal mats. Here is where we learn. Here is where time makes true *ghahreman*. No one knows this better than you, my *doost-e man*[2]."

Abbas, surveying the mounds of bodies squirming before him, said to no one in particular, "Maybe it is time for Reza to compete at Nationals."

• • • • • •

All morning in the sunlight of her kitchen, Nimtaj had rolled

2 My friend

flour and water for fresh dough. Uncovering the ceramic pot, she pushed a finger on the dough and, approving of its rising, divided the mass into equal-sized balls. She took a ball of the dough and tossed it in the air before spreading it over a cloth-covered paddle. With one hand, she gripped the wooden handle on the backside of the paddle and with her free hand she sprinkled the dough with water. She bent down to slap the dough on the hot interior walls of the well-shaped oven carved into the ground. The layers of rags wrapped around her arms, as well as years of practice, ensured that her hand wouldn't burn on the *tanoor*[3]. Flushed from the heat, her olive skin sparkled as she knelt next to her oven to repeat this motion again and again. By the time her dough covered the last empty space, the first of it had bubbled into flat bread with its alluring aroma filling the entire home.

Her two oldest daughters, Rasha and Mehri, worked alongside her, boiling rice in large copper pots, cleaning the vegetables they had picked from the garden and preparing the meat for stew. With Rasha's husband on frequent business trips, she often joined the family for dinner.

Nimtaj urged her daughters to "hurry" for "They will be hungry when they get home."

"Chashm. We know, we know, " they answered.

Mehri looked to her mother's pregnant belly and swollen feet. "Naneh, you need to sit now. We'll finish from here."

Nimtaj seemed not to hear. "Amir is joining us tonight," she said as she lifted another platter. "I hope he doesn't just ramble on about politics."

"That's all he talks about," Rasha said. "But, here, give me the platter and sit."

Nimtaj set the platter down but only to add another helping of rice. "And I know Reza will be hungry after practice. Each time I see him it seems he's grown taller."

Rasha and Mehri exchanged smiles. "Well, let's not tell him that," Mehri said. She reached for her mother's platter. "Here, let me."

"I hear their voices coming down the alley," she replied as she looked to the thin pastel curtain that blew lightly against the open window.

3 An oven, partially dug into the ground and covered with a hard clay dome.

Nimtaj let go of the platter and allowed Mehri to lift it. Holding the platters steaming with piles of rice and chunks of seasoned lamb, Rasha and Mehri followed Nimtaj into the main room.

As they entered, Soraya smoothed out the wrinkles on the white *sofreh*[4] that she had spread across the Persian rug. She took the platters and set them next to the stack of plates on the *sofreh*, taking care to cover the stain from last night's tomato sauce.

"Farah! Pari!" Rasha called. "Hassan!"

"I'm here!" Hassan said with impatience.

Reza walked in behind Abbas and washed quickly in the well. Hassan bolted to his brother. "Did you get any pins today?" Reza shook his head and looked around. He leaned into Hassan. "I think Baba will let me go to Nationals," he said in a whisper.

Hassan started to let out a yell but Reza covered his mouth. "Shhh. That's why I whispered," Reza said. Hassan nodded.

"I don't want Naneh to know just yet," Reza said. "Especially if Baba is still deciding."

"Naneh will be upset if you cut weight," Hassan said. "And then—"

"What are you two whispering about?" Soraya said in a voice just loud enough to draw attention.

"Stuff girls don't need to know!" Hassan answered. Reza only glared at Soraya and went back to washing his hands.

An evening mountain breeze blew spring through the open windows and stirred the scent of the freshly prepared meal. Amir and Mostafa came into the main room still engaged in intense political discussion. They stood under the picture of Shah that hung in its thin wooden frame.

Mostafa motioned with his chin toward the portrait. "I agree. Fear is not the way to rule. But, how is it you do not recognize his reforms of the White Revolution for the good they bring?"

Amir faced Mostafa. "What good is it when anyone who dares to speak is silenced by a visit from Sav—"

"Enough." Abbas said to his oldest sons as he looked from them to the younger children.

Nimtaj looked at her family. "*Salam*," she said.

"*Salam*," they replied.

Abbas sat at the top of the *sofreh*, Amir as the oldest son sat to

4 A spread or tablecloth placed on top of the Persian Rug for meals.

his right and the rest of the family settled into their places also on floor. Nimtaj served the adults first. Handing the final plate to Pari, she repeated her nightly plea. "Pari, finish your meat and do not fill yourself with rice and bread. You need to get healthy," she said. "And Farah, just take what you need to get full."

"*Chashm,* Naneh," they politely agreed. Pari's chocolate eyes, seeming too large for her pale face, looked at her brothers, who were already engaged in another conversation. With a push of her spoon, she tucked a piece of meat under a mound of rice. But it would be no use. Nimtaj would know.

When Nimtaj looked away, Reza pushed a heap of his food onto Hassan's plate. Proud to be part of Reza's secret, Hassan quickly added Reza's food to his own with a sly smile. Reza leaned his body over his plate, hoping Nimtaj wouldn't notice it was mostly empty. Mostafa caught Reza's eye and glanced at Reza's plate, but didn't call attention to his brothers' plan.

Pleased with her first set of gold bracelets, Soraya pushed her *alangoo*[5] up and down her arm, watching them spin and settle on her delicate wrist.

"Soraya, you've hardly touched a bite. Eat and stop playing," Nimtaj said.

Looking to Reza's plate, Soraya opened her mouth to protest when Reza changed the subject. "Did you finish your book?" Reza asked her.

She tilted her head to the side and narrowed her eyes. "Almost. Why?"

"Just looked interesting. You should read the papers, too." Reza looked to Mostafa, hoping he would begin a political conversation. It worked, and soon Abbas, Amir and Mostafa were debating Shah's politics.

"Shah weakens our economy," Amir said, "when he brings the Americans with their high-tech military equipment and foreign workers." He placed his hands on his knees and sat up a little straighter. "Shah is nothing more than a puppet to the Americans and he uses Iran's oil money to fill his palace with gold and—"

"America's puppet?" Mostafa countered. "There is no proof of that."

Hassan, eager to join the adult conversation, blurted, "Reza

5 Gold bangle bracelets

beat the Americans!" And brought the unwanted attention back to Reza, who again tried to hide his meager pieces of food. Nimtaj glared at Reza's face hovering over his empty plate. She also looked at Hassan's unusually large pile of meat.

"Reza, you must eat more," Nimtaj said. Then she scooped a mound of meat and held it to his plate. "Here. Eat, grow, become a big, strong *ghahreman.*"

He politely rejected the food. "No, no, Naneh." He let out a long, slow breath and closed his eyes. "I'm not hungry tonight."

Everyone understood the meaning behind his words, but Nimtaj felt them.

Women were not allowed at the wrestling matches and Nimtaj would never know the power, strength and skill bestowed to her son. Instead, she suffered the mother's nightmare of watching her child starve.

"Is there something I should know?" she asked.

The pain in her words forced Reza to sit up and pull his hands to his face. "Naneh, it's Nationals," he pleaded. "I could be the champion for the family and seen by everyone in Iran. I—I could—"

"And not eat? And not grow? Wither away like some forgotten berry on a vine? No, I will not have it, Reza. Not again. Wrestle at another weight. Get fatter, not skinnier. You're 13 and you have to grow."

Mostafa glanced toward his father, who in a flicker gave him permission to speak. His gentle tones cradled his mother's fears. "Naneh, he knows what he's doing. He can't compete at a heavier weight. He's too short." He stroked his beard and gave Reza a wink. "I believe he will lose the weight," he said with a smile. "And not wither away. He should compete in Nationals."

She poised her shoulders, looked only at Reza and placed her arm across her protruding belly. "How are you going to lose that much weight and still walk?"

Reza only heard Mostafa and leaned forward with added confidence. "Naneh, it's the Nationals. The Nationals. The best of the best *pahlavan* everywhere in Iran." He waited, searching his mother's face for a sign. Barely above a whisper, he said, "And I want to compete."

Rasha and Mehri set their plates down. Pari crawled into Mehri's lap and buried her cheeks into her chest. Amir rolled his head as if in disbelief such talk actually disrupted his meal. He took a huge bite of lamb, his chewing the only sound in the room. He looked at his family's faces and stopped in mid-bite.

"Naneh" Reza said, slightly above a whisper. "I need to know if I can be a champion."

Nimtaj held the silence and looked directly to her husband. Their eyes met. His face hard, he responded with a single blink. She gently closed her eyes. "Then go," she said.

"I can go?" Reza clenched his fists and shook them in the air. "I can go!" He softened his voice and looked directly at Nimtaj. "Naneh, I will be all right. Really, I will be! I promise." His words flew across the room and Hassan seemed to catch them with his huge smile.

"Reza's going to be our National Champion!" Hassan squealed.

Nimtaj looked calmly to her plate, her dark eyelashes hiding her worried eyes. "*Inshallah.*"

"I'm going to Nationals," Reza whispered, fearing that if he spoke too loud, the words might be grabbed from the air and it would no longer be real.

Nimtaj also whispered, but in a desperate prayer to herself. "God, you gave me nine beautiful children and one, one untamed warrior. You made his heart too big for his chest and his soul too big for Kermanshah."

Amir leaned forward. "Well, no sense in the rest of us wasting food. Reza, pass over that stew you won't be eating."

"Sure," Reza said, and with an illuminated face he passed the bowl of meat with both hands. *I'm going to be a National Champion.*

• • • • •

Leaving his home in the darkness of Sunday morning, Reza ran the four miles to meet Ardeshir instead of taking the bus. Their weekend trainings intensified with only two weeks until the tournament—no time for a bus ride.

The Tagh-e Bostan large rock reliefs, set in the Zagros Mountains, surrendered just enough earth to Kermanshah for its fertile fields and humble dwellings. Streams flowed with the purity of ancient rains to lace around sparse trees and abundant boulders before emptying into the reflecting pool at the base of the mountains' cliffs.

Slowing the last steps of his run to a walk, Reza greeted his friend resting under a tree. "There's a man who lives in that tree and smokes opium all day," Reza said. "And there's a huge snake that's addicted to it and just lies up there, high."

Ardeshir stood and kicked a rock toward Reza. "You lie." He attempted to reach his arms around the tree and give it a shake. Its enormous size dwarfed Ardeshir and its age rivaled that of these Tagh-e Bostan carvings reflecting the era of The Sassanid Empire. Ardeshir stood back and looked up into the thick tangle of branches. Reza half expected the snake to drop onto Ardeshir for an impromptu wrestling match. "It's the snake smoking the opium and the little man who's addicted." Just in case, Reza motioned for Ardeshir to step away.

Early rays of sun melted the mist to expose the ancient carvings presiding over the two young wrestlers. The sacred waters gushed forth from the mountain's cliff, spilled into the reflecting pool and mirrored the chiseled royal faces. Displaying prehistoric horses and riders in full battle armor, two life-sized hunting scenes flanked the reflecting pool.

"Come on, Ardeshir. If we don't get going, we'll be at the top of the mountain in the middle of the day's heat," Reza said.

"Only if you can't keep up."

The wrestlers jogged toward the engraved elephants flushing out the hunted boar from a marshy lake. In full sprint, they paid no respect to the fourth century monument made for the royalty of the Sassanid dynasty. But the eroding king with bow and arrow in hand stood eternally poised. With a frozen face and a chipped eye, he followed the *pahlavan* of his bloodline.

Running on dusty trails interspersed by trees and springs, they ended at a cliff a couple hundred meters[6] high in the mountains. Reza and Ardeshir bent over with their hands on their knees, pulled air into their lungs and watched balls of sweat fall from their faces to dissolve in the dust.

"Keep going?" Ardeshir panted.

"Left's boulders, right's trails, or we can—"

"Go up."

"Up? It's a cliff. Or we can go back down the—"

"Up," Ardeshir said. His breathing returned to normal. "Let's go up and see what's there."

Reza rolled his head, shook his arms and stretched his legs.

6 655 feet

"Climb almost two hundred meters just to see more carvings of kings?"

"Unless you're not strong enough to get up the cliff."

The veil of morning black lifted slightly to give the pinks and oranges and reds of a new day the chance to dance along the slick cliff. Untamed warmth brushed against the bodies of the young warriors as they stood at the bottom and pondered *What if?* Not *What if I fall?* But *What if he sees me as a coward?*

"Okay," Reza said. "I've been there a few times already," he lied. "It's not a big deal."

Smiling, Ardeshir began to claw up the steep face.

Hand over hand, they ascended the side of the cliff. Struggling for footholds and reaching for sturdy rocks, Reza and Ardeshir found themselves a few meters from the top.

Suddenly Reza's fingers slipped, causing a cascade of stones to bounce against the face of the cliff and shatter at the bottom. As he desperately grappled for a hold, his body slid against the jagged face. His feet struggled for a solid ledge, but he couldn't stop his slide. Just as he braced to crash to the ground, Ardeshir grabbed his arm and held him until he found a solid hold.

Now Ardeshir moved up, over to his right and just beyond Reza's reach. Reza attempted to follow, but his shorter arms forced him to go left. With extreme precision, he turned to look at his friend. Parallel, but several meters apart, the two lay flattened against the cliff like paralyzed crosses.

"Now what?" Reza said.

"You said you've come up here before," Ardeshir said, spitting out particles of dirt. "Left or right?"

Reza squeezed his eyes close to blink out the dust. "Up."

A small lizard squirmed out of his cave to sun himself on a rock's ledge. Two more followed, as if to watch the drama unfolding in their sleepy corner of the world.

Reza's fingers felt each rock several times and his bleeding feet, ounce by ounce, put weight on the smallest crag cut into the ledge. Sweat burned his eyes, but he couldn't spare a second to wipe it away. In the corner of his sight, he could make out a blur of Ardeshir's foot. A trickle of Ardeshir's blood mixed with dust and dripped onto the rocks. Reza put his head down to blink out dirt. *Stupid cocky king had to tear out the road.*

Crack! A rock bounced off his head. Ardeshir's body slid

along the face until his leg stopped at Reza's right shoulder. Reza's fingers dug into the side of the mountain and his right hand wrapped around Ardeshir's calf. "I got you," he tried to say but he could only gasp. The sounds of smashing stones made Reza squeeze against the cliff with every fiber in his body.

"Got a root on my right," Ardeshir gasped. "Just hold one more..."

The lizards ran back into their tiny caves. Reza opened his eyes. "Grab it!"

"Almost got—got it."

Ardeshir's weight pushed off Reza and he climbed right, then up, then right, then found the cliff's final ledge and hoisted himself over. Following, Reza pulled himself up. He stretched to touch the final holds, fingertips just caressing the end. *Got to get root.* Pushing his left foot over, he struggled for the hold until the warmth of human flesh grasped his hand and pulled him up. He stood next to Ardeshir on the mountaintop.

Between gasps for air, Ardeshir asked, "Why—the hell—did anyone—want to carve people—way up here? And then—remove the road?"

In shreds, Reza's T-shirt fell open on his glistening body. He tore it off, wiped dirt from his face and tied a strip around his forehead. "Kings," he said and waited for his breath to return. "They always have to be on the top." He looked at the monument. "Farid says this King Darius wanted everyone to see, so he had slaves remove that part of the mountain."

Ardeshir walked over and snapped his index finger against the king's leg. The face, eroded and timeless, bore down on him. "Couldn't have been a good king if he needed all this to feel powerful. He's got his leg on this guy's chest and these guys," he said pointing to the figures cut in stone following Darius, "got their hands tied and rope around their necks. He musta feared them." Without warning, wicked winds swept through a few nearby branches then vanished down the steep cliff.

Taking in the scene for the first time, Reza paused at every detail carved into the mountainside. "Mostafa said when Takhti wrestled the Russian Medved, he didn't shoot his right leg."

"So?"

"Medved's right knee was injured."

"Takhti lost that match," Ardeshir said. "Maybe he shoulda shot the knee."

"Nah. Takhti had honor." Reza looked back to the carvings. "Maybe these kings needed to learn his ways of *pahlavan.*"

Ardeshir picked up a branch and hurled it off the cliff. "Takhti's honor got him murdered by Savak," Ardeshir said. With a grumble, he climbed up the single tallest tree that stood slightly apart from the others.

Walking toward the cliff's edge, Reza took in the spectacular view of the Iranian pink sky bringing dawn into the cradle of civilization. He stretched his limbs and finished brushing off pieces of dirt. "I'm ready for Nationals," he said to no one in particular.

With a quick leap, Ardeshir pounced on Reza. "My fat little friend!" He pulled Reza to the ground and grabbed a fold of his flesh. "Your mother feeds you when you sleep."

"She would if she could. I think she cries every night after dinner." Reza stood and walked toward a cluster of enormous boulders.

"She'll be over it soon. But you, you've got two weeks, chubs. And with a day's bus ride to Tehran for Nationals. You better be forty-two kilos before you get on board, or you'll be dead when you arrive."

Glancing at the rough faces of the stone warriors, he generated a giant spitball and hurled it toward the sky. "There, I'm cut," he grinned.

Ardeshir posed a wrestling stance facing the tree. "You're fat *doost-e man.* You need to wrestle up. Compete with the big boys."

"When have I not made weight? Be glad I'm not heavier to embarrass you in front of everyone on TV," Reza replied.

Ardeshir followed Reza toward the boulders. "Seriously? You think it's going to be on TV?"

Arm and shoulder muscles rippled as he pulled himself up to begin the climb." Yep," Reza said.

Hurling another ball of spit, Ardeshir asked "Who's going to Tehran with you?"

Reza reached the edge of the mountain's cliff, slipped on his first hold, but regrouped and pulled himself across the second rock. "Baba has to stay to run a tournament here, so Mostafa and Hassan."

"Hassan? What's that annoying little rat gonna do?" Ardeshir said. His foot slipped on loose rocks while he struggled for a hold.

"Watch me be a National *ghahreman*," Reza smiled.

The two wrestlers worked their way down the sharp cliffs of the mountain's face. Sometimes, they were forced to climb up, over and then down. Conversation stopped as they concentrated on finding secure holds, rocks that did not slip and crevices without creatures. Finally, they reached the bottom just as the morning reached into afternoon. The rich smells of family gatherings greeted the exhausted wrestlers. Reza held his hand against the burn of his stomach as he took in the scene.

This time of day brought the Iranian families with baskets of food to picnic. Sharing the shade of the small number of trees, the women spread bright rugs. Smoke rose from the burning coals made ready for *samovars*[7] to bring afternoon tea. An old man leaned against the large tree, smoking his *hookah*[8]. Near him, two men played backgammon while small boys swung from a rope tied to the low branch of a tree. European tourist groups snapped photos of the ancient ruins, posing in their bright clothes against the fence surrounding the pools.

Reza listened to them talk, wondering if he could make out any of the American words Jimmy had taught him, but no one ever seemed to say "lamp." Ardeshir showed general disdain for the foreigners.

Noting the narrowing of Ardeshir 's eyes as he spied an American family trying to reach through the fence to touch the water, Reza diverted his attention. "Farid says there's no dirt anywhere in Europe. It's all clean, sparkling clean."

"Farid's an idiot. How can there be no dirt in all of Europe?" Ardeshir kicked a rock, sending it bouncing down the dusty path.

"Kid reads all the time. He says it's all covered in green and trees."

Ardeshir stopped at the part of the path where they went their separate ways. His large body cast a dark shadow over Reza's smaller frame. "Well, dirt or no dirt, we've got Nationals in two weeks. And you're fat."

7 Teapot

8 A vase-like device for smoking tobacco

• • • • •

Later that evening, after Reza endured another guilt-ridden dinner, he helped his siblings unroll their cotton mattresses and spread them onto the floor. The air warmed the room, signaling that soon it would be time to sleep on the roof again.

Reza rolled his mat next to Mostafa and broke the darkness with his fear.

"What if I—I lose?"

Mostafa's voice reflected his slight annoyance. "If you start thinking 'what if I lose,' you've lost."

"But, losing would bring shame."

"Reza, you could do a lot of things. Losing's not the worst," Mostafa said.

"What's worse than losing?" he whispered.

"Defeating yourself."

Reza rolled to his other side, tried to clear his mind of these thoughts and settle in for much-needed sleep. *How can someone defeat himself? He's starting to sound like Baba.* Reza gave his pillow a punch. *There's nothing worse than losing.*

"Rez. Rez." A brave little whisper came from the next mattress. "Are you sleeping?"

"Yeah, fast asleep."

Hassan reached out his small hand. "I know you'll bring home the Championship medal."

Reza searched the black air for the wide, brown eyes. He needed their faith.

• • • • •

The children were sleeping when Nimtaj found her way to her kitchen. Her sure hands carefully selected the best peaches, apples and oranges and hid them in a small ceramic pot under a bush.

Chapter Six

Spring 1976

Hassan's bare feet pounded along the stone paths in his desperate search. With the growing excitement of Nationals, also came a brutal realization. To travel to Tehran by bus, Reza would need to leave Kermanshah a full day before the tournament. That day would be a lost opportunity to train and cut weight, leaving him to arrive weak. A plane to Tehran would take just over an hour, but his family could not afford the plane ticket.

Breathless, Hassan spotted his brother Mostafa squatting in the shade of an ancient tree that grew defiantly among the brick dwellings. Commanding the circle of mostly young men, Mostafa spoke in important tones while drawing numbers in the dirt. Hassan crept behind a low wall to watch his brother and the men who listened.

"But Mostafa, you are too young to remember Mossadegh," said an older man with a deep voice and sad eyes. "He was democratically elected and for two years he challenged the British and American companies to control our own oil."

"Too young, yes," Mostafa said. "But not too stupid. I recognize the 28 Mordad coup removed Mossadegh and brought in Shah, but—"

"But nothing. General Fazlozallah Zahdi rode in on his tank," spat another man, slightly older than Mostafa. "Took out Mossadegh and put in America's puppet, Shah."

Mostafa drew the words "White Revolution" in the dirt. He stood back and let the scratched letters speak for themselves.

Then he cleared his voice. "True, Iranians should choose the fate of Iran. But we must not forget Shah's reforms. He's made good on distributing lands once held by only the clerics to all the people." Mostafa paused and the circle of eyes looked into the red dust. "Can you deny it is right that women should vote, all children go to school and to hospitals?"

Branches above their heads, disturbed by the uneasy breeze, bowed and swayed. A single leaf fell onto Mostafa's shoulder. He brushed it away and it continued its descent into the words drawn in the dirt.

"It is not right Shah removed our *ulama*[1] from important decisions and from our schools. What is to become of our Muslim identity?" said an older man in a traditional turban as he joined the circle. "Shah changed time itself. Two days ago, he changed the ancient calendar of nature's will and forces us to keep time like infidels. It is wicked he does these things."

Mostafa cleared his throat. "I understand some changes are hard. But as a nation we are moving forward, joining the modern world, exceeding expectations." He paused. "Our sisters are no longer expected to marry as young as fifteen."

The young men shifted their sandaled feet uncomfortably. A few mumbled in agreement. One said, "But you see the poor, without even their meager jobs, fill the buses to go to the cities looking for work. How has Shah helped them?"

Hearing "bus," Hassan seemed to remember his errand and burst into the circle. "*Baradar!*[2] Baba says it's too much money to put Reza on a plane! He says he has to get to Nationals on a bus. He can't do that." Silence swallowed Hassan, but he continued. "He's got to fly or he won't make forty-two kilos. He'll be so weak. We gotta get him on a plane, we've got to . . ."

One of the young men stood, leaned against the wall and looked at Mostafa. "You never mentioned Reza's going to Nationals," he said. "Why not tell us?"

Mostafa studied the men in his circle. "It is true. Haj' Abbas thinks he can compete and bring honor to Kermanshah." He allowed the importance of the matter to take hold before he continued.

But Hassan burst out, "Yeah, Rez's gonna be the *ghahreman*! And we need to find a way to get him on a plane."

---

1 Muslim legal scholar

2 Brother

Rashid, a taller man with thick hair, thicker eyebrows and a dark face, rose from his place. "Plane? Oh, isn't he the favored one. Are you hearing this, Mostafa? Put Reza on a plane?" The heavy voice took a puff from his cigarette and blew his smoke at Hassan. "Hassan, go roll a tire before you get hurt."

Mostafa slowly, slowly rose. He looked to Rashid. "Your views of politics have no bearing on my family. We can discuss these things like men or we can behave like children." Mostafa pulled Hassan to his side. "But Hassan here, he has his own cause."

Hassan glanced with fear between his brother and Rashid's equally strong body. The other young men, all standing now, shuffled from foot to foot, preparing either to stop a fight or join in.

Rashid crushed his cigarette under his dirty boot. "Nationals? Good, I hope Reza does get to Nationals. So I can watch him be destroyed on TV. That'll be the best show I've seen so far! The mighty, mighty Abedi's going to Nationals. And on a plane." He paused. He surveyed the surrounding faces to see support or disgust. Who would back him? Who would back Mostafa?

The next moment he had his answer.

The young man standing closest to Mostafa dug his thick hand into his pocket. "Here, Hassan. Your Baba's a good man. I can pitch in ten *toman*[3]."

Another voice, followed by another and another. "Here's some from me, and I'll get more from my cousin tomorrow."

"Take this to Reza."

"I've got two now but I'll be right back with more."

Soon, Hassan's grimy little outstretched hands spilled over with more money then he'd ever seen at one time in his life. And his heart heard promises for more. With his signature gentle strength, Mostafa stood over his youngest brother, holding his shoulders and smiling slightly at Hassan's trembling hands. His face stayed locked on Rashid.

And so it was. Reza would fly on a plane.

• • • • •

There is no way something that huge and heavy will ever fly. Reza wondered if taking the bus wasn't such a bad idea. Abbas gripped Reza's powerful shoulders within his own rough hands and steered him forward. They stepped into the airport's terminal and waited briefly for the family to fall in line.

3 Iranian money

Like all public places in Iran, everyone went about their business to attract no unnecessary attention. Shah's governmental rule was not tyrannical so long as you did what was expected. To stand out, to seem politically rebellious in any way, provoked a visit from the Savak, Shah's secret police, and one may not be seen again. It was best to blend in.

Draped in her loose-fitting *chador*, Nimtaj walked respectfully behind the procession, holding Pari by the hand. Rasha wore a simple, bright head scarf which crisscrossed delicately across her neck. Also in a fashionably bright *roosari*, Mehri attempted to chat with Rasha, but little Farah continually interrupted with questions of her own.

Reza's insides felt like the buzzard in a peacock parade. He tried to keep pace with the mini-posse of friends and family who came to see him off, but his legs pulled lead balloons. He took in the mammoth metal birds that glided onto the black earth. Defying all natural laws known to Reza, they scooped up their passengers and tore into the sky. Already queasy from eating just enough to stay alert, he fell prey to the noxious vapors snaking their way into his gut. He scanned the airport for the best place to puke, when his mother caught his arm. "Reza, you're sick."

"No, no, Naneh. I just—" He tried to steady his voice. "It's all a lot of noise and smells."

"What've you eaten today?" she asked, not expecting an answer.

"Nimtaj," Abbas said. "You know better than to ask that before a match. He eats what he needs and nothing more. Don't worry. He's fine." Abbas looked into Reza's pale face. "Now, there's where you get the plane. See, I bet that one's yours."

Through the murky glass waited an unremarkable silver plane on the airport's single runway. No one in the Abedi family had ever seen the inside of a plane before. Reza wasn't sure he wanted to be the first.

Hassan ran ahead and pressed his face against the glass. "It's gonna go really fast! You're going to see our house from the sky!"

Reza just gave Hassan a blank stare. *I'd rather see our house from our front yard.*

"He'll probably miss it," Soraya said as she adjusted her vibrant red roosari to rest on the back of her hair. Rasha walked over and moved it to the front, whispering, "Soraya, people are looking. Keep your hair covered."

Tight hugs and handshakes. Well wishes and back pats. Soon, Reza climbed up the staircase and into his chariot. "What if I lose?" still loomed as a larger fear than "What if I crash?" So many people had given so much to buy this ticket, to put him on this plane, to fly him to Tehran. *Better to let this plane crash right now than take me to the Nationals to lose and bring shame to my family.* He searched the crowd for his mother; he memorized her face and shot into the air. To Tehran. To Nationals.

From the sky, Reza began to see the world. So much out there. Mountains, more mountains and flat parts in every shade of brown. Ancient structures, rising cities, blue rivers and spots of green.

Reza nodded off, but sharp pains in his gut jolted him awake. He tried looking out the window to take his mind off his gnawing hunger. Tehran crawled up in the monstrous distance in uneven squares of black, brown and grey. He took in buildings and blurs of rushing cars. A popping pain knifed his ears and he held his head. *Are we crashing?*

A stewardess laid her hand on Reza's shoulder. "We're landing now." He looked up and slowly released his ears. She smiled. "Try to yawn and they will pop."

"Thanks," he said and glanced out the window. Scurrying people wove through the streets. *How will Mostafa ever find me?*

Reza took two steps into the busy Tehran terminal and stood perfectly still. Hundreds of people rushed by him, often embracing with family and friends. Most women wore the latest styles, but some still chose to observe *hejab.*

"Reza! Reza! Over here!" came a woman's voice. As promised, his Aunt Banou met him in the terminal. Her stylish dress, uncovered hair and thick gold bracelets sharply contrasted with his family's modest wardrobe.

"*Khaleh*[4] Banou, I'm so glad to see you," Reza said. "I was afraid you wouldn't recognize me." He grabbed his duffle bag and followed her down the bustling corridors.

"Nonsense. You look just like your Baba when he was thirteen. She stopped and looked at Reza. She gave him a second hug. "Except, I think you have your mother's kind eyes."

"*Merci*[5]. I just hope I get taller."

"Good thing for you height isn't a requirement for wrestlers," she said. "But I think you may need to gain weight."

4 Aunt
5 Thank you

"That's what Naneh always says," Reza replied.

They headed into the parking lot and, to his surprise, his aunt got into the driver's seat.

"Where's *amou*?" he asked.

"Your uncle is in Paris on a business trip," she replied. "Your cousins went with him and they were very disappointed to miss you. You should see how they've grown since we visited you for the holiday. Helena is becoming quite the young woman. She and Soraya will have much to discuss."

"Oh, I'm sure Soraya will think she has important news for Helena," Reza said. "And I don't want to be around to hear any of it."

His aunt laughed and continued to point out landmarks as they drove through the city.

Struggling to process all the sights and sounds of Tehran, Reza tuned out his aunt and stared out the window. The buildings were tall and packed together like rocks in a stone wall. It seemed like everyone was in a hurry, although some took time out in a corner café or store. Buses roared past and taxis sped in and out of side streets.

His aunt looked at her nephew. "It's like a lot of big cities, Reza, and a lot like Kermanshah," she said. "But with more of everything."

"I'll say. More noise, more smells, way more people. Do you know where to take me?" Reza asked.

"Of course. It's just a few blocks from my house," she said. "And everybody knows where the training buildings are in Tehran. This is a very big event in the city."

"I didn't need to hear that."

His aunt laughed and turned down the final street. She stopped by the entrance. "*Mo'afagh bashed!*[6]"

"*Merci.*" He grabbed his duffle bag and walked inside the training facilities. "Nationals," Reza whispered to himself.

Like a sticky sunset before a thunderstorm, anxiety and confidence pulsed in the air. Reza scanned the enormous area. Under poster boards tacked to the wall displaying the names of cities and towns, cots were clustered in groups of eight or ten. "The best wrestlers in all of Iran," Reza said to himself. There were a few early arrivals, lying or sitting in their assigned areas. Not rec-

6 Good luck!

ognizing anyone, Reza searched for the section sign "Reserved Kermanshah."

He walked down the main aisle, throwing his shoulders back and trying to hide his anxiety. Finally, he saw his sign and took a cot in the corner. He pushed his bag underneath and perched on its edge. He looked around once more for Ardeshir but figured he would arrive tomorrow by bus with most of the others. There would be no dinner; Reza curled up for much- needed rest.

Each cell in Reza's body starved for just one more nutrient. Bringing menacing power means weighing in at the razor's edge, within a drop of the weight allowed. This is how a wrestler lives, sweat drop by sweat drop. As if robbing from each other, Reza's blood cells bounded and searched for any bit of food ingested that day. *Hichi.* Empty. Sleep proved no match for hunger. Reza stared into the fluorescent lights and combated the fear of a humiliating loss. *I will nail every move, keep my feet, focus.* Promises paraded through his mind until exhaustion overtook him.

He twisted on his cot, moaning and groaning. Visions of drowning and dying and being sucked down deep into the depths of thick cold water rushing, swirling, suffocating. *Just paddle, just stay.* "Ahh!" Reza sprang up from his cot but a dizzy spell forced him to lie down. *I'm okay. I'm okay. Just another nightmare.*

He focused his breathing and noted the time. Ten minutes until weigh-ins. A final pee and splash of water. His tongue, swollen and parched, touched the tip of a drop before Reza clamped his lips closed. He looked back at the clock. *Six minutes.* With shaking legs, he walked toward the weigh-in line. He saw no familiar faces. Razored pains gripped his gut again as he inched his way toward the scales.

The official barely looked at Reza. "Weight class forty-two kilos?"

"*Baleh,* sir."

"Step on."

Reza blew every morsel of air from his tightening lungs and stepped forward.

"Weight forty-four kilos. Disqualified. Next."

"What? No, that's not right. No, I'm not—"

"Disqualified. Next"

"No. It can't be. I have to wrestle. You have to let me weigh in again."

"You can't lose two kilos in forty-five minutes. You're done. Disqualified."

Reza stood to his full, exhausted height. "I will be back in forty-three minutes and I will weigh forty-two kilos." The official hardly nodded.

Reza searched frantically for Mostafa in the gym now teeming with wrestlers, their coaches and a forming crowd.

"Rez! Rez! Mostafa said you look heavy and he—" Hassan had woven through the cluster of sweaty bodies and found his brother.

"Where's Mostafa?" Reza grabbed Hassan's arms and shook his body until his eyes bulged.

Before Hassan could answer, Mostafa stood behind Reza. "Over weight?"

Reza spun around. "Almost two kilos. I've done everything. I haven't eaten, I've peed gallons, and I—"

"Get your gym bag and put on all your clothes." Mostafa stopped a passing wrestler. "Where's the showers?"

"Fourth floor. Stairs through that door," the wrestler said.

"*Merci.*" Mostafa turned back to Reza. "Meet me at the showers." But Reza just stared. "*Ajaleh kon!*[7]"

Wearing layers of clothes, Reza ran up the four flights of stairs and followed the sounds of water. Mostafa had commandeered an empty stall, turned it on to the hottest setting and directed Reza to sit in the fog.

Reza had no energy to voice his questions. *What's he thinking? I'm going to puke. I can't breathe. I can't*— He collapsed in the corner.

Twenty minutes.

Mostafa leaned against a dry shower wall a few feet away, keeping exact time. Looking like a soggy shoe, Hassan stood in the steam next to his brother. His frantic eyes darted from Reza to Mostafa and back to Reza.

Through the shower stalls, Ardeshir's voice bellowed in genuine panic. "Reza! Abedi! Reeezzzaa!"

Mostafa remained still. "Relax, Ardeshir. He's right here."

"He needs to be right on the scales. Do you know he's almost two full kilos over? I knew he was getting fat. I knew it." He spotted Reza through the steam. "Reza! What the hell!? You're a mess. All that water, you must be sixty kilos! Get up!"

Reza gave no response.

---

7 Hurry!

Mostafa checked his watch while Ardeshir moved toward his friend and shouted to Hassan. "Turn off this damn shower!"

Hassan's little hands slipped around the knobs; Mostafa reached around him and shut it off.

"Reza! Reza! Let's go. You've got—" Ardeshir continued. Hassan grabbed one of Reza's wet arms in an attempt to pull him up. Slipping down his slick body, Hassan fell off the end of Reza's hand and landed in a puddle at Mostafa's feet.

Moving his head, Reza showed faint recognition. "Ardeshir?"

"Get your fat ass up!" Ardeshir crouched behind his friend, reached under his arms and pulled him to his feet. Reza's eyes rolled into his head.

Hassan stood up, looked at his brother and fainted into Mostafa's arms.

"Nice going," Ardeshir said. "You've killed them both!"

Mostafa laid Hassan on a dry bench. "They're not dead." He grabbed Reza's arms. "Come on. Help me get him to the scales. We've got three minutes."

The two dragged Reza down the stairs leaving a trail of soaked towels and clothes. Reza arrived at the scales with his underwear clinging to his shivering body.

The official looked up and raised an eyebrow. "Abedi? You have thirty seconds. Step up."

Barely able to move, Reza took two agonizing steps and closed his eyes. Ardeshir held his breath and watched the weights tip.

"Wait. His underwear's wet. Take it off. Dry him. Dry him." Ardeshir called out.

Naked, dry, exhausted, Reza weighed exactly forty-two kilos. He stepped off the scale and collapsed.

The official shook his head. "He can't wrestle," he said. "He can barely stand. Why do you waste our time? This is Nationals. You *shahrestani*[8] come here thinking you'll be somebody and you get humiliated every time."

Reza leaned on Ardeshir for support while Mostafa reminded the official of the many *ghahreman* from Kermanshah. But now it would be up to Reza and he could barely stand.

Hassan, dazed and wet, came over with the schedule. The corners were smudged, but Mostafa determined Reza's first match was in three hours.

8 People who do not live in Tehran

Blinking, Reza tried to bring Mostafa into focus. Mostafa showed him the schedule. Taking the paper in one hand, Reza steadied himself on Hassan.

"Three hours," he said.

Chapter Seven

2008

We agree to discuss the latest draft at a Persian restaurant.

"Tell me about your mom," I ask. "She's becoming a fascinating person for me."

I want to say, "My god, she was a teenager who met her husband for the first time on her wedding day, raised ten children through two major wars without Oprah or MOPS or a Starbucks and yet created a family who would risk their very lives for each other without thinking twice. Who was this woman?"

At first, Reza speaks nonstop in praising his mother and I struggle to write down every word. He stops midsentence. I finish my last notes and glance up. I look into a tear-streaked face transcending time in its sorrow. "I'm so sorry," I say. "I didn't mean to make you cry."

He takes a napkin, wipes his eyes and blows his nose. "I still miss her," Reza says. "I wouldn't be here if it weren't for her."

• • •

Tonight, all I can write about is mothers. Pages and pages and pages. I start with Nimtaj, but soon the universal cord connects me with any creature who has hugged that newborn to her chest.

My pen moves with a life of its own. I write a story my friend told me years ago about his colleague who worked with lab mice. When he took the babies away from the mother, she dashed about her metal cage and scooped up her tail in her tiny hands. She then ran to the corner and set her tail gently down as if it were her baby. "This mother mouse was going insane," he said. "This stupid little mouse."

My pen stops. I find myself wanting to write a poignant sentence encompassing the depth of a mother's love. But I cannot find the words.

Chapter Eight

Spring 1976

Brightly colored wool yarns sat in a mound next to Nimtaj in her main room. She reached for a spool, but another contraction tore through her slight frame. Gripping the loom and holding her side, she worked through deep breaths until her body relaxed. Softly chanting prayers, she focused on weaving her Persian rug. She selected the hand-died green silk yarn to form a knot and cut the surplus fiber with a knife. Another contraction ripped through her body.

"Naneh!" Rasha said rushing to her side. "Naneh. We must go now. You can finish when you come home."

Nimtaj shook her head. "I should've finished this for you a year ago. A rug is the—"

"The soul of the home," Rasha said. "We know, but the baby's coming."

Nimtaj tied another knot.

Mehri and Rasha exchanged glances and Mehri knelt next to her mother. "Naneh, it will be beautiful but it will wait. This baby will not."

"I will know," Nimtaj said. "Now watch this next knot closely. You have yet to learn this—" She stopped and clutched her side.

"What's wrong? Is it the baby?"

"No, it is not the baby. This is not my first," she said. "Now pay attention. You have another knot to learn." Nimtaj wove several yarns and directed Mehri to pull the comb and pack the row of knots as tightly as possible.

Rasha looked over to Soraya, who helped Pari with her studies as Farah bathed in the fountain-well. The usual chatter and laughter of the evening fell silent, leaving only Soraya's strained instructions to be heard. Soraya looked to Rasha. Rasha tried to smile, but worry hung a shawl across her face.

Looking out the window to the grey sky, she tried to judge if it would be the spring rain or the baby that came first. After burying her last baby, she feared damp weather. Both would be coming soon. Once again labor pains ripped through Nimtaj, making her clutch her side.

Rasha rushed to her mother's side. "The baby could be coming early."

"No, not yet." She smiled into her daughter's face, rubbing her belly. "I just hope your brother's eating," she said.

"Reza's fine. Can you think about you? At least the baby?" she said.

Nimtaj squeezed her face through another contraction and returned with a reassuring smile. "I will know."

Seeing Nimtaj would not listen, Rasha looked to Mehri. "Let's finish this row."

"No, no, I can—"

"Naneh. What is it?" Rasha held her mother.

Mehri went to the door. "Soraya. *Zood bosh*!"

• • • • •

Reza's eyes opened and he leaned against the wall in a daze. No one seemed to notice Hassan and Ardeshir struggling to bring Reza to his senses. Ardeshir slapped Reza several times and even hung him from his feet. He looked at the clock. "My match," Ardeshir said. "I have to go prepare."

"What do I do?" Hassan asked. "I wish Baba were here."

"Well, he's not. So, try to get him to—to talk or something. I have to see coach or he'll kill me."

Hassan nodded and Ardeshir took one last look at his dissolving friend before he disappeared into the bodies of the gym. Quietly, carefully, Hassan took out the small bag his mother had given to him. "Here, Rez. I have some apples and pears and some rice. Naneh said to eat the fruit first, though. Here, just try one."

Reza opened his cracked lips and focused on the apple Hassan held. Within minutes, he devoured each piece, in the order Nimtaj had instructed.

With renewed strength, he used Hassan's shoulder to steady himself. "Did Naneh give you anything else?"

"No," Hassan said. "Just that, but you don't look so dead anymore."

"Where's Ardeshir?"

"Over there." Hassan pointed. "After he hung you upside down, he said he had to go warm up."

"I better go show him I don't look so dead, anymore." He gave Hassan a brotherly smack on the back and set out on a jog in perfect tempo around the gym. Spotting Ardeshir, Reza paused, shot his huge smile and waved. Ardeshir stared.

"Smart ass," Ardeshir mumbled.

Jogging around the perimeter of the mats, Reza surveyed the several hundred men cheering, coaching and wrestling. Bodies slammed to the mats, limbs twisted in unnatural positions and faces displayed colors meant for a sunset. Reza pulsed with the energy. The heavyweights lined up and collided like buffalo in a powerful tangle of muscle and bone. Throughout the gym, hands rose in victory and faces fell with defeat.

Stopping near two opponents of his weight class, Reza studied their moves and looked for weakness. His eyes scanned every fiber of every muscle.

Hassan charged up to Reza's side and pointed to the young men on the mat. "You can beat 'em, Rez! They're not even as strong as you! Look, you could pin him right—there. See that Rez? That's a pin for you."

Reza continued to stare at the entwined bodies in front of them. *I don't know about a pin, but maybe I could—*

"Don't let them see you looking worried. Do you want them to sense that fear and crush you?" Mostafa said, startling Reza when he came up.

"Do I look scared? I'm not. I'm as good as these guys. This guy here," he said pointing to an opponent who lay flattened under the sweating body of another young man, "he could do a reversal and he's just lying there."

"Make one mistake, you'll pay," Mostafa said.

"I know."

The clock on the back wall, under the large portrait of Shah, reminded Reza he had one hour until his first match.

• • • • •

The contractions were more frequent and intense. Rasha pleaded with Nimtaj. "Please, Naneh. If the baby's coming early, we must get to the hospital."

Smiling, Nimtaj simply pointed to the ball of beet-red yarn. She separated the two strings and passed the yarn first under them and then between them to form a knot. After a tighten and cut, she repeated the process. "Rasha, this will be beautiful in—" Her soft brown eyes closed through another contraction. For a moment, her daughters witnessed the perfect lines of her face contort and take her to another place. The ancient place of birth and of death. In a flash, her eyes opened and shone again with the beauty of Nimtaj. "I will be okay. Like this rug, we bring the soul of yesterday into tomorrow."

Rasha took her hand and pleaded. "*Baleh,* but please let us take you to the hospital. It's not good for the children to see you like this. It scares them."

Looking through the checkered glass, Nimtaj let a small smile grace her face. "We will go now." She waddled awkwardly to her room and returned in her *chador.* The long, loose-fitting black cloak completely encased her large pregnant belly.

She fought through another contraction. "Soraya, you stay and take care of Farah and Pari. Don't let Pari outside without shoes and a coat and be sure Farah doesn't help herself to the winter nuts." Nimtaj said. "Baba will be home shortly."

Soraya gave a wide-eyed nod.

• • • • •

At the modest hospital, her daughters continually wiped Nimtaj's reddened face while she murmured prayers to bring a healthy life into her world.

A midwife approached them. She smiled and asked, "Another beautiful baby for your family, Nimtaj? Blessings."

Nimtaj tried to answer but was caught by a furious contraction.

"Is this number ten?" the midwife asked.

The darkness moved across Nimtaj's face in remembrance of the baby she had laid into the earth.

"No, this will be our eleventh child. *Inshallah,*" Nimtaj replied in perfect tempo.

"Of course, Nimtaj. Your eleventh perfect, beautiful child. Well, let's bring this baby into the world. *Inshallah.*"

Nimtaj was led by her daughters to a small room at the end of the short hallway.

They placed her carefully on the cotton-stuffed mattress and Rasha lifted Nimtaj's feet onto wooden slats that held her up on either side. It would be anytime now.

• • • • •

As the referee lifted Reza's hand in *piroozi*, a huge smile crossed Reza's face. *I'm going to take Nationals!*

Mostafa nodded thoughtfully, while Hassan stood and cheered. Reza jogged off the mat and prepared for the next opponent.

"He crushed him!" Hassan said. "Rez's gonna win the whole tournament. It took him only one minute to pin him. And his next guy's really weak. I saw him earlier today and I—"

"Slow down," Mostafa said. "It's a long tournament and finals are late tomorrow. Reza might last, but will you?" Mostafa stood and surveyed the matches in the gym. Tomorrow, each weight class would compete one at a time, to the cheers of the crowd here, and those watching on TV at home.

"Who's Reza wrestling next?" Hassan asked, sensing Mostafa's thoughts of victory.

"I think that guy there." He pointed out a small young man, with long arms and stocky legs.

"Have you watched him?"

"He's good."

"Not good enough to beat Reza. He's going to be National Champion!"

"Maybe, Hassan. Maybe."

They moved to the side of the gym where Reza would compete in his next match. A short hour later, Reza matched his skill against another foe.

Moving in a predator's circle around his prey, Reza's fingertips twitched while bare feet scraped the slick surface. His hardened feet grasped for the catches of the rougher, burlap practice tarp. Twice, he almost fell to his back.

Reza sprang at his opponent first and held him by a half-headlock with one arm while his leg hooked the left leg.

"Keep your weight on his head!" Mostafa yelled through cupped hands.

Hassan sprang to his feet. "He's pinning him. He's gonna win!"

Mostafa nodded.

Then Hassan became concerned. "The guy's blue—he's—he's not moving. Did Reza— did he—kill—is he dead?"

Mostafa pulled his young brother to his side. "Ancient Iranian wrestling, in Farsi, is *koshti*[1], which means to—"

"To kill," Hassan said as his eyebrows raised his new realization. "But you really don't still kill people, right?"

He laughed. "No. Now you just score points by looking like you're killing him. So Reza can score by a takedown, escape, reversal, near-fall or a—looks like—a pin. Reza pinned him!"

Reza's hand raised in victory; another huge smile crossed his face as he looked into the camera.

Hassan jumped up and down cheering Reza's name. He followed Mostafa down the bleachers, looking for Ardeshir. "Ardeshir likes to throw his opponents. I've seen him."

Mostafa smiled. "Ardeshir's a strong guy. Better stay on his good side."

"If he has one."

Ardeshir snuck up behind the two and, hearing Hassan, he hunkered down and lowered his voice. "Wrestling is pain," he said as he twisted his face for Hassan's wide eyes. "How much pain the body can survive as bones crush, muscles tear, ligaments snap, skin stretches before it rips off your skull—"

"All right, Ardeshir," Mostafa broke in. "You guys are tough. We get it."

Ardeshir slapped Mostafa on the back. "Oh, we're tough and we're about to be *ghahreman*! Can you handle that? Me and Reza are gonna wrestle tomorrow, on National TV, and we are going to win!"

Hassan stood and craned his neck to search the crowded gym for Reza. Mostafa rubbed his chin.

• • • • •

Rasha pulled her thick black hair into a knot and wiped the sweat rolling down her neck. Something was wrong. The contractions arrived in spastic jerks and too much fluid had been lost. All through the night, Nimtaj floated between screams and unconscious states. Mehri had gone home briefly to check on the family and returned to the hospital.

Her first look at Nimtaj and she flew at Rasha. "What's the doctor said? Are they giving her medicine? Has Naneh slept? Eaten? Has she—?"

Rasha held her finger to her lips and motioned toward Nim-

---

1 To kill

taj. Mehri pulled Rasha into the hallway to get a straight answer. Rasha whispered, "No, they can't give her the medicine or she'll sleep and not push the baby out."

"Why doesn't the doctor turn it? Why's she waiting? Naneh's too weak for this. I saw the blood."

"Shhh. She'll hear you. Stop it now. You're no help. Go back home."

"Rasha? Mehri? Is Reza home?" came a delusional cry from inside the room.

"No, Naneh. Not yet," they answered as they swiftly entered the room and fell into place coaxing and preparing. How much more could her body endure before life—or death—was brought into this world?

• • • • •

Reza had dominated his opponents and qualified to compete in the final National Championship match against the fierce contender Mashadi Aghee. Reza and Ardeshir stood with their strong arms crossed and eyes fixed on him in a warm-up match.

"He's good, Reza," Ardeshir said. "A takedown wrestler. Quick and strong, like a—"

"Like a what? A bear? A tiger? I'll kill him," Reza said.

Silence filled their space.

Ardeshir punched his friend's arm. "Run the mountain."

"You, too."

Reza's confidence had grown with each pin and he knew he was National Champion caliber. He could almost hear the cheers of those watching at home. With the pace of a caged animal, Reza isolated himself in the gym's corner. *No mistakes. Be strong. Be swift. Be patient.* He craned his neck and swung his arms in a circle. *Win Nationals. Make the team. And travel. This is my ticket to see the world. I can't screw this up. Focus. Focus.*

Each weight class had a separate championship match. All eyes watched with the brutal expectation that two warriors would meet and only one would survive. A wrestler wins alone and loses alone. Defeats came with pain, with shame and with no second chances.

Ardeshir's championship match happened just before Reza's. He struggled with his opponent, finding himself behind on points going into the final period. With seconds left, Ardeshir drove his opponent, turned him and pressed his spine into the mat. The wrestler tried to sprawl, but Ardeshir's menacing strength held him. With a double leg lift, he slammed his opponent to his back and had the pin. First Place.

Now pulsing with his own adrenaline, Reza circled his opponent, Mashadi Aghee, to the deafening cheers of the gym. Deep, husky voices raged for the warriors to begin the battle. Mashadi had watched Reza in two previous matches and planned his assault. In seconds, he shot a double leg on Reza forcing Reza to his back. Mashadi scored the points, but Reza could regroup for the second period.

In the crowded bleachers, Hassan buried his face in Mostafa while Ardeshir clenched his fists and shouted commands to Reza. Gripping Mashadi around his left arm, Reza scored points on his fireman carry but he could not finish him for a pin. Mashadi shot a high crotch single leg and lifted Reza up and straight to his back. Arching his back, Reza bridged to keep space between his flesh and the mat. After a long struggle, Reza turned to his belly. Mashadi Aghee dominated Reza, winning 9 to 3. For a moment, Reza feared he could not move, but somehow he rose to his place of defeat.

• • • • •

"One, two, three, push. Push, Nimtaj. One, two, three, puuuuussssshhhh!" Rasha and Mehri said along with the midwife, who also feared the worst.

Every muscle, every cell, every fiber of Nimtaj's being became birth. She craned her neck to see if there was a small, fragile head this time, please this time, but no. Only more blood, only more pain.

"Nimtaj, it's okay. You're almost there. Squeeze this towel," the midwife said. "Here we go, here we go, one more time."

"Ahhhh, ahhhh, noooooo." And then the bodies of two baby girls.

One tiny little blue baby lay weak and bloodied in Rasha's arms and the other the midwife took immediately from the room. Nimtaj rolled to her side and vomited into a bucket Mehri held. She wiped her mouth and called, "Bring my babies."

"The nurse took one, and...here, just take a drink of water."

Nimtaj struggled to straighten her body and held out her arms.

"My baby."

Mehri's voice gurgled in her own nausea and she pressed her body against the wall for support. "Naneh, please, I don't think she—"

Rasha's tear-streaked face looked at the grey infant she held in one arm. She pleaded. "She's too tiny, Naneh. I must to take her to the nurse."

"Rasha. My baby."

Placed in her arms, the small daughter shivered with each difficult breath. Nimtaj worked in sure, quick motions to explore her baby. Rubbing her back and belly with rhythmic strokes, she chanted the ancient prayers to bring life. Please, bring life.

• • • • •

The corner of the torn bus seat poked at Reza's leg. He reached down, ripped off the edge and tossed it onto the littered floor.

"At least Kermanshah took third in Nationals," Hassan said, but with no response from Reza. Hassan returned his stare to the swaying of Mostafa's shoulders directly in front of them. Reza's muscles ached with each bump of the ride. But his crushed spirit bore the most pain.

Although Mostafa had told Reza right after the tournament that he wrestled a good match, Reza's haunted eyes could only relive each painful moment of his defeat. Reza had congratulated Ardeshir, who humbly thanked his friend and then boarded his bus. Now Reza felt the distilled loneliness of the ride home. The only thing he felt more than the need to be home was the dread of actually arriving there. He doubted he would ever wrestle again. All his dreams of making the National Team lay crushed under Mashadi Aghee.

After several silent hours, Hassan again tried to start conversations about the excitement of Tehran or the funny looking people on the bus or what Naneh would cook when they got home. "At least now you can eat whatever you want Rez and now—"

"Hush, Hassan! Just, just stop all your stupid talking."

"Rez, you're not a loser. I know you'll beat him next time, Rez. You'll be the *ghahreman.* Maybe even a *pah—*"

"Shut up. I'm not wrestling him or anyone and I lost and I—"

Waking from his nap, Mostafa reached around to gently grab Hassan's arm and lead him to his lap. Hassan's head rested on Mostafa's scratchy beard and he stared out the dirty window. "I only thought Reza should know he can beat him next time."

Mostafa patted Hassan's arm. "He knows, Hassan. He knows."

• • • • •

The crowded old bus thumped and bumped into Kermanshah just at sunset and only an hour behind schedule. Aching legs and backs departed into the arms of waiting family or grabbed a dusty bag and walked off to the next destination.

With the halting of the bus, Mostafa jerked awake. Some of the other wrestlers from Kermanshah's team, the victorious ones, hurried out to be greeted by cheering family and friends. Reza stared out the soiled window. *I didn't make the National Team. I came home a loser. How can I face Baba?*

Mostafa sat next to Reza and looked out the same, opaque window. Reza turned his face and slowly shook his head. His hurt carried beyond tears, and leaving the bus assured the reality of his loss. Mostafa patted Reza's shoulder, then stood and made his way down the aisle.

I can't believe I lost. He crushed me. He stood up and grabbed his bag. *I hope nobody sees me.* Reza stepped off the bus, planning to evaporate into the night. And in the crowded corner stood his family, holding signs and cheering for Reza. "Reza! Welcome home, Reza!" They applauded as he wobbled down the bus steps.

Reza steadied himself and, despite his proud resolve, the sight of his family made him smile. Abbas was the first to approach his son. "All the way to the championship match!" he said. He moved in to greet his son and whispered, "I noted that last move. We'll practice an escape." Reza nodded and regained bits of the dignity beaten out of him on Tehran's mats.

"Where's Naneh?" Reza asked.

"Waiting for you with piles of meat," Abbas answered.

"And a baby sister!" Farah said. With her pudgy hands, she formed a small circle. "But she's really, really tiny."

"Barely bigger than a sack of potatoes," Pari added.

The Abedis trudged home in the modest parade of a proud family. Farah looked to Reza with her round face and announced she had told little Pari that surely Reza would be dead. Pari's soft brown eyes swelled in tears under her black curls as she reported she feared that Hassan was dead and maybe Mostafa, too. She coughed out sobs as Reza tried unsuccessfully to reassure her that he would never die in a wrestling match, at least not in the way they were thinking. Pari soon lost all interest in the wrestling part and wanted to know if Reza's airplane could go to the moon and stars if it wanted to, like Hassan said.

"Nah, it's nothing like that," Reza said. "It's loud and it makes your stomach into soup."

"Could you touch the clouds? Could you touch the sky?" she asked.

"Nah—I mean—yes, but don't tell anyone." He leaned into their wide-eyed faces and whispered, "I touched a cloud." He smiled. "And the sky. And I wanted to bring a puff of the clouds home, but the cloud fairies came and took it back so you can see the clouds in the sky tomorrow."

"Oh, that's good they put it back. I like clouds." Their voices chirped and sputtered, lost in their world of fairies.

Moving in next to Reza, Soraya tossed her hair and removed her *roosari*. "Oh, please. A puff of cloud."

"Put that back on. Baba will give you the look." Reza said, swiping her bright green scarf and attempting to tie it in a knot on her head.

"Stop, Reza," she said, taking it off. "You don't know what it's like to cover your hair all the time." She placed the scarf back on her hair. "Half the girls at my school don't even have to observe *hejab*."

Reza looked into her face and tried to read why she was so upset. *It's just a scarf.* "Well, Baba says you have to," he said. "Maybe Naneh should wrap her *chador* around you until you learn!"

Surprised a beautiful face could shoot such a dirty look, Reza actually took a step to the side. "Come on, Soraya, I was just kidding. You look—look nice in your *roosari*."

A single tear rolled down her cheek. She wiped it away and joined her sisters.

A few brave stars punctured the sapphire sky in the piece of time where each day ends before night begins. The fullness of the fresh moon matched the satisfaction as the family approached their home.

Reza scurried ahead and burst through the door, through the courtyard and into the main room. His mother rested against the wall, cushioned by large square pillows. Locks of her midnight hair dropped in spoonfuls atop her shoulders. Seeing Reza, she straightened her back a bit.

"*Salam*, Naneh," Reza said and then he hung his head. "I lost."

"I know," she said, but her face illuminated with promise. "It wasn't your time."

Reza paused for a moment and then sat by her side. She reached her arms to him with the little bundle. "Meet your baby sister Mariam," she said. "Here, hold her." A tiny pink face, bundled in a hand-woven blanket, peeked at Reza.

Reza approached the tiny bundle with the gentle moves of a deer. The powerful hands that only hours earlier focused to crush life now lifted his baby sister to his chest. "I will always keep you safe," he whispered. She began to whimper. He held her tighter to his chest. *Please don't cry.* "Why is she doing that?"

"Just hold her tight so she knows you're there," Nimtaj smiled. "And she'll know she's safe."

Reza gave his baby sister a small hug and handed her back to Nimtaj. He looked around his home, as if seeing it for the first time. "I wanted to come home a champion," he whispered.

"Maybe you did."

The rest of the family entered the home, greeted Nimtaj and set into motion for a special evening meal. Hassan, still stinging from Reza's unusual anger, seemed lost between the little kids, the older kids and the cold shoulder from his best friend.

Nimtaj reached softly to touch Reza's arm. "Is your brother okay?"

"Hassan? He's fine."

"I'm not so sure." She motioned toward Hassan, who sat near the fountain-well and moved a small stone under his foot.

"What? Is he mad that I lost? I'm sure he's worried he'll be teased at school tomorrow. He's worried—" Reza babbled with his own fears.

"No, that's not his worry."

"No? Then I don't know. He's probably tired. That bus ride's awful."

"He's not just tired," Nimtaj said as she stood up and moved with slow steps toward the kitchen. "It's not the bus ride."

Mehri laid out a bright *sofreh* on top of the Persian rug and hurried to set out the steaming ceramic platters and woven baskets of bread and apples. Setting baby Mariam on a warm blanket in her basket, Rasha assisted Mehri, all the while trying to convince Nimtaj to "sit down and rest a minute." It was no use. Nimtaj had her family and nothing would stop her from preparing this feast.

Hassan went into the back through the alley and Reza followed. Reza touched his arm. "I'm glad you were there."

Hassan stumbled with what to say. "I'm sorry you lost, Rez."

"Me, too." Reza paused to see if anyone else was close enough to be listening. "But I have to tell you a secret you can never tell anyone."

"What? I won't ever tell. What?"

Reza paused again and then cleared his throat to take his secret to a whisper.

"I saw—I saw Mashadi Aghee's eyes—but they weren't eyes, they were—"

"Weren't eyes?"

"No. They were—"

"Were what?"

"They were—pure red. Like fire!"

Hassan tilted his head slightly, wondering if this were a joke. Reza's face held no humor. He continued with a greater sense of importance. "I looked into his eyes, and you had to be close to see 'em. But, brother, they were a demon's eyes!"

"*Shayton*[2]'s eyes?"

"*Baleh.* The devil came to wrestle me, Hassan. But you can't tell anyone. Never. You hear me?"

"I will never, ever tell anyone." Hassan swelled in the importance of the secret that Reza trusted only to him. "Wow, you wrestled the devil."

The two brothers entered the warm, lively home. The complete family sat comfortably on the rug, passed the bowls, broke the bread and shared their stories. The older men dominated the conversation, but now and then Reza added some choice bits of discussion. Even though he didn't talk at dinner, Hassan ate with a noticeable sense of satisfaction and Nimtaj caught Reza's eye with a smile.

Reza pulled the mattresses onto the roof while Hassan grabbed their woven blankets. The brothers then lay under the salted sky. Hassan, still weary from the excitement of the adventure, struggled with sleep. But sleep won.

Wrestling with his visions of humiliation, Reza dreaded both dreams and consciousness. Although he felt no shame from friends or family, he could not stop the hurt. Nearby, his name

2 The devil or evil one

was voiced into the night and he searched the darkness for the familiar face.

"Farid?" Reza propped up on one elbow, scanning the rooftop for his cousin. "Shhh, don't wake Hassan. He'll never stop talking."

Farid's scrawny arms pulled him onto the rooftop. "Don't I know it." He sat next to Reza. "Saw you on TV."

Reza looked hard at his cousin.

Farid continued. "Except for that last part, you looked good." He scanned his notebook in the darkness. "Can't believe you weighed forty-two kilos. You must've been dead."

"I don't even remember half the stuff that happened," he sighed, "except for that last part." Reza rolled his shoulders and stared at his hands, wondering how everything could have failed him so quickly, so completely.

Farid held a few moments of the silence. "Remember when Muhammad Ali and Frazier battled the third time?"

"The Thrilla in Manila? Course I remember. Frazier got crushed." Reza looked into the night. "Like me."

"No, he really didn't. Frazier's trainer made him quit. Trainer said Frazier was near death, couldn't even see anymore, so he wouldn't let him go the last round. Frazier begged to fight, even beaten and blind, but he was . . ." Farid searched for just the right words. "He was sentenced to shame when denied his right to finish his battle."

"I'm in no mood for your riddles. Muhammad Ali is the champion of the world because he beat Frazier to a bloody pulp. Just like I was beaten."

"No, not like you. Not like you. That's my point. You battled. But Frazier's dead now. Not dead-and-buried dead. But dead to himself. Dead to the world. I read that he just sits in the dark and watches his old boxing matches on TV." Farid turned to face Reza. "When the trainer stopped the fight, Frazier's life was spared but his soul was imprisoned."

Taking a long, slow breath, Reza looked up into his timeless sky. "Then his trainer does not know the ways of *pahlavan*."

"But you do."

Lying on his back, Reza pulled his blanket to his chin and let warm tears have their way down his face. He wiped a trail of snot from chin and tried to sob in silence. Farid lay next to his cousin, giving him space to grieve.

Reza's voice cracked into the endless darkness. "I didn't make the National Team."

"I know."

"I wanted to see Europe. That was my only chance."

"No, Reza. That was your first chance."

Chapter Nine

January 1978

An uneasiness crept on its belly down the frozen mountains, up the icy rivers and across the barren fields. It swept into homes, snuck into schools and slunk about the gym. It skirted along the outside, waited in the corners and watched from the rafters. Like a ghost, it begged to have a body and searched to steal a soul.

But Reza did not notice. Instead, he stood in front of the locker room mirror and patted his washboard stomach. In the two years that had passed since Reza lost his Nationals match to Mashida Aghee, he recommitted himself to even more grueling training. His fifteen-year-old physique, although barely reaching the height of Abbas at 168 centimeters, reflected the muscular build of an elite athlete. His thick mass of black hair stuck out in a mismatch as if it couldn't decide whether it wanted to be straight or curly. Across his chiseled jaw lay the landscape of dark sprouting whiskers. Only his dazzling grin, which now caused his impish eyes to squint and his forehead to wrinkle like a cloth, remained from his boyish days of falling from rooftops.

Reza walked back into the gym, where the wrestlers engaged in routine warm-up matches while Abbas shouted commands.

"That is good," Abbas said to the wrestlers. "You may take a two-minute break." The wrestlers jogged over to the water cooler and Reza joined them. He kept a steady gaze on his father, wondering why he hadn't yelled for him.

Standing to the side, Abbas rubbed his rough beard as he

counted the wrestlers who missed the day's practice and looked once more to the door. Seeming to absorb the wrestlers' hallowed blows, Shah's portrait hung slightly crooked below the winter-frosted windows.

From behind Abbas, one of those missing wrestlers touched his elbow. "My pardon, Haj' Abbas. I have been absent." The wrestler shot out both his swollen hands to grasp Abbas's. He repeated, "Haj' Abbas, again, my apologies."

"You need to be here. You're one of our best wrestlers," Abbas said. He touched the wrestler on alternating cheeks and held his hands. "Why have you been gone?"

When the wrestler looked to his feet, Abbas noticed a discolored lump on his head. "Kaveh. Have you been fighting? How did you get this large lump? And your hands—"

Touching his head, Kaveh fought tears. "My family, we've been so many days without flour, no meat for my brothers . . ."

"Why didn't you ask—"

"You have been so generous to my family and to so many families here. I know you have your family and . . ." Sobbing finished his sentence.

Abbas put his arm around Kaveh and led him to the back of the gym. "Tell me what happened."

Leaning against the wall, Kaveh wiped his dark eyes. "You know of the article in the Ettela'at newspaper? The one that said . . ." He paused and leaned in closer to Abbas. "Said that—he—is of Indian descent, indulges in wine and those other awful rumors? The ones I cannot speak."

"I am aware of the article, *baleh*." Abbas crossed his arms and tilted his head. "How does that affect you?"

Two tears dripped off Kaveh's chin. "I heard that in Qom there would be demonstrations. So I went yesterday. I thought, if there was enough confusion, I would have a chance to break into a store—to get food. I've never stolen anything before, Haj' Abbas. Please don't think I'm wicked. We've been so hungry and . . ."

Abbas reached his hand to Kaveh's shoulder. "I do not think you are wicked."

Kaveh closed his eyes.

"What did you see?"

"Thousands of people gathered there, mostly students just a little older than me. First, it was peaceful. People were chanting and screaming for Shah to retract what was said. His police were everywhere. Then there were pushes and clubs—even the women they beat—then some men bared their chests toward the police and dropped to their knees. I heard the guns—the bullets—the blood—" Kaveh pushed his body into Abbas's chest and trembled. Every sound in the gym stopped. Only his sobs filled the space.

Looking to the frightened faces staring at them, Abbas commanded, "Finish your workouts and go right home. Go home to your families!"

• • • • •

Later that night, Abbas brought Hassan and Reza to the yard. "I want you to be careful about who you talk to and who you are seen with," he said.

"Baba, did Kaveh tell you this? He went to Qom." Reza checked his father's expression to see if he could continue. "That's not going to happen here. And if it does, I'm fifteen. I can handle myself."

"Reza, this is serious. You must be more careful. And you," Abbas said turning to Hassan, "you will stay closer to home."

The weight of their father's words began to take hold. Reza squinted his eyes and studied the lines of his father's face.

Hassan pressed his father. "But, Baba, I go to see my cousins. They're family. How can we not trust family?" He pushed his shoe into the snow.

"Hassan! There are things you don't understand, so I will understand them for you. Go to school, wait for your sisters and then come straight home." The harsh edge in Abbas's voice widened Hassan's eyes, and Reza shifted his feet. Hassan dug his shoe further into the grey snow and made a small cave.

"Baba," Reza asked in a quiet tone. "Can I still—go to English school?"

After months of their quiet self-sacrificing, Abbas had enough money to pay for the exclusive after-school English class. Reza never directly asked to go, but he welcomed the rare opportunity to increase his chances to be accepted into the university and to travel.

Baba hesitated but couldn't escape Reza's insistent stare. "For now. But be alert. You can't wrestle a bullet."

"A bullet?" they chimed. Hassan brought his hands behind his back and pushed his snow cave with a toe. But Reza took a step toward his father.

"Really, Baba?" He waited for his father to retract his statement. "Shah's police will shoot us in Kermanshah?"

Their father nodded. "And now you will listen to the BBC[1] with me," he said. "It is time you know."

"Know what?" Reza said, not expecting an answer. He looked into his father's face but Abbas looked away.

Beloved stars hid behind night's dark canvas where grey clouds filtered the glow of a full moon. Reza watched his father, stooping with a heavy walk, trudge through the dirty snow back into the house.

"What's such a big deal about the BBC?" Hassan asked.

"I'll have to ask Farid to be sure," Reza said as he rubbed his biceps, reassuring himself of his strength, "but since the news from the BBC comes from Britain, it's not just what Shah wants us to hear." *So, what does Shah not want us to hear?* He turned to his brother and placed his hands on his shoulders. "You come right home after school."

• • • • •

With constant glances to the door, Nimtaj sang her prayers and prepared her family's meal. Her *chador* hung slanted off her slender hip and her hands moved with a robotic sureness, chopping and slicing. Her hair bounced and swayed as she scurried about her kitchen. Any sound suggesting footsteps or children's voices made her stop. Another glance at the door. Silence. With a mother's imploring voice, she filled the space with her prayers, soft and low.

"Hassan, Farah, Soraya and Pari coming home from school yet?" little Mariam asked as she followed her mom.

"One more hour, *azizam*[2]. We'll get the blanket warmed up for their chilly toes." She knelt under the *khorsi*[3] and felt the heat from crackling embers. "I think there'll be more snow tonight."

Mariam stood on tiptoe to peer over the *khorsi* and look directly into her mother's face. "Reza coming, too?"

"*Baleh*, but—later."

1 British Broadcast Company radio station broadcast from Britain and not censored by Iran

2 Sweet heart or dear

3 A low square table-stove used to heat blankets to be placed over legs.

Mariam froze at her mother's voice catching on the word "later." But Nimtaj continued. "Come. Let's spread the blanket."

Nimtaj bent carefully and placed her last pieces of coal into the brazier under the small, square *khorsi*. Feeling the heat with her palm, Nimtaj nodded. They laid the thick blanket on top of the centered *khorsi*, and soon the warmth spread through the wool.

"I hear them!" Mariam said.

Her mother answered by singing a quiet prayer.

The four children entered, peeled off their wet coats and handed them to Nimtaj, who spread them near the stove. Mariam brought them their nightshirts in a heap she struggled to see over.

One by one, they stuffed their legs under the warming wool and snacked on bread and cheese. Mariam cuddled with them until her insistent chatter made them banish her to "go play."

Quietly, Mostafa snuck in through the back. He stood a minute to enjoy the sight of his siblings huddled under the blanket, savoring their snack. Taking two small steps toward them, he leaped and then landed on his siblings with a thud.

Nimtaj screamed, dropped her basket of fruit and pretended to come at Mostafa with a wooden spoon. When her children's giggles subsided, she looked at Mostafa. "Really, you can't do that to me anymore. It's—I just worry so much now."

"When have you not worried?" Mostafa asked as he rolled off the pile.

She shook her head and went back to the kitchen. She returned with her *samovar* and poured two cups of piping hot *chai*[4]. "Mostafa!" she cried out. "What happened to you? Those bruises on your hands and face—is that—what happened to your ear?"

Mostafa took his favorite tea and smiled. "See, again you worry." He looked to his siblings with a grin. "I got into a fight with some of the big kids at school today."

Hassan sprang from his spot to get a closer look. "You don't go to school! Who did you fight with? Wow! That's a big one there. Do you have more?"

"Hassan! Don't ask your brother these things. Go finish your homework." Nimtaj let out a long slow breath and then took a sip of her chai. "Did you bring us more news? More awful pictures

4 Tea

and more talk of burning and chanting and shooting the young people in the streets?"

"Well, this time the violence erupted in Tabriz and hundreds were killed." He touched the dried blood on his ear but quickly removed his hand when he saw the sadness in his mother's face. "I'm sorry, Naneh. It is bad news I bring."

"Is it Savak? It seems every man I pass looks like he could be one of them."

"I don't think it's that bad, yet. It's mostly the uniformed police. When will Baba be—I think I hear him."

Mariam rushed to the door to greet Abbas. He shook the snow from his boots and patted her head. He embraced his son and exchanged two touches on alternating cheeks. Then, he noticed his wounds. "You were in the streets yesterday."

"*Baleh,* Baba," Mostafa answered, bringing his eyes humbly to the floor.

Nimtaj pulled off Abbas's wet, tattered coat and shook off the last bits of snow.

Abbas blew into his hands. "It was bad?"

"*Baleh,* it was bad. There were many cities burning yesterday and many students ..." He lowered his voice. "Shot."

Nimtaj froze in the midst of hanging up the coat. She shook her head. "When will they stop? Tabriz is such a beautiful city. I pray for it to stay that way, *inshallah.*" She left the two and softly chanted her prayers.

Mostafa joined Abbas on the rug, at the opposite end from the kids. He waited for his father to have a few sips of chai. He made his voice low. "Baba," he said, "the students are showing no fear of Shah's forces, not even Savak. They want change."

"At such a cost as this? I fear that *Ayatollah*[5] is not being very honest with our people. We are fighting and burning and yelling." Abbas took a sip and continued. "But when all the smoke is gone, the dead bodies cleared from our streets, how will Iran be any stronger?"

"Many are saying these things. Ayatollah Kazem Shariatmadari is a strong voice for a peaceful discussion about government." Mostafa touched the side of his head. "I guess some didn't get the message."

---

5 Title for high-ranking religious leader in Shi'ite Islam, similar to a Catholic bishop.

Pressing a cloth soaked in herbs to Mostafa's mangled ear, Nimtaj spoke in quiet, measured tones. "I fear for our children, Haji Abbas. What kind of life will they lead? I had such hopes for Shah's reforms—for our girls to finish school."

"The Iranian people, we're strong. And the West won't let us fall into chaos," Abbas said.

The siblings fell quiet, trying to overhear. Nimtaj looked to them. "You'll finish your studies later. Come, let's prepare for our meal."

Soraya's long, slender arms smoothed out their brightest *sofreh* and Nimtaj set her steaming platters in the center. Each time Mostafa took a bite, Nimtaj heaped another helping onto his plate. "Naneh, I won't be able to fit out the door," he said, followed by the laughter of the kids.

"Good!" she replied. "Then you should stay here and not go out into the madness."

While Nimtaj and the girls brought the dishes to wash in the fountain-well, Abbas turned on the TV. The single, state-run channel showed alternating pictures of the Iranian flag, Shah and other dignified government officials.

"Is everyone mad at Shah," Hassan asked, "because he doesn't give us our share of the oil money?"

"Hassan! Where did you hear such talk?" Abbas said.

"School. That's what some of the kids say. Even some teachers say there's going to be a change. I hear them talking in the halls."

"Well, those teachers," Mostafa said, "better be careful what they're saying. There's still a lot to be decided." Then he spoke in a serious tone. "Did Baba tell you to come right home?" Hassan nodded. "And only tell *me* those things you hear at school, okay?"

Hassan looked to the floor. "I will. And I do come right home."

"Good, and where's Reza?" Mostafa asked, looking to his father.

Abbas glanced at the clock. "Usually he's home by now. Sometimes, he's a little late. But no one is going to mess with Reza." He stood, looked at the door and rubbed his eyes with his fingertips. "Here, Nimtaj has tea and *khorma*[6]. Let's go talk these things out." Abbas headed toward the kitchen.

Mostafa had slipped back out into the night before the family even noticed he was gone.

---

6 Dates

• • • • •

Waiting until all the other students left in their warm cars, Reza set out on his humble trek on foot. Knowing the financial strain his family endured to pay for the class, he never asked for additional money for a bus. He just walked the three miles home. Tonight, he mumbled the English words he had just learned, trying to forget the biting cold.

He never saw them coming.

"Stop! What are you doing out so late? And what are you saying? Foreign words?" Two men in black trench coats blasted flashlights into Reza's path.

"What? I'm Reza. Reza Abedi and I are walking home from school. I'm only two blocks from home. I live—"

The taller man stepped into his path. "School? That's a lie! School ended many hours ago. Where are you really coming from?" Stale cigarette breath cut through the crisp winter night and burned Reza's eyes.

Reza took a step back. "No, no really. It's a school. A school after regular school, where you learn Eng—learn more studies."

"Those schools are for the rich kids, with cars and boots. You're nothing. We'll ask you one more time before we take you in for real questioning. Where are you coming from?"

Reza took a step back. *Take you in for real questioning?* He tried to speak, but he couldn't think of what they wanted him to say.

"Well? You have no answer! I heard those foreign words. You're a spy! Huh? You're making plans to kill Shah. That's your late errand!"

Shuddering, Reza heard his voice say, "No, no, I'm no spy. Here, look at my books. My name—it's here—my name at the top. It's all schoolwork. It's all—"

The men dumped his papers and schoolbooks into the falling snow. Reza's heart melted as his diligent work dissolved under the harsh beams of the light. Books ruined, papers soaked, expensive supplies all gone.

A large, powerful hand gripped Reza's bicep. "I don't believe you. You're coming with us. Turn around. Let's go."

When Reza struggled, the taller man twisted Reza's other arm behind his back and pushed him down the darkened path. Stumbling, Reza tried planting his feet on the slushy ground. Feeling the cold metal of a gun pressed into his side, he begged for his words not to fail him again. "No, no, I'm telling you the truth. I'm telling you—"

No one heard the other footsteps. "Good evening. Is there a problem?"

The taller man turned his head just enough to face the stranger. "There might be, but it's none of your affair."

"You are holding my *baradar*. This is my affair."

Reza squeezed his eyes closed. *Mostafa.*

The men glanced at each other.

Mostafa's steady voice continued. "I am sure his crime is something we can discuss between us—here."

Tightening their grip on Reza, they slowly turned around. Reza watched snowflakes fall from the blackened sky and stick to the mangled flesh of his brother's ear. The officer took a long drag from his cigarette and tossed the orange butt onto Reza's book.

Sensing their hesitation, Mostafa persisted. "My friends, my young brother Reza here, he is sometimes ignorant, and he makes mistakes. Please, let me—compensate you for his mistakes."

Shifting his boots, the tall officer released the only sound in the night: the soft, crunching snow. Reza tightened his body and slightly bent his knees. Slowly, slowly, they released Reza's arms. In a swift, practiced motion Mostafa pressed precisely the correct amount of *toman* into the tall officer's hand.

Reza looked desperately at his brother and then toward his schoolwork scattered in the snow.

His gaze not leaving the inevitable black steel weapons at the men's sides, Mostafa motioned to Reza. "Get your books and let's go home."

Grateful for the command, Reza knelt in the snow and shook the flakes from the soggy materials. The officers quietly walked off into the night.

"Reza, get up. You must get up. We have to go." Mostafa pulled Reza upright and grabbed both shoulders. "Look at me. Get whatever you can, right now, and let's go. *Zood bosh!*"

Reza tried to speak through the full realization of what could have actually happened. He choked out his words. "My books, the expensive books, and my papers, and all my—"

"I know, but Savak always comes back."

• • • • •

The next day, fear touched each of Reza's steps as he walked to Kazazi high school with Farid and Hassan. Talking about girls, wrestling and some politics usually dominated Reza's and Farid's conversation, but today Reza spoke little. So Farid started talking about Reza's favorite topic: going to Europe. Hassan listened nervously and occasionally popped in with "How are you going to get there?" Or "It's so much money to get there." or "Why do you want to go there? I forgot."

Farid ignored Hassan, but Reza addressed his little brother's concerns. "It's just different in Europe."

"You don't know that. It could be a lie, like Amir says," Hassan said.

"Oh, Amir doesn't know," answered Farid. "He should read more before he says these things."

Reza continued, wearing his blank stare. "Well, Mr. Mehdian knows, because he's been there."

"Well, Mr. Mehdian could be lying, too," Hassan said, "to make you dream about going, even though he knows you don't have money."

"Why would he do that?" Farid said, cracking his notebook on top of Hassan's head.

"Teachers do that to us because they hate us," Hassan replied with absolute certainty.

Reza shook his head as they drew close to Kazazi. His sisters had been several steps behind and Reza waved them to the girls' school. He glanced around, adopting the anxiety of his town, and lowered his voice. "Mr. Mehdian's different. He treats his students like humans. We ask questions and he talks to us, not like we're idiots but like we can think." Walking toward the school, he added, "That's why they made him department head."

Reza looked around for his favorite teacher. The tall, thin man with pleasant eyes, who often spent his office time with Reza, fielding his spray of questions about leaving Iran. "How can you get a job? Do you miss your family? What's the cheapest way to get there? Can you go to any university?" And Mr. Mehdian always had time and answers for Reza and any other brave student who would sit in the office, which smelled of crowded books, sketchpads and paper piles. With no sign of Mr. Mehdian, Reza followed Farid to class.

But last night's events haunted Reza and he couldn't concentrate. He asked his teacher if he could use the restroom and bolted to Mr. Mehdian's office where he unloaded the events of prior evening.

"I see," Mr. Mehdian replied, pushing his wire rim glasses to the top of his thin nose. "Mostafa is a good man."

"*Baleh*, we're so lucky. With his dark beard and the way he looks at people, he just gets them to do whatever he wants. I think he saved my life. I should have listened to Baba. I . . ." Reza looked at his feet in shame.

Mr. Mehdian caught Reza's glance and redirected his disgrace. "What happened to you last night was not your fault. You have to believe that. Things are going crazy in every direction right now. And it's bound to get worse."

Reza lifted his eyes to read the teacher's. *Worse?*

A small group of teachers walked by the tiny office, peered in and walked on. Mr. Mehdian stood up, closed the door and turned the key.

Mr. Mehdian leaned in close to Reza and lowered his voice. "The lines of right seem to be disappearing. The perception of corruption is catching up with Shah and the people are tired that so few have so much and so many have so little. We are not willing to give Shah's reforms time to take hold, it seems."

Hearing footsteps, Reza held his breath. The footsteps came to the door, stopped and walked quickly away.

"Why?" Reza whispered. "Why's everyone going mad?"

Mr. Mehdian considered how to answer the question on every reasonable Iranian's mind. "Why indeed," he said. "When were you born?"

"February 1963."

"Well, think of Shah's Iran as your rebellious twin sister. In 1963, Shah proposed a plan of liberal reforms, including voting and other rights for women. He modernized atomic power plants, increased oil production, added 8,000 steel mills, created education and health programs to include the previously forgotten families like yours and mine."

Reza leaned forward. "The White Revolution, but those are good things, right?"

"They are," the teacher nodded. "But too many people see him as a corrupt puppet for the West. Persia is a proud culture of thousands of years and we don't welcome foreign governments taking—"

Hearing footsteps, they both stared at the door handle. The pause was longer this time but echoing steps went quickly down the hall.

Reza shifted in his wooden chair.

The teacher continued. "Shah seems to be a bit naive and forgot that some adolescents rebel against control they don't understand." Mr. Median smiled and Reza cautiously replied with a grin.

"Control never seems like a good thing," Reza said. He kept an eye on the door.

"That's very insightful," his teacher said. "And to add to Shah's problems, his regulation created inflation, which didn't seem right to the merchants or the new middle class. And then he really upset some people when he changed the calendar. Going from the Islamic calendar to the new secular calendar, that was more significant than a lot of people realize."

"I remember Mostafa talking about that. He said Savak murdered the cleric who spoke against Shah changing the calendar."

"He may be right about that. You don't want to be on the wrong side of Savak."

The dark shadow crossed Reza's face. "I know."

The teacher leaned over and patted Reza's knee. "You're fine, Reza. These riots, these demonstrations and shootings in our streets, it's like an adolescent rebellion, just on a really big scale. Historically, youth often think they should have more freedom and more rights and more money, but they don't think through why or how. They just want more and they want it now."

"Like the American hippies you showed us in *Life* magazine? The ones with weird names and face paint?"

"More like the ones who were marching in the streets with Dr. King. But we could be moving in a different direction for we have the issue of another, very significant man in Iran's past."

Reza leaned forward. "I think I know who you mean. Mostafa showed me these grainy photos of an Ayatollah. His name was something with a Kh—"

"Khomeini," the teacher finished his sentence. "The mystery Ayatollah's name is Khomeini. Most Iranians don't even remember him, but he and Shah had major differences. Shah finally had him arrested in 1963 and hundreds were killed for protesting his arrest."

"But those people support Khomeini and say he's going to share Iran's oil profits with everyone."

Mr. Mehdian leaned back in his chair and studied Reza for a moment. Reza got the same feeling he usually got when his father was about to tell him something that he probably wouldn't understand. As Mr. Mehdian took a long, slow breath, Reza tried to focus.

"I realize that many people and even many intellects support Khomeini," Mr. Mehdian said. "But I have read his lectures on the *Vali-ye Faquih*[7], and he very clearly asserts that only the *ulamas* and *ayatollahs* should rule under a strict Shia Islamic law. Even a Shah must submit."

Reza hesitated, slightly ashamed of his failure to fully grasp what his teacher had just told him. "And, that would be different from Shah's White Revolution?"

His teacher gave him a smile. "Very different. For you have to remember that—"

Fast footsteps, insistent pounding and the click, click of someone trying to open the door. A voice. "Reza. Reza Abedi. Are you in there?"

The teacher rose and whispered into the door crack. "*Ki eh*[8]?"

"They're looking for Reza. I'm coming to warn him. It's Farid. Open up."

In one motion, Mr. Median opened the door, pulled Farid inside and locked the door behind him.

Reza bolted to his feet. "Is it Savak? They've come back for me?"

Farid's eyes sprang open. "Savak? Savak's looking for you? Reza, what the hell have you done? You must hide, and not here, and—"

As Reza frantically gathered his books, Mr. Mehdian gently grabbed Farid's arm. "Farid, who is looking for Reza?"

"Well, the principal and, now, Savak! Reza's not in class and you know Reza. Mr. Studious, who never misses class and always sits in the front and—"

Reza froze. "The principal's looking for me? Why didn't you say so? You had me crapping my pants!" Reza sat down in a heap on the chair, balancing his books on his lap. *The principal!*

The teacher rubbed his eyes under his glasses, made a phone call to the principal and then stood so Farid could sit in his chair. The two cousins faced each other in puzzlement. Finally, Reza spilled the whole story of last night's events.

Farid leaned back and clasped his hands on his head. "Wow,

---

7 Khomeini created this document to assert that Muslim Shia religious leaders should govern with absolute authority.

8 Who's there?

that's intense. You're so lucky Mostafa came home last night. If they took you to prison, they would've—"

"Enough, Farid," Mr. Mehdian said as the blood drained from Reza's face. "Now, can I give you boys a bit of advice and maybe a book or two?"

Reza's face brightened at the word "book," but Farid still seemed to be absorbing the shock of Reza's meeting with Savak.

The teacher reached into his bookshelf, removed several books and then reached even further back. He pulled out books with plain burlap covers and no titles, no writing anywhere on the front, back or sides. Farid looked in fear at Reza, but Reza had already reached for the first stack and called out the authors and titles while flipping through the pages. "Marx, Jefferson, Revolutions of the Twentieth Century."

Mr. Mehdian handed a stack to Farid. "Gandhi, Henry David Thoreau, Freud—"

Peeking at Farid's stack, Reza said, "Anne Frank? I've heard of her. Here, I'll trade the writings of Walt Whitman for Anne Frank."

"Deal."

The teacher smiled. "Just tuck them away. They're not a problem now, but things are changing every day."

The cousins exchanged confused glances.

"Keep them as long as you want," Mr. Mehdian continued. "And I'll see what else I can find in the meantime. I think it's time you boys get to class. I know Savak is tough, but the principal can be pretty tough, too."

"Thank you, Mr. Mehdian."

He stopped them at the door. "I said books and advice." They smiled. "So, here's my advice from two well-known Americans: Alexander Hamilton and more recently quoted by Malcolm X." Clearing his throat, the teacher stated: "If you stand for nothing, you will fall for anything." The boys nodded, gathered the precious books and headed to class.

Mr. Mehdian sat at his cluttered desk and located his sketchpad. Seeming to search through his ideas of how to explain Iran, he began to draw. His hand swam across the pages, sketching image after image. He sketched Iraq with a rebellious spirit issuing demands to overthrow Shah. The spirit twisted into the image of Khomeini rising from the dungeons of the damned to bleed back into Iran as a rancorous sore. Using darker pencil, he created shadows and a phantom bearded face that ordered work stoppages that swept the mutinous nation. Deep into his art, he didn't see the principal's face peering through the door. "Mr. Mehdian?"

Jumping and then quickly covering his sketches with his spread fingers. "*Salam.* I didn't see you there, I—"

"Apparently," the principal said, craning his neck to see the sketch. "Are you preparing for a class?"

Mr. Median closed his eyes and sighed. "Just trying to sort out—recent events."

The principal nodded. "I see," he said as he tried again to steal a glance at the covered papers. "Recent events can be complicated." He closed the door and walked down the hall.

Mr. Mehdian lifted his pencil and then rubbed his eyes. Slowly he returned to his sketches. He depicted a large turban with shark-dead eyes that promised better wages, the destruction of Savak and overthrow of Shah. He outlined thin lips shrieking for an immediate return. He drew demonstrations that rocked Iran and spilt her blood among the smoke and the fury and the flaming pictures of Shah. His tears dropped, slightly smearing the sketches of his beloved Iran. Iran in her adolescent years fumbling between hate for authority, the cry for an undefined freedom and the want to grow up without the responsibility of adulthood.

Chapter Ten

Laguna Niguel, 2009

Surrounded by stacks of books, newspaper articles, timelines, photos and a laptop blinking with YouTube videos, I struggle to untangle this whole revolution business. Using poster board, I have drawn a timeline of Reza's life and worked for days to match it with the political events of Iran. I'm stumped, so I pick up the phone.

"The Shah seemed like he was doing so many good things for Iran," I say, with my pencil hovering above my yellow pad waiting for the answers. "I can't wrap my head around why millions of Iranians would want this Ayatollah Khomeini guy."

"But we didn't know about these things," Reza says. "My dad and my teacher were suspicious. But I thought, 'They're old. They don't understand.'"

"What did they see that the others missed?"

"Greed," he says. "So many rumors about Shah taking the oil money for himself and we were told if Shah was overthrown, a check would come with our share."

I hear the sadness. "And that never happened?"

"No," he says. "Khomeini stole the revolution."

I write those words down and darken the letters of "stole."

"What about Savak?" I ask. "What's it like to live with a secret police?"

"Nobody liked Savak, but," he clears his throat, "they didn't come after you unless you were involved in politics somehow."

I pause and jot a few notes, but I still feel there is a gap. I go for a simple question.

"What do you remember the most about the revolution?"

In the silence that follows, I hope I haven't overstepped my bounds. I know he suffered during those years.

He takes a deep breath. "So many things. Fear. Hunger." He sighs. "Everything we knew was lost, just gone."

Chapter Eleven

March 1978

"Reza, if you're not going to help," Soraya said as she lifted the broom and began to jab it at Reza, "then go outside and get out of the way."

"We're helping," Hassan said. "But cleaning is girls' work. We're going to—"

Whap! Soraya smacked Hassan on the top of his head with her broom. He covered his head with his hands as Soraya went in for a second whack.

Reza lunged for her and began to wrestle the broom out of her hands. "How about we sweep you out of the house?"

"Let go!"

"You let go!"

"Both of you let go right now!" Nimtaj said. "We will never be ready for *Nowruz*[1] at this rate. Whatever is Shah's crazy new calendar, my *haft-seen*[2] will be set tonight for New Year. Now, Reza, you and Hassan go to the Zandi's house and pick out a goldfish."

Without another word, Nimtaj left the room and went back to the spicy aroma of her kitchen that had been brewing for days in preparation for Iran's most celebrated holiday. Beginning tomorrow and continuing for most of the next twelve days, the house would be filled with friends and relatives bringing trays of fresh-baked sweets and crisp dollar bills for the children. The ceremonial setting of the *haft-seen,* which consists of seven

1 Iranian New Year celebrated on the first day of spring

2 Traditional table setting for Nowruz of seven symbolic dishes

symbols displayed with other meaningful objects, is prepared to bring in a happy and healthy new year. One of those objects is a goldfish in a bowl.

"You heard Naneh. Go get the gold fish," Soraya said, giving the broom a twist.

Reza pulled it back, making Soraya trip a few steps, but still she held on. "We'll pick one out that looks just like you and name it Soraya, the impossible fish." He yanked the broom from her grip with a firm tug and then handed it gently back to Soraya with a warm smile.

Hassan burst into giggles. "Yeah, we'll get the one where the eyes are sticking way out and they look in ten different directions at once and swim in a big fat circle and—"

"Enough, Hassan," Reza said. "Let's go."

The two brothers walked to the door, Hassan still immersed in the chatter about the goldfish.

"Hey," Soraya said. "Be careful."

May 1978

The sun wasn't as warm, Reza thought, as he walked to school with the usual brood. His sisters' constant chatter, along with Farid and Hassan's nonsensical bickering, grated on his nerves. He sped up his pace but Soraya broke from the clamor and caught up with him.

"Are you going to walk us home today?" Soraya asked as she avoided a fallen tree in the road. "I think you should."

"Why? You're fine with Hassan and Farid."

She looked behind her and back at Reza, her face showing no confidence in the two who babbled nonstop in circular arguments. "No, we're not." She paused for emphasis. "Not anymore."

"You've been listening when Mostafa comes over. You shouldn't and you wouldn't be scared." Reza wouldn't look at her; he pretended to focus on the uneven ground. *I wish this would all just stop.*

"Of course I listen. It's not as if they're quiet, with all their tapes and talk. And Baba lets me listen to the BBC with him. I know everyone's saying Shah's leaving so that Ayatollah Khokhomeni—"

"Khomeini," Reza corrected her.

She sighed. "So Khomeini will come and then everyone will get checks for the oil. But if it's such a good thing, why is there so much violence and strikes and people going into the streets and the police shooting at them? I know you're scared, too."

"I'm not scared and it's not as simple as you think," Reza replied, avoiding her eyes.

"And," Farid butted in, taking out his notebook. "The English and the Americans will not be coming to save Shah this time. If you ask me, Shah tried to be too Western and moved too far from his Shiite identity."

"Shhh!" Reza said. He looked around at the trail of students heading toward the school. "Not so loud."

"Maybe Savak took out Shah's enemies before," Farid continued, "but now Shah finds himself with a lot of student protests and overflowing prisons. If you ask me, Shah's reforms are being lost in the—"

"Nobody asked you and nobody cares." Soraya said. She looked at Reza, pursed her lips together and placed her hands on her hips.

Reza looked to the chalk blue sky. *Here we go. She's going to be impossible.*

"Well," Farid replied, "if you'd listen more, you'd see Shah has brought a lot of this on himself, and Khomeini is really just taking advantage of people's fears, a fairly typical political strategy."

She turned from Farid to directly face her brother. "Are you going to walk us home?"

"Not today," Reza answered.

"Reza!" Soraya said, fighting her tears. "I don't feel safe anymore."

"Okay, Soraya calm down. You're being such a girl. Fine, I'll walk everyone home. We'll meet here after school, but don't be late. I have to run back for practice."

Soraya had already headed with her sisters to the girls' side after his first "okay" and Reza could only shake his head. He headed to his favorite teacher's office to clear his thoughts before school started.

Mr. Mehdian greeted Reza with a single raised finger, indicating a minute of silence while he finished writing an idea. Putting down his pencil on the swell of papers stacked atop a mountain of books, he waved his hand to Reza. "Come in. Sit. Where are

Hassan and Farid this morning?"

Reza cleared a heap of sketches from the only other chair in the tiny office and settled in with a sigh. He shook his head and looked down at his feet.

"I see," Mr. Mehdian said turning his full attention to the exhausted boy before him. "It was a difficult walk this morning?"

If you only knew. Reza welcomed the benevolent face behind the wire-rimmed glasses. The face that held all the answers to any question ever posed. He and Farid had come more frequently to his office to piece together the latest events, untangle the rumors and build a case for Shah to step down. "Caution, my students," Mr. Mehdian would say. "All is not what it seems. Old and young people need to understand Shah has done many good things, too, and we are an impatient people. Sometimes too impatient."

"The morning was difficult, *baleh,*" Reza said. "But, I've been thinking, do you think they will open the university to accept more students?"

"Perhaps," his teacher answered.

"Do you think the price to get to Europe will come down after Shah leaves? Even just a little?"

"I think a lot of things will change, some for the better and some for the worse."

"But the price to get to Europe or maybe even America. That has to get better, right?"

"Nothing has to get better, Reza."

"Even if it gets just a little cheaper, say 1,000 less *toman* and then maybe another 1,000 less the next year and . . ."

Mr. Mehdian rested his chin on his thumb, as was his habit when studying the thoughts of his students. Reza recognized this gesture and tried to refine his question to be worthy of his teacher's time. "I'm just so tired of all this. And now Soraya won't go anywhere unless I'm with her, and Mostafa with his cassette tapes and papers. Naneh doesn't always have enough flour and who knows when they will shut everything down again and—"

"And so your answer is to go to Europe."

Slumping his shoulders and dropping his chin to his chest, Reza sighed. "Not just to go to Europe, but to go to Europe and to go to a university," Reza said. He lifted his face to meet his teacher's gaze. "I've been thinking about maybe being a teacher, too, but it's not going to happen, is it?"

Mr. Mehdian leaned toward Reza. "It's hard to say what more changes there might be, especially in the universities. As you know, the clerics and *ulamas* were traditionally the only recognized teachers and now—"

The sound of footsteps in the hallway stopped Mr. Mehdian's words. Squirming a little in his chair, Reza looked everywhere but at his teacher. Such conversations used to be common, but now Reza felt like the walls were listening.

"Sorry, maybe I shouldn't ask these things," Reza said.

"No, please, go on."

"Well, I know Shah and his father made changes. I've heard my mother and aunts talk about being little girls and the police enforcing the law of women not being allowed to wear *chador* or even veils."

"Ah." The teacher seemed to perk up at the opportunity for a lesson. "Religion and politics. A struggle as old as good and evil."

Reza settled in his chair.

"You know," Mr. Mehdian continued, "that roughly eighty-five percent of Muslims are Sunni. And Sunni believe that successors to the prophet Muhammad should be elected."

"But most Iranians are Shia," Reza added.

"Correct, and there's the conflict. Since Shia believe that the leaders who follow Muhammad should be direct descendants of Muhammad, Islam has been divided."

"But that's religion, not politics."

Mr. Mehdian gave a warm smile. "I wish that were so," he said. "Since you started with questions about the West, let me give you a Western example. Christianity, like Islam, is divided into many sects. The Catholic sect and the Islamic Shia sect share a belief system that recognizes a strict religious hierarchy. For Catholics the top of that hierarchy is the pope and for Shias it's the grand ayatollah."

"And politics?"

"Think politics, think power. Religion can be used by some as a vehicle to gain that power. When the belief system recognizes a supreme leader, that can be significant in terms of power. That's not to say religion or faith or any belief system is bad or good or better or worse. Just to say when religion is mixed with politics, history has shown that it—"

Mr. Mehdian glanced with apprehension out his open office door. Reza followed his gaze and saw several other teachers, those whom Reza held in little regard, speaking in whispers as they passed the doorway. "It's time to go to class, Reza."

The last words stung, for class did not begin for several minutes and Mr. Mehdian never hurried a thoughtful conversation. Reza realized that his teacher's movements had become uncharacteristically short and hurried, including frequent glances to the hallway.

Reza took a few steps out of the office and then looked back. "Oh, I was wondering if you had more—"

"Shhh! Reza, not now." He closed the door and Reza heard the click of the lock.

* * * * *

On the last day of school, Reza told Hassan to walk the girls home so he could say goodbye to Mr. Mehdian. He increased his pace as he hurried down the hall, hoping he wouldn't miss him.

Mr. Mehdian's office was empty. His books lay untouched exactly as they had been the day before, but several papers were ripped out of his sketchpad. Reza stood confused and searched for an explanation for the teacher's absence. Other teachers walked by, paused and hurried on.

Reza ran his hand through the thin dust across the cover of a book. His heart thrashed within the cage of his chest. *This isn't right.*

Summer 1978

"Baba, what's martial law?" Farah asked.

Abbas's thick eyebrows furrowed over his deep-set eyes. He pressed his finger to his lips. "Shhh, not now."

Even though night's gentle darkness descended on Kermanshah, the summer's high temperature lingered. In the main room, the sealed windows trapped the day's desert warmth and the family glistened with heat. And fear. Pressed too close together in order to hear the low crackle of the forbidden radio, Soraya, Reza, Hassan and Farah huddled next to their father.

Nimtaj paced in the room. Mariam laid her head on Soraya's lap and the older girl smoothed her sister's soft curls and reminded her to be a "quiet girl." Mariam's once-happy, high-pitched songs became poignant hums. In her pacing, Nimtaj looked to the window and then to her family, to the door and then to her family. She knelt next to Pari and brushed back the bangs that stuck with fever to her forehead. Pari's small body stayed motionless, except for the shallow breathing that raised her chest in uneven heaves.

Soraya followed her mother's movements while trying to listen intently to the BBC. The voice crackled in and out, becoming inaudible for a few seconds. Reza reached for the tuning knob, but in the darkness turned up the volume. Loud static raged through the home. Abbas lunged for the radio and snapped off the power button. They sat motionless, silent.

"I'm so sorry," Reza whispered.

"You're going to get us all arrested," Soraya hissed.

"Silence. Both of you," Abbas said. He walked to the window and peered into the sticky night. Painful, still moments passed. With each breath, Pari's rattling lungs became the only sound. With a wave of his hand, Abbas motioned for Reza to turn the radio back on. Using a surgeon's precision, he turned down the volume and tuned to the BBC. Hassan reached over and patted Reza's arm and the two nodded. Soraya responded with an eye roll as she scooted over to make room for Abbas to sit. Farah left the circle and curled up next to Pari.

The voice repeated the events that rocked Iran that August. On August 6, Shah pledged free elections, but the violent demonstrations continued. Thousands took to the streets and those thousands faced bullets, batons and tear gas. On August 16, the government declared martial law, forbidding the people to listen to any news other than the state-run news channel. Martial law also made it difficult for families to get food, kerosene and medicine.

The BBC's voice picked up the pace. "Prime Minister Amuzegar resigned and has been replaced by Jafar Sharif-Emami."

Abbas shook his head, but the kids remained puzzled. Hassan leaned to Reza. "Why's that a big deal?"

"Sharif-Emami has different ideas than Shah," Reza whispered back. "It shows Shah is feeling pressure to move toward an Islamic government."

The voice continued. "The new prime minister and ruler of Iran, Sharif-Emami imposes his will. As a devout follower of Islam, Sharif-Emani has ordered casinos to close immediately and he has—abolished the secular calendar—" Crackles interrupted the voice. "He has declared the party of Islam—will have the right—to rule Iran."

The voice cut out and static filled the darkness in the Abedi home. Abbas turned off the radio. Hassan studied each face and saw no answers.

"Baba," Soraya leaned forward. "Does that mean we can take Pari to the hospital?"

Abbas shook his head. "Men will only listen to those whose fists hold money."

The clink of Nimtaj's *alangoo* echoed in the darkness as her gold bracelets dropped into the center of the family. "Haji Abbas, tomorrow you will buy medicine for Pari."

He took her *alangoo.* "Nimtaj, take this back. We will go to the hospital in the morning and—"

She shook her head. "Please, Haji Abbas. I beg you. These are *hichi,* nothing. Pari needs medicine to get well. I know tomorrow you can find the men who have this medicine."

Pulling the *alangoo* from her arms, Soraya added them to Nimtaj's. "Mine, too."

Abbas reached to the gold and rubbed the smooth surfaces in his rough hands. Pari's cough filled the silence.

• • • • •

The next night, Reza accompanied Abbas to a part of the city known for having a black market. As they approached the end of the dark alley, Abbas turned to his son. "I will speak. You will listen."

"*Chashm,* Baba," Reza said. At first he felt a rush of anticipation, much like he did before a match. But as his mouth went dry and his breath froze in his lungs, he recognized the feeling he hated. Fear.

The men, some as old as sixty and others as young as twelve, cautiously exchanged rumors and other precious bits of information. Some had come from Tehran and other cities where the violent protests commonly erupted. One man was showing the scars burned into his feet by Savak.

"Burns!" yelled a large man with thick grey eyebrows protruding over his deep-set eyes. "I come from Abadan. I will tell you about Shah's burns."

Reza leaned in to Abbas. "What's he talking about?"

"Listen," Abbas said.

"You speak of Cinema Rex," said a shorter man. He looked much older to Reza, maybe sixty. He wore a pressed dress shirt and fine shoes. Reza immediately wondered why this man would be at a black market.

"What is it you know about Cinema Rex?" said the grey eyebrows. "I can tell you the truth. Shah ordered Savak to lock the doors and then . . ." He lifted both arms to the blackened sky. "And then Savak lit the theater on fire! Four hundred or more innocent people screamed as they were burned alive!"

Several men shook their fists and chanted, "Death to Shah! Burn him!"

Taking a step closer to Abbas, Reza whispered, "Would Shah do that?"

"No," Abbas answered. "Mostafa said theaters were burned during *Ramadan*[3] because some mullahs thought the films were too modern, but—" Abbas's sentence was cut short.

"This is to be considered," said the older man in the fine shoes as he pointed to Abbas. "Shah has not been burning the theaters and restaurants. We know those orders are from the Islamic militants protesting what they see as Western modernization." The circle of men shifted a bit. Some spit in the dirt and a few turned and walked away. "Know this!" the older man continued. "And remember you heard it here. There are trained guerrilla warriors, those who speak Arabic like many of our Iranian brothers, but they are not Iranian. They are from Palestine sent here to—"

"You lie, old man!"

"You are a Savak spy!"

"End of fifty years of Pahlavi tyranny!"

As the shouts answered the old man, Abbas pulled on Reza's arm. "Come. We get what we came for."

Fall 1978

Students' desks sat vacant. Banks boarded their windows and bolted their doors. Once bustling bazaars shut down. Instead of students and shoppers, the streets filled with demonstrators and the police were ordered to stop them. The boiling summer days morphed into autumn nights of looting, protests and violence.

The struggle to secure medicine for Pari solidified the danger

3 A Muslim holiday that takes place during the 9th month of the Islamic calendar. It is a time for self-reflection and devotion to God.

families faced in obtaining basic supplies. Like those of most cities and towns across the nation, each street in Kermanshah formed a band of young men who both protected their neighborhood and raided stores for food and provisions. With the help of Mostafa, Reza recruited the strongest young men, mostly wrestlers, in the neighborhood. They first planned a blockade to secure their street. Reza gathered with the young men at the end of an alley and looked into their frightened but determined faces.

"There's a burned-out bus on the next alley," he said. He pointed to four wrestlers leaning against the wall. "You guys lift where there's a missing wheel and the rest of us will push it." He drew a line in the dirt with a stick. "We'll wedge it here and then police will not be able to get past this point." He pushed the stick further into the dirt, making the line deep and defined. "This will keep our street safe." *For a few days at least.* Afraid to actually voice it, he remained silent. *Just enough time to get more food.*

The next night, illuminated with spastic bits of explosion and gunfire, Reza led his neighborhood band on a raid of a nearby marketplace. The group of ten strong young men wove through the alleys toward the violent sounds. Struggling with the weight of his backpack, Hassan fell to the back of the group and almost became lost altogether. A hand reached out and grabbed his arm. "Hassan, your brother wants you."

"What's the matter?" Hassan asked, panting as he caught up to Reza.

"Where'd you go?" Reza asked. "Why're you sweating?"

"You made me carry all the rocks, remember? The Molotov cocktails are lighter, let me carry those."

Reza reached to pull off Hassan's backpack. "No, those explode sometimes."

"I'm almost the same size as you," Hassan said, moving away from Reza's reach. "Just not as—"

"Strong is not about muscles," Reza said. "Can you carry the rocks or not?"

Hassan nodded.

"And keep up?"

"I may even pass you," Hassan said as he resettled the heavy backpack. "But I'm carrying the rocks."

"You can't stop," Reza replied. "You stop, you quit, you—well, you just have to keep up!" He increased the pace. "I have to look for a place to meet."

"Go!" Hassan repeated with certainty. "I'm right behind you."

Reza motioned for the group to gather behind a low wall and they sat in a small circle. Reza again drew the plan into the dirt. They moved their faces close to see in the moonlight and nodded.

"And we meet here and go back together," Reza said. He turned to Hassan. "Stay behind me and stay low."

Other men had already started the raid on one market; Reza's group joined in by throwing rocks at the police and hurling Molotov cocktails. As the explosions blew out glass and crumbled brick walls, the young men ran into the filthy air and returned with random supplies.

Less than an hour later, the group met behind the wall. Reza took stock of the supplies and ensured each man had returned. "Let's go," he said

A wrestler spoke up. "Are we taking this to the mosque?"

Reza hesitated. True, they had been taking supplies to the mosque with the reassurance from mullahs that the supplies would be distributed to their families. However, these wrestlers had yet to see their loot shared. Reza took a chance. "Not this time. Let's bring these to our families." He searched the darkness, looking into the blackened faces and noting their eyes shifting uncomfortably. He added, "The next raid will be bigger and we'll bring those supplies to the mosque."

The young men nodded in seeming gratitude for the permission to bring food home to their hungry families.

Reza and Hassan walked through the door as the morning sun struggled to break through the black. Powerful sobs came from a figure huddled in the corner next to the radio.

Reza and Hassan dropped everything and rushed to their mother. "Naneh—why—are you okay? Are the girls—" Reza said as he counted the figures sleeping under a blanket near their mother.

Nimtaj looked at her sons and pulled their bodies into hers. "You're safe! You're home safe!"

"Of course we are," Reza said. "Why are you crying?"

Taking a deep breath, Nimtaj pulled herself into a seated position. "When Baba left to meet his people, I continued to listen to the BBC."

The boys exchanged glances.

"And the BBC reported Shah ordered the use of his gunships and helicopters—to shoot the peaceful protestors—to kill the students and women—maybe even tens of thousands—maybe children."

Cries rocked her body and Reza held her. "It's okay. We're right here. We're safe. These reports aren't always accurate, like Mostafa tells us. Shhh, Naneh, shhh."

"Yeah, maybe it was too dark to really know," Hassan said. He scooted a little closer and lowered his voice. "Did they say anything else, Naneh?"

Reza furrowed his eyebrows and shot him a look.

Nimtaj wiped her eyes. "They said today will be called Black Friday."

"Black Friday?" Reza said. He shook his head. "Well, it's not a black Friday for us. Come and see what we were able to get tonight." He looked for a sign of comfort from his mother. She slowly turned her head toward the meager pile they had dropped by the door.

"Hassan, go get Naneh's favorite little grapes," Reza said. "I grabbed two handfuls."

As Hassan hurried to the pile, Nimtaj's lips braved a small smile. "In this season? You found grapes?"

He nodded. "They're probably sour, but—"

She reached up and touched the rough skin of his face. Hassan scurried over, his blackened hands holding two bunches of the tiny, bitter fruit.

"These are for *you*," Reza emphasized. "And next time we will get more."

"Next time," she said, taking the wilted bunches, "I will go to the market and fill my basket with fresh fruits and berries for the family."

The brothers exchanged a worried look. Hassan raised an eyebrow.

"I will hope so, too," Reza said.

• • • • •

The evenings to follow repeated the same struggle. When the electricity worked, the Abedis gathered in front of the TV. It sputtered the Iranian national anthem with the still portrait of Shah and his wife posed in front of the Iranian flag.

On November 5, 1978, Shah entered millions of homes as a man whose eyes swelled in fatigue and suffered a hundred years beyond the face that hung in every home. His rhetoric ebbed and flowed with cries for peace and promises for reform, tempered with the threats of military involvement. In a quaking voice that caught and cracked, he promised not to repeat past mistakes and to make amends saying: "I heard the voice of your revolution. As Shah of Iran as well as an Iranian citizen, I cannot but approve your revolution. Let all of us work together to establish real democracy in Iran. I make a commitment to be with you and your revolution against corruption and injustice in Iran."

The Abedis received his message in silence. Huddled together under a single blanket for warmth, Mariam sat in Pari's lap twisting Pari's curls around her tiny finger. Farah's chubby face pressed next to the other two and she pulled the blanket around them. Soraya and Reza stood with Hassan between them. Mostafa leaned against the door, stroking his beard.

The screen faded back to the Iranian flag. Nimtaj turned off the power and pointed to the platters set in the center of her *sofreh.* The platters that once brimmed with steaming piles of rice and lamb now sat sullen with bits of meat and wilted vegetables.

Mostafa pulled open the door but Nimtaj grabbed his arm. "Whatever it is, it will wait. You must eat."

Abbas pointed to Mostafa's place on the rug and Mostafa sat. In the silence, they passed the platters. Mostafa's eyes seemed to harbor their own thoughts as they darted from one place to the next.

"Why do you look so worried?" Hassan asked. "Shah will leave and Ayatollah Khomeini will make sure we all get our share of the oil profits."

"Hassan!" Mostafa barked. "Do not speak what you do not know!"

"Easy. He's just a kid," Reza said. "He's just repeating what we've been told." He looked to his father, who remained oddly quiet. One by one, all the children's faces turned to Abbas. He set his spoon down and looked at Mostafa.

"Son," he said. "If Shah leaves, what will become of the good people of Iran?"

"I don't know, Baba," he said. "I really don't know."

Winter 1978

The late-December storms tore with bitter anger through the unheated homes. Nimtaj had used the last of the kerosene Reza had brought from their hiding place at the gym. To store kerosene in the home invited looters or beatings from police demanding to know the source.

As Nimtaj struggled to glean more heat from the last few drops, Pari's haunting cough echoed through the home. Reza stood up and paced about the room while his father watched. Nimtaj sung her prayers and held her daughter.

Reza approached Abbas and sat next to him. "Baba, let me go to the gym and get more kerosene." He blew into his hands.

"We can try tomorrow," Abbas said. "You cannot go out at night."

Pari's cough rattled through the dark house. Hassan joined his brother. "We can both go, Baba. We know the best way. No one knows we've hidden the kerosene tank there, so no one will be near it."

Reza nodded. But Abbas shook his head. "They're everywhere," he said. "It will not be safe for you to go."

"I know you think we're safer in our large numbers, but we're not. We're a bigger target that way. This way . . ." Reza looked at his father. "This way, we sneak through the dark alleys and we're back in one hour."

Nimtaj secured the last blanket around the girls. Pari's fit of coughing was followed by the cries of Mariam. Abbas looked at his sons and nodded.

* * * * *

Hunger burned in his stomach and cold bit at Reza's uncovered hands. Hassan struggled to keep up. Each sound made them freeze while the bright, terrible moon illuminated the red plastic containers they held. Those containers, implying they might hold precious kerosene, would invite the clubs of the looters or the bullets of the police.

Hassan scanned the area as Reza took out his father's keys and entered the gym. They stepped inside and held still for several minutes, listening, listening. Reza's eyes adjusted to milky light seeping into his beloved gym. He mourned his mats that lay like a graveyard of his hopes and dreams. *God, I want to wrestle again.*

"Rez, let's go."

They poured the precious fuel into their cans and then stepped outside. Hassan turned his face to the moon and whispered, "Remember a few weeks ago when everyone thought they saw Khomeini's face in the moon so they were crying and jumping and thinking it was some sign?"

"Yeah, bunch of crazies."

"Well, tonight I think I see Ardeshir's face."

Reza looked back up to the moon and gave Hassan a half grin. "Don't ever tell him that."

The two slid into the shadows for the icy trek home. Hassan slipped and his container skidded for several feet, leaving a trail of putrid fumes. He scrambled across the alley after his container, picked it up and started to return to Reza. Reza was about to scold him when two bright headlights slithered down the alleyway. A nearby doorway hid Reza, but Hassan had nowhere to go.

The car's tires momentarily lost traction and light beams stayed plastered to the bits of a broken wall. Reza dropped his containers and slid on his belly to Hassan. Tires crunched in the snow and the beams of light once again crept along. In a few feet, they would highlight Reza's red cans.

Grabbing Hassan's container, Reza pushed Hassan with the other hand down the alley until they could hide behind the remnants of a car. Their icy breath sent smoke signals and forced them to bury their faces in the snow bank. They huddled blind and helpless.

The heat of the engine sprayed across their backs amplifying the smell of the spilled kerosene. Lurching along, the car struggled for footing in the snow, sending the headlights in a chaotic pattern along the walls, ground and sky. And under the moon of Ardeshir's face, the headlights barely missed the red cans and the brothers cowering in the snow bank. The car turned into the next alley.

"I'm so sorry," Hassan said. "I'll hold on tighter. I promise. I'm so sorry, Reza. I'm—"

"Just pick up your can."

Hassan reached down, grabbed the handle and then collapsed into the snow bank with a flood of tears. "I'm so sorry, Rez. I could have gotten us killed. They almost saw us, and we would have gone to prison, and we—"

With a brisk yank, Reza pulled Hassan out of the snow. "You can't cry about it. They didn't see us, so grab your can and let's go." He took two steps down the alley. "Tears are for cowards, Hassan. Whatever happens, you have to stand up and keep moving." He gripped his container and turned his back.

They returned home in silence.

• • • • •

A few nights later, Hassan sat shivering on the roof, pouring black gunpowder into a jar previously filled with cucumber slices. He added kerosene and torn rags for a wick exactly as Mostafa had taught him. His smudged face looked at Reza. "This makes ten. How many more do we need?"

Reza gathered the latest Molotov cocktail and added it to the others in the cardboard box. "Make ten more, just in case we raid the bank." He shook off a chill and blamed it on the brisk winter winds.

Hassan's face lit up. "The bank?"

"I said, just in case," Reza answered. "There's always rumors. If we go out tonight, we need to be ready."

Each night, the ginger sky pulsed with gunfire and explosions. The ancient breezes that once caressed the humble homes now swept through towns only to spread their ashes. In daylight, the girls would collect rocks and leave piles for their brothers. Without weapons, rocks and Molotov cocktails became the only defense against the firepower of Shah's police.

Hungry, tired and desperate for normalcy, Hassan hoped to engage in conversation to take him far from the suffering and uncertainty of their daily lives. "Could you beat Ardeshir if you wrestled today? I mean, if you got bigger," he asked.

"Ardeshir? I saw him two weeks ago. I always kick his ass." Reza added more jars to the box. "I don't care what he says."

Grateful for the invitation to talk, Hassan continued to sputter. "He said he's going to be on the next National Team. That's what he told me. And he said you are too, Rez. He said you can make it this time." Hassan leaned in closer to Reza, as if he were sharing a secret Reza knew nothing about. "He said you're going to be *ghahreman.*"

Reza feigned interest until his little brother's voice hummed like a gnat that he needed to swat away. "Stop saying these things. Ardeshir and his National Team. He just says that to impress girls."

"No, Rez, he says the National Team travels to Europe. He says they stay in hotels and eat in fine restaurants."

"I'm sure he says all those things, but—"

"You don't think it's true? I knew it! He's such a liar. His tongue will shrivel up and fall out!"

"What are you talking about? I didn't say he was a liar," Reza said. He blew into his stiff hands. "There's just a lot involved in being on Nationals. And who knows if there's even going be a National Team anymore. Even if there is, you don't just show up and say, 'I'm good, pick me.' Every year you wrestle a lot of matches all over Iran to qualify, and now you'll have to be in the military and then—it's just complicated, so drop it." Reza's voice was harsh and biting. *I don't want to think about it anymore.*

Punctuated by distant explosions and bathed in a sulfur haze of kerosene, this night offered little hope. As Reza struggled with tears he could not explain, Hassan predictably had one more thing to say. "If Ardeshir can make the team, I know you can. Then you can go to Europe, too."

Reza stood up and paced about the roof. He swung his arms and cursed under his breath. Following him with wide eyes, Hassan whispered, "I'm sorry, Rez."

"I hate this," Reza said looking into the murky night. He hung his head and slowly shook it from side to side. "I used to think being a champion wrestler was the only thing that mattered. But now," he turned to Hassan, "it hardly seems important."

Hassan let out a heavy sigh, just like his brother's, and watched for the falling stars he depended on for his wishes for Reza. Only the nomadic moon burned behind the grey sky. "Well, if there's a National Team, you'll be on it."

"Oh, Hassan," Reza said. "Let's just finish this up and go inside. I don't want to talk about it anymore."

Winds swirled around the brothers, burning their ears and biting their necks. Their hands trembled as they fought to bend their fingers and grip the last slippery jars. It was a low noise, but Reza jumped to his feet. He grabbed a huge rock and aimed toward the sound. "Who's there?"

Mostafa's battered face peeked over the edge from the ladder. With his swollen hands, he signaled to come down and then disappeared into the blackness.

Mostafa's visits were always short, unannounced and in the middle of the night.

Sometimes the men he brought supported Khomeini, sometimes Shah and sometimes they were men like him. Men who worked with the side that best suited their purpose at any given time. Reza and Hassan were careful to listen first before speaking. They went to join the circle of men.

"No, kid, you stay by the windows and circle the house every few minutes to see if someone's coming," a man commanded as he pointed in the direction of the door.

"Why can't I listen, too?" Hassan asked.

Mostafa waved Hassan to his side and whispered, "Reza'll tell you everything. To be the lookout is the most important. If someone comes, we need you to warn us."

Hassan looked for confirmation from Reza, who didn't hear Mostafa but didn't need to. Reza nodded. Hassan took his post by the window.

Tonight, Mostafa came with cassette tapes, a bundle of rolled-up documents and an envelope of grainy pictures. Thick clicks pushed one tape after another into the recorder. Measured speeches from Ayatollah Khomeini crept into the home, spinning spider webs of promises: "I will serve as your leader for the time necessary to complete a peaceful and plentiful transition to a government that would share all wealth with all people . . . ."

Reza watched the faces of his father, his older brothers and a few "friends" of Mostafa's whom he didn't recognize. They all sat motionless, all staring at the machine unleashing Ayatollah Khomeini's voice. Pictures, newspaper clippings and assorted documents spread across the rug. The men held them to the kerosene lamps, mumbling, nodding their heads.

Abbas looked blankly at a list and scanned the room for more pictures. Reza understood and went to his side to read the words for him. "Here, Baba, let me."

Nodding, Abbas held a lamp close to the paper. Reza's dark eyes, usually warm and mischievous, narrowed. "First, it lists all the dates of the strikes in '78 and then some places of the riots. And here is a list of Shah's government officials who have been killed or have left. And here it says that on September 25 the Rastakhiz party collapsed and on October 3 Khomeini left Iraq for Kuwait but they wouldn't let him in."

"I fear he is a madman and his intentions are not for the good of Iran. Kuwait must have seen that too," Abbas said.

"But, Baba," Reza whispered, "he says he will make the foreign oil companies share their money with all the families."

"A man who wants power will say what the people want to hear," Abbas answered.

Reza heard a grumble from the far side of the room. He

looked at a man who held Khomeini's picture and kissed the image. Their eyes met. *Maybe Baba's too old to understand.* He ran his finger down the list looking for other important dates. Reza continued, "Well, the French didn't see it that way because on October 10 they put him up in a chateau and he's being interviewed everyday by reporters from everywhere."

Mostafa looked over. "Keep that article away from the lamp. It's important."

Reza placed the article back in the pile. A soft voice from behind him whispered, "Reza, let me see that."

Reza twisted around to see Soraya's face hidden under the black *chador* of their mother. Through clenched teeth he hissed, "What are you doing? You shouldn't be here."

Soraya looked to Abbas, who quickly glanced around to see if any of the men had noticed her presence. He then nodded to Reza to give her some articles. She huddled behind Reza and peeked over his shoulder to share the flickering orange glow.

"Impossible," Reza muttered.

Abbas lit a cigarette and squinted at his son in the darkness. "Is there something there about Black Friday?"

"That's what the latest talk is about. It is said some of those people were even killed in the mosque of Kerman." He read directly from a wrinkled section of newspaper: "In memory of those murdered on Black Friday, a rapid succession of strikes cripple almost all the bazaars, universities, high schools, oil installations, banks, government ministries, newspapers and seal Shah's fate. Some people in the protest were severely injured."

A deep voice barked in the darkness. "Those *some people* got beaten by chains and bars. Those *some people* were marching in a peaceful protest to honor those killed." Reza turned to the voice and saw that it came from a disfigured face.

The face turned to Mostafa. "Turn on the BBC. This paper says there will be more news tonight."

Fielding looks of concern from his friends, Mostafa looked at his younger brother. "Hassan, be certain the area is secure. Circle the house slowly while we hide these articles and photographs."

"*Chashm.*" Returning moments later, Hassan reported, "We're clear."

From the small black radio, the crackling voice carefully entered the room and repeated reports as they came in. Bloody riots. Army raid at Tehran University. Students participating in demonstrations are killed.

One man lit a cigarette. Another man wiped his eyes.

The sounds of a truck engine entered the neighborhood. Reza turned to his father. "Baba, someone's coming. Someone heard." In a swift, practiced motion Abbas hid the radio in a hole under the rug while Mostafa and his men retreated into the night.

The engine stopped and heavy boots pounded up and down the street. Reza and Hassan didn't have time to climb the ladder and so they lay flat on the floor, near the door. The boots continued in a pattern of walking, pausing, walking. Flashlight beams pierced the darkness and ripped through windows. Reza felt warm tears on his arm and went to wipe his eyes, but his face was dry. The tears were Soraya's. She pressed herself to his back as she fought to suppress her sobs. In the single, signature move of a champion wrestler, Reza pulled Soraya underneath him and embraced her. "Shhh. You've got to be quiet."

Her body trembled as her chest lifted with sobs. Reza covered her mouth and whispered, "Do you want to be arrested?" She tried to shake her head. He pressed his full body on her slender frame. He took in a deep breath and pressed his lips to her ear. "Shhh. You're okay. I got you. Just breathe. Breathe."

After the deadening weight of several minutes, the engine drove off. Reza pulled Soraya to her feet and led her into Nimtaj's room to rejoin the other sleeping sisters. She began to say thank you, but Reza turned his back and walked away.

He rejoined his father as one by one the men returned. Reza suspected there would be further conversation, but fatigue drew him to his soft mattress in the second room. Hassan followed and Reza arranged his wool blankets.

"Are they going to burn down Kermanshah?" Hassan asked.

"I'm going to sleep," Reza answered. "If I catch on fire, let me know."

Hassan returned to his mattress and tried to get comfortable, tried in earnest to go to sleep. "Rez, you asleep yet?"

"Yep, fast asleep."

"If Ayatollah Khomeini comes here, do you think things will be back to normal?"

Reza rolled to face his brother. "I wish I knew," he said with a tired sigh. "But Baba doesn't think so and Mostafa's not really sure. But, it's going to be different." He rolled to his back and patted his solid stomach. "I just want to get my last year of school done and get into the university."

* * * * *

One by one, as millions continued to take to the streets, Shah's appointed leaders slipped out of the country. On January 16, 1979, Shah and his wife left Iran for "vacation" and "medical treatment." They would never return.

Gypsy winds whipped through the ruins they left behind. The Iranian people waited.

Chapter Twelve

January 1979

"Oh, Naneh!" Soraya exclaimed as she ran into the home just before sunset. "Did you hear?"

Nimtaj held the *sofreh* folded in her arms. "Hang up your coat and help me with dinner."

Soraya stopped in her tracks, snow dripping from her coat, which hung too large on her body. "They put flowers in the soldiers' guns. Flowers! And the soldiers were hugging everyone!" Her mother showed no reaction. "Did Reza already tell you?"

"No, he's still away with Hassan." Nimtaj held the cloth to Soraya. "But that is wonderful news."

Soraya reluctantly took the *sofreh* and followed her mother into the main room. "Well, it is being spoken all through the streets. Everyone's talking about it. I hope Mostafa comes again soon. I have so much to ask him."

"I hope so, too."

Soraya scurried about the kitchen, and while she helped her mother she repeated the strings of rumors circulating in the streets. "I hear the National Democratic Front will be rewriting the constitution. I think Mostafa knows a lot of those people." She lowered her voice and came close to her mother's ear. "And Ayatollah Khomeini is going to come to Tehran. Probably in just weeks."

Nimtaj froze. For several seconds she did not move.

"Naneh?"

"May this bring peace to Iran, *Inshallah.*" Her voice whispered with uncertainty.

• • • • •

Great excitement buzzed around Kermanshah for days; the Abedis pressed their ears to their forbidden radio every night awaiting news from a BBC broadcast. Tonight, February 1, they gathered once again and listened.

"People of Iran," the BBC whispered. "Great people of Iran. I am pleased to report to you that the five million people are lining the streets of Tehran to witness the homecoming of the Ayatollah Khomeini. They chant *Esteghlal Azadi, Jomhouri Eslami.* Independence, Freedom Islamic Republic. May this bring peace to Iran, *inshallah.*"

"He's here!" Hassan said.

"Shhh!" Abbas told him.

"He will deliver his first speech in the Behesht-e-Zahra Cemetery," the BBC continued. "And it will be a marking place for Iranian history."

Shaking his head, Abbas clicked off the radio.

• • • • •

But in the days after Khomeini's return, brutal demonstrations rocked Tehran and many cities throughout Iran. Banks, government offices, schools and the bazaars tenuously attempted to remain open, but orders of curfew and martial law disrupted routine.

Since it was too dangerous for Amir, Rasha and Mehri to come to the Abedi home, the families relied on unpredictable phone service to stay in contact. Mostafa's visits were fewer and farther between. Nimtaj paced anxiously at night or sat by the radio until the BBS's accounts of violent demonstrations and numbers of the dead she could no longer bear hear. Reza and Hassan continued to conduct raids for food and kerosene, but the increased aggression and firepower of the different factions fighting for power made each raid more dangerous than the last. The girls never left the house.

Abbas and Mostafa sold most of what they owned on the black market and bartered for food and medicine. They had not yet resorted to straight theft, but they had scarcely anything left to trade.

During these dealings, Mostafa learned about a riot at the prison. Such a raid meant not just food but guns and bullets. Now Reza discussed the plan with Mostafa while sipping hot water meant to simulate afternoon chai.

"Some of those prisoners are real criminals but most . . ." Mostafa paused to take a sip of tea. "Most are political prisoners."

"I'm just getting supplies," Reza said. "I'm not stopping to ask who's for Khomeini and who's against him."

"Do you understand the danger?" Mostafa said. "Once those guards have taken over the prison, they will throw open the gates and we will be facing the fires of hell."

"I understand," Reza said. *I feel like I've been there already.*

"It's important that we're with people we can trust," Mostafa said. He finished his last sip of chai. "We must know. Can we trust them with our lives?" Mostafa's last words pressed weights onto Reza's chest.

"Hassan is strong and I will find Ardeshir."

Mostafa nodded.

Reza took a last sip of the hot water. *Trust with my life. My life. What is my life coming to?*

• • • • •

In the still darkness just before the moon gives way to the sun, Reza drove the stolen truck with Hassan next to him in the front. Ardeshir and Mostafa rode in the back. Before they had left, Reza needed to convince Ardeshir they'd be safe with Hassan. "We'd be safer with your sisters," Ardeshir protested.

As the truck left the paved city roads and rolled onto a single dirt lane, it slipped and crunched along the slushy path. Heaps of snow covered the charred remains of overturned cars that littered the path to Dizel Abad Prison. Reza kept his steady gaze forward. Just as the sun clawed her way above the barren landscape, Reza saw the tip of the prison guard towers cut against the horizon. He shivered.

Hassan had been dozing off, but woke up in the screams of a nightmare crying out that the wicked walls were calling his name and chasing him with fire and chains.

"Rez, no! Stop! They're coming for me!"

"Hey. Relax. It's a nightmare, that's all. This is the prison. Did you think there'd be flowers and trees lining the streets with a huge welcome sign?"

"No, just had a dream that—no, it's nothing. *Hichi.*"

"Yeah, *hichi,*" Reza said. "You've got to stay alert. You've got to—"

"Ahh!" Hassan cried out. "Stop! Why are there more cars and trucks? Is this an ambush? Are the police there? Who is the—"

"Hang on, hang on. Come on, you're a mess. You're not being locked up. We're here for food and some weapons and it's gonna be messy." Reza looked sideways at his brother, who glistened in rivers of sweat. "Can you handle it?"

"Yeah, Rez, of course I can handle it." Hassan took a few deep breaths. Then he gripped the dashboard. "Why are you slowing down?"

"Relax. I'm pulling over here to these cars. These are good guys. Look, I know that one from wrestling. We need to find out what they know," Reza said. "And I think you need to stay in the truck."

Reza pulled the truck to where the men gathered. He saw a few familiar faces and felt security in numbers. They, too, had heard that the guards inside were no longer loyal to Shah and planned to overthrow the prison. This scene had been repeated across the nation and always ended in violence. And death.

Mostafa jumped out of the back and motioned for the others to get out of the truck. They joined a circle of about thirty men who stood shifting their dirty boots in the snow, their hands stuffed in coat pockets.

A spooky tension mingled with the smell of smoke and the spastic yells from behind the walls. Reza shivered and rubbed his hands for warmth. *I hope Mostafa got his information right.*

Hassan could not peel his eyes from the huge cement walls.

Reza placed his hand on Hassan's shoulder. "It'll be anytime. You sure you can go through with this?"

Hassan continued his gaze. "Rez, how high do you think those walls are?"

"Ten, maybe twelve meters."

"Do you think a prisoner ever sees the sun or do they just sit in cells all day?"

"Why do you ask these things?"

"Just wondering, Rez. Just wondering."

Reza brought both hands to his brother's shoulders. "We're coming out, Hassan. We're going in, taking what we need and coming out. You've got to be ready."

"I am, I am. I may not be an almighty *pahlavan,* but I can hold my own."

"Almighty, *pah*—what the hell is that supposed to mean?"

Before Hassan could answer, shouts of "Get ready! We're going in!" roared across the desert.

A crashing wave of angry men gushed through the terrible gates of the terrible walls. Some bled, some wore only shreds of clothes, some carried a stick or a stone. Many voices shrieked, "Death to Shah!" and others simply cried out. Running out of the gates, they slowed, almost in surprise that there were men to greet them. The waiting men stood paralyzed in a silent shock, desperately taking in the surreal scene unfolding before them. The briefest moment of an eerie silence hung. What now?

The answer came in shots fired into the crowds of escaping prisoners and waiting men. Prisoners and guards fled together like beasts escaping a forest fire. Every man grabbed any semblance of a weapon he could and used it to wield a sword of falsified power.

Hassan followed Reza into the hordes of charging men. No longer a place of prisoner and guard, the entire fortress collapsed into Shah and Khomeini. Stronger than most, Reza pushed bodies aside and cleared his path into the guts of hell. Smells of human feces, burning bodies and rot tore through the brothers.

Reza found himself in the storehouse of clothes and shoes. Scanning the piles, he saw nothing that would fit his sisters, but grabbed armloads of shirts and shoes and turned to run back to the truck.

"Hassan! Grab some— Hassan? Hassan?" It would be impossible to find him in the chaos, so Reza ran back to his truck, locked in the supplies and rushed back into the prison. He watched a few guards approaching a locked back door and cautiously looking around. *It's got to be the guns.*

His instincts were rewarded. An entire room was filled with weapons of every kind and bullets. Lots of bullets. Reza grabbed an armload and headed back to his truck. Almost to the gate, he heard, "Rez! Rez! Hey, look what I got!"

Reza turned to see Hassan running after him carrying an AK-47 and wearing a child's tremendous grin. Reza smiled himself in a twisted sense of pride for his little brother.

SMASH! A crushing blow came down on Hassan's head by the butt of a gun.

"Hassan!" Reza dropped his weapons and ran to him. Within an instant, both were covered in Hassan's blood.

"Hassan! Hass— Okay, I'm going to carry you out of here. Do you hear me? Hold on! Hold onto my neck. That's it. Hold tight now. I'm going to get you out of here. Hold tight."

Reza laid Hassan on the front seat of the truck and leaned his head out the passenger window so the blood would drain to the ground.

"Rez, Rez, I'm gonna—"

"You're okay. Don't—"

"Throw up. Open the doo—"

The puddle of vomit mixed with the rich red blood seeping from his skull. Hassan threw up violently, holding his stomach in one hand and his head with the other. His spasms stopped and he closed his eyes to lean against the seat.

Reza pulled off his shirt and pressed it against Hassan's head. The cloth became instantly crimson, but soon Hassan's bleeding slowed to a steady ooze.

"Can you wait here for a few more minutes?"

He nodded and Reza ran back into the prison.

The frenzy had slowed to a modest hum. Guards stood protecting the piles of flour, canned food and weapons being gathered at the front.

Reza spotted Mostafa in the fray, who also seemed to be examining this guarded heap of food. "What's that pile all about?" Reza asked

"Trucks. The big trucks are coming to take the supplies to the mosques."

"To the mosques?" Reza said. "We need to get some more stuff into *our* truck."

Mostafa nodded. "Follow me."

Reza trailed behind Mostafa, who took him through two back doors, a tunnel and up a narrow staircase. He turned to Reza. "Where's Hassan?"

"He's, uh—he's waiting in the truck."

"Good. I told Ardeshir to wait for me on the backside." Mostafa continued to climb to the top of a small guard tower. Sounds of gunshots and tortured screams faded into thick echoes seeping from the cement walls.

Mostafa pushed open the door that led into a small guard tower. He turned to Reza. "I saw a pile of supplies at the end of the next hall." They entered the tiny room. "We'll hide them here and you'll wait until I bring the truck."

Reza peered over the half-open cement wall of the guard tower. "Just drop them over?"

"And then run to the backside. We'll pick you up there."

Reza followed Mostafa back down the steps to get the supplies. "No, get the truck now. I'll get the supplies to the tower." He grabbed Mostafa by the arm. "Then leave as soon as the truck is loaded."

"Don't be foolish."

"Hassan has to get home," Reza said. "Load, then go. I'll find a way back."

Mostafa nodded and headed back through the darkened prison tunnels.

Thirty minutes passed. Reza could not drop the supplies without Ardeshir and Mostafa to catch them. And guard them. But he couldn't wait much longer without being discovered. Several times boots thumped past him, but no one had turned up the last narrow staircase leading to the guard tower. Depending on who found him, Reza would be shot, captured or robbed. *Maybe Ardeshir got to the truck and Hassan was dead. Maybe he got caught on the way out and couldn't make it to the truck. Maybe someone had already found the truck, shot Hassan and stolen it.* The maybe demons paraded through Reza's head and time dragged daggers down his throat. *I am a fool. How did I think this could possibly work?* Boots again, voices this time, running boots, loud voices, gunshots, silence. *I'm going to die here, next to bags of flour and barley. And three pairs of shoes.*

Tires in the dirt and two honks floated to him as the sweetest sound Reza had ever heard. He peered over the tower wall and met the sight of his truck. Within minutes, Reza threw huge bags and cans of food to his waiting friends below. One flour bag exploded on top of Mostafa creating a surreal feeling of freshly fallen snow, but their strength brought all the other supplies safely into the truck. Reza barely had a chance to check on Hassan, who lay dazed against the side.

"Jump!" Ardeshir shouted.

"What?"

"Jump! Now! You'll never get out. They've closed the gates. The whole backside's burning. You have to jump. *Zood bosh! Zood bosh!*"

Figuring he'd break at least his ankle, Reza tried to shimmy down the guard tower to get as close to the ground as possible. "Jump! There's no time. A truck's coming. I think we've been spotted. Just jump."

Reza landed on Ardeshir in the back of the truck and it sped furiously down the dirt road. The shrinking sight of men loading large trucks, supervised by the mullahs, made Reza smile.

The shroud of night veiled the four young men as they drove back into town. Abbas met them in the back alley and directed the unloading of the supplies. Ardeshir kept his share in the truck and left in the night. Mostafa carried Hassan into the home and Nimtaj descended on her son with an arsenal of herbs and medicines.

Pulling Reza into the corner of the room, Abbas hugged his son. For a moment, Reza thought Abbas might be crying. He released him and spoke with soft, clear words. "You did well."

Spring 1979

"Reza, tomorrow you will go with Hassan to the Zandi's house and pick out a goldfish," Nimtaj said as she cleared the dinner dishes. Her voice tried to bring hope into the home with the promise of the *Nowruz.* The girls followed her into the kitchen with the platters and only Mariam's face had brightened with the mention of the goldfish.

"No, not to the Zandis," Abbas said.

"Really, Baba?" Hassan said. "The Zandis are bad now?"

Reza looked quickly to his father. *No, not the Zandis, too.*

"I didn't say they were bad," Abbas said. "We just have to be very careful."

Only Soraya came back into the room. Pari, Farah and Mariam remained in the kitchen to help Nimtaj.

"Careful of the Zandis?" Soraya said. She pointed to a basket and Reza handed it to her. "They've been our friends since—well—since before any one of us were even born."

Reza studied his father's face. Deep lines of sadness wrapped around Abbas's eyes as his lips struggled to form the right words. Hugging his knees, Reza rocked slowly and waited for his father to explain this new world. The one where friends who knew him before he was born could no longer be trusted. Even for a goldfish.

"They are still good people," Abbas said. "But I don't like some of what I heard at their home the other night."

"About Ayatollah Khomeini?" Hassan asked. "I heard them talking, too. They think that he's going to better for Iran than Shah."

"Hassan," Abbas started and then let out a long sigh.

"What Baba is saying," Reza said, "is that no one knows who is better for Iran, but everyone thinks they know. And there's a lot about this Khomeini that we don't know. So we just have to be careful until the right people are back in power."

Hassan and Soraya looked to their father. A smile came to his lips, although it was not the smile they remembered as children. "We must hope for the right people," he said. "Until then, we will do without a goldfish."

* * * * *

A few weeks later, Reza met Farid behind a pile of boulders near the mountains where they connected in secret to share bits of news.

"You look tired," Farid said.

"Who sleeps anymore?"

Early April breezes stirred the trees. Birds seemed to struggle through songs they used to belt out with happiness and hope. Although the sky hosted no clouds, the blue hung dull and listless.

Farid reached into his coat. "Mostafa's friend brought these envelopes to my house last night." He opened one and dumped the contents onto the flat, grey boulder.

Reza looked at the little pile. He did not reach for it. "We've not heard from Mostafa. And we've had no electricity, no batteries for the radio. Sorry, I come with little news."

Farid opened the first envelope. "I am afraid I am the one with the news today and it's not good," he said.

Reza shook his head, mirroring the motion he had seen so many times from his father. "Let's hear it."

Farid made little stacks of newspaper articles and notebook paper. "This article claims that on February 11 Shah's regime officially collapsed, making the revolutionaries victorious and—" Farid showed Reza a tattered sheet of paper. "It says that there's been a Foundation of Islamic Republican party by revolutionary clerics led by guess who?"

"Khomeini."

"And he's not wasting any time. Khomeini replaced Shapur Bakhtiar as prime minister with Dr. Mehdi Bazargan."

"But Bakhtiar had also opposed Shah."

"I think Khomeini saw Bakhtiar's position as the former leader of the National Front, not to mention his secular ties, as a threat."

"Politics, religion and power," Reza mumbled.

Farid pointed to a wrinkled newspaper article. "But Bazargan has spoken to the importance of democracy." He neatly folded that article and took out a piece of notebook paper with scribbled words. "See these names?"

Reza looked at the paper.

"The Revolutionary Tribunals, under the rule of the *ulama,* are executing hundreds of senior army officers. Rumors are that former Prime Minister Amir Abbas Hoveyda and his entire cabinet are next."

"Says who?"

"The hanging judge," Farid said as he mimicked the gesture of being hung. "Ayatollah Sadeq Khalkhali. And you better be careful. That little organized group of wrestlers you led might get you arrested."

"For what? Getting food for my family?"

Farid looked around. He unfolded another article. "Read what—"

Reza pushed it away. "I'm done with all this."

"You need to hear this," Farid said. "And I'm quoting Khomeini now, 'Civil rights and legal procedures are nothing more than a reflection of the Western sickness among us. The people on trial are criminals and should be killed.'"

"But you said Bazargan is prime minister and he's—"

"He's not in control, Reza," Farid said. "You've got to be careful."

"Careful? I get food for the family. How's that a crime?" Reza looked away from the paper and into the silhouette of his timeless mountains. He had nothing more to say.

"Have you heard of the Islamic Revolutionary Guard Corps?" Farid said as he dug through more articles.

"The what?"

"Or maybe you heard them called the *Sepah e Pasdaran*[1]."

Reza shook his head.

"Or *Sepah* for short."

"I got it. What the hell are they?"

Farid pulled up a picture and showed it to Reza. "Well, it seems Khomeini is concerned that the military and police may still be loyal to Shah or Democratic Front or other groups looking to have a say in the new Iranian government."

---

1 Khomeini's military force

"So? Khomeini said he's going to Qom to be the religious leader and let the politicians do all the government decisions."

Farid handed a photograph to Reza. "That's Yasser Arafat kissing Khomeini. He showed up here just a couple weeks after Khomeini did."

"Arafat from the PLO?" Reza said. He thought back to the old man at the black market who claimed the Palestinians locked the doors of Cinema Rex. He shook off a chill and gave the photo back to Farid. "I'm done with all this. When will school start?"

Farid carefully tucked the photos and articles back into the envelope. "In some places, the stores and schools are already starting to open. I imagine by September everything will be back open."

"Great," Reza said flatly. He sighed. "I wonder what Mr. Mehdian will have to say about all of this."

Farid's movements froze. "I've heard another terrible rumor." But, he couldn't look at Reza.

"What rumor isn't terrible?" Reza answered.

"I heard something last week. I didn't think it was true, you know, like you say, there're so many rumors." He looked to the sky. "But this I heard about Mr. Mehdian."

Reza snapped his face to Farid's. "What rumors? Did he leave the country?"

"No, that's not what I heard."

Reza searched his cousin's face with the familiar feeling of fear that always closed his throat.

Farid leaned into Reza and held him in his gaze. "Reza, they—"

"They who? What did they—"

"They took him out of his house and—in front of his family—"

"What? What happened?"

Farid took a deep breath. "They shot him."

Reza dropped to his knees and cradled his head in his hands. "No, no, no, no! Not Mr. Mehdian! Why? Why him? He's a good man. He's a—what would he have to do with any of this?" Before he could stop himself, Reza dissolved in a stream of tears.

• • • • •

Spring melted most of the snow, but the grey skies seemed to remain in a state of winter.

Reza's mind swirled with the conversations he had had with Mr. Mehdian. He wanted to ask Mostafa about politics, power and religion, but he couldn't form the right words.

On April 1, the Abedis gathered around the radio. The BBC sputtered with news of widespread riots and violent clashes using weapons of war. News that Iranians had come to expect, but tonight there was an added message. In the darkness, the radio declared, "Ninety-eight percent of the votes have been tallied in favor of an Islamic Republic."

Abbas snapped off the radio. "So it is true what Mostafa tells me. The world will think we voted to be an Islamic Republic."

"But," Hassan asked, "but that means Khomeini will put people in charge to run the government who will share the oil profits, right?"

"We'll see," Abbas said. "Khomeini made a lot of promises."

Violent images of Mr. Mehdian's bloody body invaded Reza's mind. He shook his head to clear the picture, but the kind eyes of the teacher looked right through him. *If you stand for nothing, you will fall for anything.* "Baba," Reza said. "Things have to get better. Right?"

"Nothing has to get better."

Summer 1979

"I've heard there will be more demonstrations tonight," Reza said. He drove the old car with Ardeshir, Farid and Hassan through the streets of Kermanshah. Warm, dusty winds blew in the open window and offered no relief. "Mostafa said some members of the National Democratic Front are protesting Khomeini's failure to consult them in governmental decisions."

Farid pointed to a young man who stood in the back of his truck on a street corner. "Let's go see why he's calling people over."

"Park behind this building," Hassan said. "In case we need to drive away fast."

"And both of you, keep your mouth shut," Ardeshir said looking to Farid and Hassan. "I'm not jumping in to save you this time."

Reza gave his friend a grin. Like Reza, Ardeshir had continued to work out daily despite the political uncertainties. Although everything about Ardeshir was twice the size of Reza, Reza's fierce athletic build gave him an equally formidable appearance.

The four young men stood toward the back of the crowd. Ardeshir and Reza inched forward, with Hassan and Farid standing close behind them.

The man in the back of the truck waved a newspaper. "Light

it and then wave the smoke in front of your eyes to stop the burn of tear gas."

A younger man grabbed the paper. Reza stood on tiptoe to see what would happen next. He cringed at the sight of three mangled stubs of flesh where fingers should have been. With his good hand, this man smoothed the paper across his dirty car hood. "Of course! You bring us *Ayandegan*[2]. Khomeini would love to see us burn this!" He held up his disfigured hand and yelled, "His *Sepah* took these fingers two weeks ago when we protested the closing down of this paper. I will not see it burned!"

Men shifted and the dust rose around their filthy clothes. From behind him, Reza heard Farid's voice and turned to see him pulling out his tattered notebook.

Farid flipped several pages and pushed his glasses up through the sweat. "I believe you are referring to when Khomeini ordered *Ayandegan* closed after they printed an article against his *Velayat-e faqih*. . Yes, I believe it was an act of his newly formed Revolutionary Guard."

"Whose side are you on?" The man of the disfigured hand called to Farid.

The dust settled and not a soul moved. To call out someone's loyalties in these turbulent times could mean an immediate and violent death if you were with the wrong crowd. Reza tried to anticipate which men from this crowd might attack them first. Ardeshir growled and shot Reza a sideways glance.

"Side?" Farid asked. "I am merely pointing out that if Khomeini insists on using *Velayat-e faqih* as the basis for drafting a new constitution then it will—"

"Will what?" said another man as he took a step toward Farid.

"Will make Iran completely Islamic," Farid finished. "As ordained by God himself."

"And you have a problem with that?" another voice bellowed.

"I might," Farid answered. "It reinstates the *ulama* and *grand ayatollahs* as a ruling class. Even though Bazargan is prime minister, his decision-making powers are reduced."

With his larger-than-life smile, Reza stepped forward. "And it could all be rumors."

Farid glanced at Reza, flipped another page and continued. "Of course. I just wanted to note that *Ayandegan* was the first

2 One of the major newspapers in Iran

newspaper to call out *Velayat-e faqih.*" He looked at the glistening faces. "Really, it is something we should have seen in Khomeini's earliest writings and—"

"And what?" an angry voice asked.

Farid flipped to another page. "And it is very significant to note that no one had really heard of *Velayat-e faqih* before. *Ayandegan* did the right thing to question its validity. In my opinion, Khomeini should not have called the people at the paper wild animals." He looked up briefly. "And I'm quoting Khomeini now, 'we will not tolerate them anymore . . . that . . . after each revolution several thousand of these corrupt elements are executed in public and burnt . . . that . . . we will close all parties except the one . . .'"

The shadow of a face bearing fresh scars crossed Farid's notebook. Farid looked into the dark eyes of a man twice his size. "You done?" the man bellowed.

Ardeshir and Reza took a step closer to Farid.

Farid peered into the shadow. "I mean no disrespect. I simply want to dispel rumors."

The man pulled his shirt over his head to expose a road map of bruises and welts and a cascade of crumpled flesh. He turned his back to Farid and barked, "Do you see your rumors there? Do you see the marks of burning oil poured onto us by Khomeini's guard? Can you read his *Velayat-e faqih* in the folds of my flesh?"

The man turned back around to face Farid but found himself staring into Reza's narrowed eyes. "My cousin said he means no disrespect," Reza said. "You do not suffer alone. My *baradar* also bears such scars."

"As do many of us," said another voice.

Ardeshir stood behind Reza. "We are finished here."

The men nodded and grumbled, then broke into smaller groups to continue their discussions. From a car several feet away, a few men gathered and Reza could hear Khomeini's voice coming from the cassette deck in the car.

Ardeshir yanked Farid's arm, and his notebook landed in the dust. "Put that damn notepad away before I make you eat it," Ardeshir said.

Fall 1979

On a crisp Saturday morning, Reza and Ardeshir finished their run through the streets of Kermanshah before arriving at the gym for the day's workout. Ardeshir's weekend training sessions resumed, as did school, but under the regime of Ayatollah Khomeini. Abbas's earlier warning to "be careful who you talk to, who you are seen with, what you say" fell like a hammer on their daily lives. Daily lives that seethed in the cauldron of the unknown.

Just before approaching the gym, the wrestlers slowed to a walk. Like the life they once knew, their white breath cut into the air and slowly dissolved away. Reza placed his hands on his hips and tried to feel comfort in the sun rising over the mountains.

"Have you heard anything about the American Embassy?" Reza asked. "I thought they were supposed to let those people go by now."

"Khomeini got involved," Ardeshir said. "What does Mostafa say about the vote in December?"

His question slightly startled Reza. Ardeshir usually didn't discuss politics, especially since his father had quickly moved up the ranks of Khomeini's Revolutionary Guard.

"Well," Reza said, after he looked around to be sure the streets and alleys were clear, "he thinks Khomeini purposely chose the day after the *Ashura*[3] holiday and he's using the fact that Carter allowed Shah into the United States to prove Shah was a puppet of the West."

"He was."

"I guess," Reza said. "Mostafa thinks there will only be the one choice of Islamic Republic on the ballot anyway."

The young men began to walk toward the gym.

"It's only a matter of time before the documents are discovered in that den of spies to prove the Americans and English pulled off Operation Ajax," Ardeshir said. He took a large stone and threw it over a wall. "They took out Mossadegh and put in Shah."

"Mostafa said it's all about the oil profits." Reza shook his head. "Power and politics."

"Does Mostafa know if they're going to kill the American hostages?"

Reza stopped his pace. "Where'd you get that idea?"

"Just asking."

They turned up the alley to the gym. Ardeshir stopped, interlocked his hands and placed them on top of his head. His thick

3 Islamic holiday recognized differently by Sunni and Shia Muslims.

arms bulged out on either side, but Reza thought his face looked like that of a lost child.

"I heard my father say Bazargan quit like a coward," Ardeshir said. "Khomeini just appointed him and now he's trying to flee."

"Farid had articles where Bazargan talked about wanting more of a democracy," Reza said. Just before he reached the gym door, he turned to Ardeshir. "Nothing makes any sense anymore."

Ardeshir moved closer to Reza. "The only thing that makes sense to me," he said, pointing inside the gym, "are those mats."

• • • • •

Later that afternoon, Reza listened to Ardeshir and Farid argue whose town had the best-looking girls. Despite the cold, the young men preferred to sit on Reza's rooftop so their discussions would be away from the others. Making due with several layers of clothing and a few rough blankets, they tried to piece together the fraying edges of their world.

Ardeshir's weekend visits often came with his stories of the array of delicious girls just ripe for marrying. Finishing a set of pushups, Ardeshir huffed, "and all of them wanna be paired with a *ghahreman*, so I'll not get one who looks like the butt of a goat."

"How lucky for your children," Farid responded, adding Ardeshir's wool blanket to his legs. "They'll have only half a chance of looking like you."

Ardeshir reached over and reclaimed his blanket. "Each night, after you wed and bed the goat's ass, just think of my beautiful face."

Farid grunted in a response signaling this verbal sparring was over, and he turned his attention to Reza. Sitting cross-legged, Reza stared into the sunset, absorbed in his dreams for Europe. "What about the girls in Europe?"

"Well, you're not going to meet any," Ardeshir said. "You're Iranian, you're poor and you're going to marry someone who looks like Farid's goat's ass and raise little goat-ass children." He pulled his blankets and secured them tightly while tossing a warning glance to Farid. Then he rested his interlaced hands under his head and closed his eyes.

"I may be all those things," Reza responded. "But someday it'll be different for me."

"No it won't," Ardeshir answered. "Accept it."

"My wife," Reza said, to no one in particular, "will be no one's goat's ass. And she's sure not going to look like Ardeshir. No, she's in a land far from here." He blew into his hands. "Far from these crushing laws and paranoid rules. She's where you can be who you want to be, where the only thing stopping you is you."

Neither boy responded, perhaps each hoping the other would. Because, somehow, when Reza said these things, they seemed possible.

After many minutes, Ardeshir stood and walked toward the ladder. "Well, she's not going to be an American. They think all Iranians are evil villains since those Muslim students took over their embassy."

Farid scooped up the blanket pile and followed Ardeshir. "Most Iranians don't even know there are American hostages," he said. He looked at Reza. "The Americans probably don't know about it either."

Reza stood up and walked to the roof's edge. He looked into the last ray of the setting sun. "I'm afraid Ardeshir's right. Holding those Americans hostage is going to really piss off the West," he said. But nobody heard him.

Chapter Thirteen

2009

I remember waking up as a small child and screaming for my dad. He would check under my bed, again, and promised there were no monsters. Forty years later I'm ripped awake with the same feeling. My husband tells me I'm working too much on this book. "It's all you ever do," he says.

"I know," I admit. "I'm sorry. Somehow it went from a hobby to a project to a—calling."

"What calling?" he says. "Just write Reza's story."

"It's more than that," I whisper.

It's 4:00 a.m. and nothing makes sense at the hour meant for the unconscious. I sit up and pull the covers up to my chin. "At first it was Reza's story. Then it was his family's. And now I feel like there's so much more to tell."

My husband has already drifted back to sleep so I slip downstairs and pop open my laptop. I replay YouTube videos of the American hostages and I remember. I remember my mother standing in our living room and then moving slowly to perch on the end of our gold couch. The rabbit ears poke into the olive drapes and she directs me to bend them toward the macramé plant holder. I do so and, although the picture is not clearer, I sit next to her. Bleeding onto our screen is the image of an American hostage, his face wrapped in a dirty white cloth, surrounded by dark-eyed men raising their guns.

My mother twists her dishtowel. "Those damn bastards."

Chapter Fourteen

Spring 1980

Although families used the New Year *Nowruz* celebration to try to bring a sense of normalcy, Khomeini's promises of riches were being replaced with increasing repression. The girls were forced to observe *hejab.* And each day Hassan would run to the mail and look for the oil money check, and each day he came back empty-handed.

At their usual meeting place, Hassan and Reza greeted Farid before walking into the school.

"*Salam,*" Reza said with a tired sigh. "Big test in math today and I didn't finish my studies."

Farid put his hand on his cousin's shoulder. "I'm afraid you have bigger problems than that, my *dooste-man.*" He pulled out his notebook. "And I quote from Khomeini's New Year's speech: 'We must rail against imperialist universities where those cloaked with the West teach and study. All universities in Iran must become completely Islamic.'"

A thud echoed as Reza's books hit the dirt. "When did he—why would he—what does that mean?" *All universities must become completely Islamic?*

"It means you're going to have to become a devout follower of Islam or you're not going to be accepted into any of the universities in Iran," Farid answered.

Picking Reza's books out of the dirt, Hassan held them out to him. But Reza stood frozen. Hassan took a step toward his brother. "You're smart enough, Rez, and strong enough. Just memorize some of those prayers Naneh's always saying."

Reza grabbed his books. "It's not that easy." He looked at Farid. "Devout follower of Islam? He said that? Those exact words?"

"*Baleh*, Reza. With *Velayat-e faqih* in the constitution, Iran is now an Islamic nation. Better start growing a beard."

"A beard?" Reza said. "Somehow a beard is going to make me more—I don't know—more Muslim? I can't live like this, Farid."

"You don't have a choice."

Rubbing his hands together, Reza stared off into the silhouette of mountains that sliced into the sky. "Is Joe Frazier still dead?"

"Is who still—you mean the American boxer?"

Reza nodded, his eyes not leaving the mountainside.

Farid stood next to his cousin and joined in his stare. "Still dead," Farid answered.

Placing a hand on Farid's shoulder, Reza whispered, "Well, I'm not."

• • • • •

Darkness descended on Reza's books. Each night, he sat on the rooftop surrounded by stacks of texts—closest to him lay the precious pile of those without titles on their covers.

"Naneh wanted me to bring you this plate," Pari said as she placed it on the rooftop and hoisted herself over. "Since you missed dinner again."

"Thank you, *azizam*," Reza said. "Did you finish your dinner?"

"*Baleh*," she said. "Is your big test tomorrow?"

Reza nodded.

Pari looked around. Her eyes grew wide in her pale face. "Do you have to read all these books to pass?"

Smiling, Reza took the plate. "Every word in every one."

"Oh. Well, I'm glad Naneh says prayers for you every night." She flipped open a few books. "That should help."

"It always has," he said.

Pari gave a small giggle.

"What?"

"My friend's sister said you're cute."

"Really?" Reza said, setting his book aside. "Who's that?"

"I promised I wouldn't say. But, I hear it, too, in the bathhouse when I go with Naneh."

"Cute? Is that all they say?"

"They think you're strong and smart and have a nice face."

Reza rubbed his chin with his hand. "What's a nice face?" he mumbled to himself, realizing that this world of women would be even more difficult to understand than all the books that surrounded him.

With another little laugh, Pari pulled at a lock of Reza's thick hair and stepped over the books toward the roof's edge.

"Well, thanks again for the dinner," he said.

Pari started down the ladder, then she stopped and came back to the top. "I really hope you get into the university."

Reza spoke through a mouthful of rice. "With Naneh's prayers, I'm in for certain."

• • • • •

His academic and physical qualifications were stellar and each day sowed increasing hope for the opportunities that come with higher education. The final interview in the screening process rested with the mullah to ensure Reza's deep devotion to Islam and the Ayatollah Khomeini.

After his final interview, Reza waited on the thick wooden bench in the barren stone hall. The office door opened and he snapped to his feet. The mullah walked to Reza. "Denied" is all he said. And he walked away.

Reza sunk to his knees. Tears would not come. He clenched his fists and held his breath with a fear that if he so much as breathed, he would curse all the mullahs to hell. Biting his lip, he damned the day Khomeini was born. *You will not stop me. I will be more than your slave!* Blood trickled from his mouth and he let it drip onto the stone floor.

He turned and ran. He tore through the streets of Kermanshah until he found himself pressed up against the cliff he had climbed with Ardeshir. Pain shook his body with unnatural rhythm as rippling muscles pulled him up the cliff. Darkness plastered the mountainside and the moon did not share her light. His hands and feet seemed to be on separate paths as he neared the top. Cascades of stone crashed against the cliff to mix with the blood dripping from his feet.

His right hand grabbed a rock that came loose and plummeted to the hard ground below. As he hung perpendicular from the cliff's face, swinging like an old gate, Reza felt the hot breath of death on his neck. *Let go* it breathed. *Just let go.*

"Nooooo!" his voice boomed off the carvings of kings.

• • • • •

Ardeshir found Reza at the top of their mountain sitting cross-legged and staring into the carving of Darius. In the fading moonlight, the ghosts of the fallen warriors hovered and ached. As if commanded by his ancestors, Ardeshir stood silent for a moment before he sat alongside his friend. "Your family's worried about you. Nimtaj's convinced you've been arrested."

Reza's face bled tears. "I know. I'm sorry to worry her. I just couldn't—I couldn't— What can I say to them?"

They stared into the carved faces of the immortal warriors. A tiny black bug approached the puddle from Reza's bleeding bare feet. Its shiny wings sparkled as it hovered over the blood. Ardeshir crushed it.

"Too bad we weren't born with them. They got it," Ardeshir said. "The strong ruled and the rest listened. All these rules and laws now, they are the ways of the paranoid and the cowardly."

Reza nodded.

Ardeshir took a deep breath. "I don't know what you're going to do. But my life has been chosen for me."

"Chosen for you? No one can choose a life for you." Reza grasped for words to match the fears whisking through his mind like the wicked winds.

Ardeshir looked into the empty, dark sky. "My father, as an officer in Khomeini's Elite Revolutionary Guard." He stopped. His lips formed the words before his breath could say them. He looked away from Reza. "He has bid me to join him."

Reza grabbed his friend's arm. "No! He cannot make you be a *Sepahi*! How can you support Khomeini and be a part of his lies? He's a coward. You said so yourself."

"Shhh! You want to be slaughtered right here?"

"In the mountains? They'll follow us in the—"

"Shhh, they're everywhere," he whispered. "And next week I will report to be with them and sent to Beirut."

Reza took a stick and drew lines through his blood puddle. There was nothing more to say. *Ardeshir's a Sepah e Pasdaran and I—I will be next.* Reza lay on his back and pressed his hands to his face. He glanced at his friend's shaking body, also silent in its sobs.

The damp chill of morning woke the young warriors and they descended the mountain. Revolutionary Guards paced the monuments and no families came to picnic.

Ardeshir pointed to something under the enormous tree. They cautiously approached the long, grotesque figure rotting under the branches.

"He is dead."

• • • • •

At dinner, Reza shared the news his family already knew, that his admission was denied to the university. He took another bite and chewed in the silence before he said the words his mother couldn't bear to hear. "In four months," he said, "I will join Amir in the Air Force."

Nimtaj set down her plate and touched her heart.

"Why?" Soraya said. "You can wait and apply to the university again in—"

"I'm tired of waiting!"

"Can you try out for the wrestling team?" Hassan asked. "Like Ardeshir said?"

Reza looked to his mother who still held her heart, gently rocking. "That's my plan. Amir can get me privileges on his base and, after I complete the boot camp, I'll train to compete for a place on the wrestling team." He turned his attention to Hassan. "I've worked it all out with Amir."

Hassan nodded with satisfaction. "You'll make the team."

"Naneh," Reza said. "I'll be fine."

"You leave this winter," Nimtaj said, with the quiet voice of a mother's heartache.

"Just before the snows. That's when Amir can get me on his base. I won't be on the front lines because I'm going to wrestle for the National Military Team," he paused. "Really Naneh, I will be—" Reza saw that his words brought no peace so he quickly scanned his mind for what might. "But I will take you to Qom before I leave, like we've talked about."

Nimtaj nodded and left for her room.

Reza watched her go. *I don't know what else to do.*

August 1980

"Look, his foot twitches," Reza said to Farid over the chanting of the bloodthirsty crowd. "I think he's still alive."

The four bloodied men, their hands and feet bound in dirty ropes, stood on the hanging platform as cords were tightened around their necks. The cords attached to a monstrous crane recently erected over the main square in Kermanshah.

Mullahs pointed to the condemned men and then yelled "These men are evil!" to the repeating roars of the crowd. "They defy God in their abhorrent ways! He—" said the tallest mullah, whose flowing black robes gave him the appearance of floating above the others. "He is a homosexual and his unnatural act must bring him death. God is great!" The pulsating crowd directed its hate toward the man in the middle, who yelled and spat in protest.

"I think he just peed himself," Farid said. "Look, isn't it wet right there?"

"Don't point!" Reza pulled Farid's hand to his side. "What if someone thinks you are pointing at someone we know? Are you mad?"

"You're right. Just thought when the sun hit it, you could see the wet spot."

Reza and Farid, looking foreign to each other as their mandatory beards sprouted from their seventeen-year-old chins, separated themselves from the sweating masses and crossed through the dusty alleys for home. In years past, such a walk would have been accompanied by energetic conversation or maybe a smile to a passing girl. Today, in the raging summer of 1980, Reza and Farid walked in fearful silence, as though the uneven mud-covered walls directly reported their activities to the Ayatollah Khomeini himself.

Turning down an obscure path that led the two from the town through the fields, Farid cautiously began a conversation. "I wonder if they'll do that every day, until the town is rid of all the—"

"Rid of all what? People? Who knows what things those men actually did?" Reza took a leap over a fallen tree in the path and crunched down in the arid grass.

"Shhh, don't be so loud," Farid said, stepping over the same log. Despite the desert heat they both wore long-sleeved shirts over their pants, now bearing the sweat marks of a long day.

"This *Velayat-e faqih* is a death sentence," Reza said. "That's all it is, an excuse to terrify and murder people."

Farid nodded in agreement but offered no answers.

Reza continued to speak, his voice wandering as his thoughts crisscrossed through questions and ideas. "Those books and pamphlets Mr. Mehdian gave us." He paused to reconfirm the silence around them. "I've been reading them again, slowly this time, and made some notes. It makes me think about all these things. This crushing control. It's not how it's supposed to be."

The path brought them closer to town and Reza could see the rooftop of his home among the patchy flat browns in the distance. He stopped, turned toward the thick orange sun descending into the timeless Middle Eastern sky and fingered the wisps of his unwelcome beard. "I can't live like this."

September 1980

Nimtaj's hand lightly brushed the magnificent prayer rugs that hung in a row in the bustling bazaar of Qom. Reza hovered near his mother, absorbing the occasional bumps from the other escorted women who mimicked a trail of black ants along the merchants' path. Staunch faces peering from the dark frames of flowing chadors became one. Merchants, who once called out and bartered, now tempered their voices and rolled prayer beads in their fingers.

Careful not to smile or speak loudly, Reza leaned toward his mother. "That's a nice one, Naneh."

She waved her hand. "Not as nice as the ones in Kermanshah," she said. "Our rugs have soul."

"Of course. But it's nice to see things from other places sometimes."

Nimtaj nodded and made her voice barely above a whisper. "*Baleh*, and when you go to Europe, you will see nice things there too," she said. A smile perched on her lips. "But there is dirt."

Reza stopped. *She knows I think there's no dirt?*

Finding himself and his mother in an isolated doorway, Reza tried to begin a thousand sentences and came out with, "I figured there probably would be."

"Dirt," she said. "And all the opportunities that come with it. You're too smart not to go to the university and you were not born to be a soldier."

"Naneh, I'll be fine," Reza said. "Amir will get me a tryout for the Air Force's wrestling team."

Two *Sepahi* from the Revolutionary Guard approached them. The shorter man's thick green uniform was wrapped too tightly in an attempt to fit around his lazy belly. A filthy smell, mixed with splashes of rose water, met Reza and Nimtaj just ahead of the guards. The taller man's dull, wide-set eyes pierced into Reza. Nimtaj bowed her head but Reza returned the stare. The white glove of the taller guard caressed his gun as he squinted at Reza, smirking.

The boots stopped in front of the mother and son. Reza's jaw tightened; his judgment firm in his face. *Cowards. Your uniform means nothing.*

By stepping to the wall, Nimtaj gave the guards room to pass. A pause, a breath and they walked on. It was several moments before Reza found his voice. "I will not be them," he said. "I will never be them."

"I know," Nimtaj answered. "I've known from the day Haji Abbas brought you to his gym."

Fond memories of the gym flowed like cleansing waters through Reza. "You wanted me to play soccer," he smiled.

"I did, but even I could not keep you from those mats."

"Those mats," Reza said. "Do you know how much I miss those mats? That's the only reason I'm in the Air Force. Really. I know I can make the National Team. And travel. And—"

Nimtaj looked at her son. "And follow your heart."

He looked at her and took in every line, every freckle and the very curve of her face. Imprints from years of sun and cold winters caressed her skin, leaving a map of memories. Beside the wrinkles of worries, her cinnamon eyes sparkled with hope.

They approached the large open courtyard paved in eggshell-like stone and stood to absorb the majestic grandeur of the four looming towers marking the vast golden top. Qom, the second holiest city in Iran, gave Reza anything but a feeling of peace.

Leering over the gentle pilgrims, Revolutionary Guard watched for an escaping strand of a woman's hair, a hint of lipstick perhaps, maybe an uninvited smile to a man unknown to her. Reza kept a wary eye on his mother and tried to feel the beauty of the moment, but he couldn't escape the ever-present feeling of being watched, being analyzed, being suffocated.

Nimtaj scurried into the shrine and prayed with her whole heart and soul. Reza had tried to do the same in the section devoted for the prayers of men. *I pray you to watch my family. I pray these paranoid control freaks get thrown out of Iran. I pray I can get into a university and I can become a teacher and I...*

And then the whispers began. Whispers at first, always there were whispers. Reza and Nimtaj regrouped in the courtyard where the words were clear and audible now. Iraq had dropped bombs on Iran and sent soldiers across the border. Kermanshah, a border and oil-rich city, would be a primary target.

"Naneh, we must get to the car," Reza said grabbing his mother's hand. "We have to leave now!"

Reza's foot pumped the gas pedal, willing the old car to fly to Kermanshah. Reza understood his hometown, only sixty miles from the Iraq border and graced by surrounding oil fields, would be a prime bombing target. Driving through the endless night, Reza and Nimtaj were greeted by a wicked orange glow across the horizon of their beloved Kermanshah. Iraq's bombs had landed on their oil refinery targets, giving rise to a furnace raining an ooze of oil.

• • • • •

The war shortages strangled the families and Reza worked every day to secure food and basic supplies. The sounds of bombs crashed with vengeance and rocked them with greater firepower than the days of the Revolution.

Soon after their return from Qom, Abbas and the men of the neighborhood worked with a false hope to secure their homes. The humble brick dwellings lay exposed like the soft underbelly of a turtle to the Iraqi fighter jets that would roar overhead.

• • • • •

A few weeks after their return from Qom, Reza lay exhausted on the mattress in the main room. Since many of the panes of glass had been shattered, he could hear Nimtaj patting the flour for bread loaves in the kitchen. He turned to watch his mother in the light of the clay stove and marveled at a woman who never did anything for herself. Next to her, Pari helped roll the dough while Mariam sang softly.

Reza peeled himself off the floor and went to sit next to his sisters. He could think of nothing to say, so he simply asked, "Naneh, do you have enough flour? Should I go out and get some more?"

Nimtaj kept her rhythm and shook her head slowly. "No, no. We've plenty. Why don't you rest? It's quiet."

"*Baleh,* it is. Where's everybody?"

She stopped her patting for a moment and looked at Reza with a smile. "Iraj, Mostafa's best friend—"

"The wrestler, right?" Reza felt a tightness in his chest.

"*Baleh.*" She resumed her patting. "The arrangements are being made for him to marry Farah in three weeks' time."

"Three weeks!" He lowered his voice. "Why so soon?"

She focused on her dough. "Farah is happy and you should be too."

"Iraj is a good man." He continued to watch his mother in silence. *Farah's happy. Happy.* He bit his lip. *I can't even remember what happy feels like.*

"So," Nimtaj continued, "Soraya and Farah went to Mehri's for a visit and Hassan's with Farid." She slapped the round dough against the warm oven's dome.

"Who escorted the girls?"

"Haji Abbas took them in the cab and will bring them home. Soon, *Inshallah.*" She rested her powdered hands on her knees.

"Next time," Pari said as she scooted over to sit next to Reza, "I get to go, too."

He brushed a long curly lock of hair back from her pale face. "In Baba's cab? Maybe he'll let you drive and—Naneh, did you hear?—the planes!"

Shaking with uncontrolled violence, the tender house exploded in deafening waves. No longer able to be heard, Reza motioned to Nimtaj to take Mariam and Pari into the back alley. He tried to cover the oven's burning coals, but a blast smashed him against the wall, and plaster crumbled from every part of the house.

"Naneh! Naneh! Are you okay? Can you hear me?" Reza struggled to get to his feet but was knocked down by several more blasts. He crawled toward the courtyard and called for his family. No answer. He stood up and started to go down the alley when he heard Pari.

"Help me!" she cried as she stumbled into the street. Above her, two more Iraqi jets slashed through the sky. "Help me! Please!" She pulled her hands over her head and waited to die.

Reza scooped up Pari and ran back toward the house. Holding her shivering body, he called for his mother. "Naneh!"

"Here!" Naneh said. Mariam clung to her side at the end of the alley. Another shattering roar rocked them to their core.

Not knowing where to go, Reza ran toward his mother and they huddled next to the side of the house. Looking up, Reza saw the detail of the Iraqi flag on the sides of the silver bombers as they flew off to their next target.

"Wait here," he said. He climbed to the roof for a better view. From this vantage point, he clearly understood the specific targets: the schools, major highways, oil fields, the market place and the hospital. Like a bizarre scene from hell where fire mixed with snow, his beloved city lay covered in dust and flames. Billows of black smoke dotted the horizon and fire spit into the sky.

To clear his head, he closed his eyes—and for a moment he remembered hopeful families, bending their antennas this way and that, calling down to children waiting below, "Now? Can you see anything now?" He saw himself fall from the roof. With a swollen foot, he watched two warriors refusing to stay down, their sweat and blood splashing behind the thick wall of glass.

"Reza! Do you see anyone?" Nimtaj burst into his thoughts.

Reza rushed to the side of the rooftop, half afraid his mother's voice was still in his dreams. "Naneh. Are you okay?"

"You have to find everyone!"

He climbed down the ladder and looked at his mother. He didn't know what to do next. Shaking the house, a second wave of distant bombers announced they would soon be near. Nimtaj, holding Mariam and with Pari clinging to her side, stood without wavering. "Walk toward Mehri's," she said. "And watch for Baba's cab."

He had only gone a few blocks before Abbas's cab came bouncing down the torn-up street. Farah opened the door and he slid inside. "Where's Hassan?" he asked.

"We don't know," Soraya answered. "We've been driving all over, but no one's seen him."

"Did you find Farid?" Reza said as he climbed from the back seat to the front.

"I'm taking the girls home," Baba said. "Then we'll look."

The old cab bumped over holes and swerved around fallen debris. They pulled up in front of the house. "Do not go outside," Abbas said. "Stay with your mother."

Reza was about to scold Soraya and add that she should "listen for once" but she spoke first. "We will, Baba." She looked at Reza through a current of tears. "Please bring Hassan home."

Hours of darkness and there was still no sign. Too many parts of the road were impassable, so they parked the cab and continued on foot. Broken, blood-stained families stumbled along the streets, also in a quest to reunite with loved ones. People moved in either a blank trance or a panicked rush, as mothers went to one another saying the names of their children. A young woman, her face blackened and bloodied, carried a limp child.

A pang gripped Reza's gut and he realized he hadn't eaten for almost a day. Abbas's steady pace showed no hunger. Judging by the moon, Reza figured it to be close to 4:00 a.m. and almost twelve hours since the first raid. They had found Farid at his home around midnight. He said Hassan had already started to go back home just after the first wave of bombing. Reza and Abbas criss-crossed along all the possible alleyways. Now, in the mostly vacant streets, the homes of Kermanshah cowered like beaten dogs.

A pounding sound came from the street behind them and Abbas pulled Reza to hide behind a toppled wall. An Iranian army caravan crushed along the road. Reza looked to his father, his face puzzled. *We're hiding?* His father looked straight ahead.

In the butchered light, Reza spotted a small figure wandering in the street. Behind him, the continued rumble of the caravan was heading right toward the child. Abbas followed Reza's eyes, Reza's thoughts, and, before he could stop him, Reza leaped over the wall.

The engine's heat burned Reza's back as he scooped up the little girl and dove into a bush. He looked up to see a soldier flick a lit cigarette butt at them and laugh.

"You bastard! You dog!" Reza yelled. He stood up to hurl more biting words when a rough hand touched his arm.

"Reza, no!" Abbas said. "The child's safe. That's enough."

The little girl rested her head on Reza's shoulder. "Naneh," she whimpered.

Reza squinted his eyes as the final cloud of dust settled. "We'll find your Naneh," he said. He looked around the desolate street. "Where do you live?"

"With Naneh and Baba," she answered.

Reza let out a long, slow breath, set the little girl down and knelt next to her.

"What's your Naneh's name?" Reza asked. But she answered in cries.

Abbas also knelt next to the child. "Tell me your name."

"Darya," she said.

"Point to where your house is," Abbas said. She pointed straight ahead.

Abbas took Darya's hand and they started to walk along the rubble-strewn sidewalk. Reza watched their silhouette. Without warning, an ice cold rage twisted within him. He clenched his fists and swung his arms. "What's going on?" he spat. "What the hell is happening?"

Without stopping, Abbas answered, "We're taking Darya home."

"No, Baba." He didn't want the little girl to cry again, so he forced an even tone. The struggle burned his eyes with the tears he hated. "Nothing is right anymore. Everything in my life is a—a lie!" He dropped to his knees and wanted to cry, but the words bit at his heart with more anger than sadness.

"Darya!" A woman's voice cut into the night. "Oh, Darya! My baby!"

Looking up, Reza saw a woman desperately trying to keep her *roosari* on with one hand while she ran to her daughter.

Reza got to his feet and walked toward them. Darya ran to her mother and the two sobbed in each other's arms. "The nice men took me to find you," she said. A face, a mother's face where tears cut through blackened blood, looked at Reza. Her dark eyes said thank you in ways words never could. Reza nodded.

Abbas and Reza escorted the two to their home. The woman insisted they have some rice and a cup of chai. They ate on a low wall just outside the door. Reza scraped his plate and, although hunger still lashed at him, he told the woman he was full.

"We will go home," Abbas said. "Hassan may be there by now." He rubbed his forehead and looked to the horizon. "It's almost morning."

They walked into their home and saw Nimtaj kneeling next to Hassan. She massaged herbs into the cuts on his arms, legs and head. Abbas stood above his son as Reza fell to his side. "Hassan!" Reza said.

"Shhh," Nimtaj said. "You mustn't wake him."

"He's okay?"

She nodded.

Abbas surveyed his home, patting the cracks in the walls and seeming to make mental notes of the damage. He didn't speak but rather grumbled at each discovery. Reza found his father staring at the pile of smashed clay where the oven should have been.

"Baba," Reza said. "How can I serve in the Air Force?"

Soiled smoke and scattered fires barred light from the rising sun. Abbas threw the clay against the courtyard wall. "When you stop, you quit, you die," he said.

Reza picked up a piece of broken wall and sent it hurling into the alley. "I'm not eight!" He touched his clasped hands to his forehead and closed his eyes. "We're not on the mats anymore, Baba."

A brave ray of morning struggled through the smoldering town and cast a burning glow on Abbas's face. He placed his firm hands on his son's shoulders. "Reza," he said. He waited for Reza's eyes to open. "No medal you win, no uniform you wear, no oath you take—"

"But, Baba, I can't, I can't." Reza's words caught in his short, shallow breath.

"And no God you pray to or flag you bow before or man of power will ever, ever define you."

• • • • •

"Give brother a hug, Mariam," Nimtaj said, wiping the stream of tears from her own face.

"*Doset Daram*[1]," Mariam's voice cooed as she wrapped her thin arms around him.

"I love you, too," he whispered.

The entire family stood in the blackened, dilapidated bus station to bid him farewell. Hassan's brave whiskers grew in tendril shoots across his teenage face, reflecting this age of no-man's land. Fighting back child-like pangs of sadness, he simply broke from the crowd, embraced Reza, and hung his head as he blended back into his family.

"Please, please don't be a hero, Reza," Soraya whispered as she hugged her brother. "Stay in the back for once and . . ." Her sobs drowned out her last words.

The last to say goodbye, Abbas touched his son on alternating cheeks. "Listen to Amir," he said. "Do as he tells you and you will come home."

"I will," Reza choked out. He boarded the bus.

The military bus secured its human cargo and pulled away from the weeping families. To the people of the border town of Kermanshah, the war with Iraq ground in a daily reality of violent destruction. And Reza was headed right for it.

---

1 I love you

Through the drone of the military bus packed with fresh soldiers, Reza tried to pull in the surrounding beauty of the mountainside, awash in its colors of fall, but the tear-stained face of his mother bled into every image of his mind.

• • • • •

His blessed stars dulled above the bright city of Tehran and left only the surrounding Alborz Mountains to offer memories of simpler times when Reza climbed trails with Ardeshir. He spent weary nights untangling the sounds of honks and shouting in the pulsing city. Days passed in a brain-numbing routine of feats of strength and vows of loyalty to the Ayatollah Khomeini, neither of which Reza found particularly inspiring.

As arranged by Amir's position in the military, Reza was granted permission to stay with his aunt while he completed his training in Tehran. In times of war, compounded by military rations, finding food became Reza's biggest challenge in the barracks. Staying with his aunt, he enjoyed meals he could chew and taste. She only asked that Reza sleep each night on her expensive silk Persian Rug to deter the growing numbers of looters.

• • • • •

In late November, Reza passed by the American Embassy still under siege. Since the takeover, the embassy became the unofficial place for demonstrations, political discussions and general chanting. He eyed the Revolutionary Guards pacing the steps in their falsified stride of power. Intrigued by rumors that Ayatollah Khomeini had the finest Persian carpet weavers dig through the shredded documents to reconstruct secret Western papers, he tried to walk up the steps and peer inside. An AK-47 pointed in his face cured that curiosity.

Pieces of a burnt American flag blew against Reza's leg in the swirl of political flyers denouncing the West and its evil ways. Fingering the blue cloth, he thought of Mr. Mehdian. *What would you make of all this madness? I'm almost glad you didn't live to see it.*

Tucking the cloth into his pocket for no apparent reason, he continued to his aunt's house in anticipation of dinner. Instead, the house stood dark, silent.

"Aunt? Are you home?" Reza looked immediately to the silk rug, still there. He continued through the house, room by room, listening, asking, watching. Until he found his aunt sitting on her bed.

"Why are you so upset? What happened?" Reza sat next to her and put his arms around her trembling body. "Did the police bother you today? Please tell me."

"Be so glad you're a man. Be so glad." She wiped her face in an attempt to gather her thoughts for her nephew.

"Why are you crying? Tell me who did this. I'll find them and I'll kill them."

"Find them? Find thousands of them? Kill them all? I wish you could. The damn bastards. The mullahs and those little idiots, the *Basiji*[2], and their wicked sister group. Barely a beard between them, yet the Basiji roam our streets looking for a rogue strand of a woman's hair, or the glint of lipstick—any excuse . . ." her voice trailed off indicating there was more.

Reza had seen the *Basiji,* Iran's answer to the Hitler Youth, driving through the streets enforcing the laws of Islam. Since men could not touch a woman, they often traveled with a group of women who carried out their vile tasks.

"Did they hurt you?" Reza asked in a softer voice, looking for marks or bruises. "Please tell me what happened."

She slowly stood up and walked to her bedroom window. Her stooped silhouette looked over the city she once loved. "No, they didn't hurt me," she said. "But this little girl, this young girl. She had to be maybe fifteen, sixteen at the most. And with the most wondrous brown eyes like a deer."

"They didn't . . ."

"I heard them come up to her and they were yelling at her. Who knows what they were saying, really." She paused and returned to sit next to Reza. "She had the most beautiful brown eyes, just naturally amazing. That's why I noticed her when she passed me. You know, sometimes you just notice these things."

Reza felt his throat closing as he feared what would come next.

"Two of the women grabbed her arms and a third held her face and yelled and yelled. I could see spit flying. And she was twisting her head by her chin. The whole city passes by and no one, no one stops them." Tears poured without apology for a girl she had never even spoken to.

As she turned to face Reza, he stood to go to her. But she held up her hand.

---

2 An offshoot military group of the Revolutionary Guard whose primary function is to enforce Islamic Law

"I don't even think she knew it was coming—who could?" she said. "Who could think such a thing?" Her mouth first formed the words before her voice could speak them.

Reza squinted his eyes in a studied focus of her lips, trying to discern the final piece. "Put what in her face?" he whispered.

"Acid." She looked down at her hands and then shook with sobs. "They flung acid in her face! And she screamed! And cried! I ran to her and held her, but what could I do? No one else came to help. Her eyes were still as beautiful, but—but the flesh on her face bled and bubbled and—and became colors skin should never . . ." She finished the sentence with exhausted cries.

Raw anger and undefined shame rocked Reza. His insides raged, his body shook. But in the end, he could only cry with her. Cry until he lay drained of all emotions, save one. The one he had tried to banish all his life. Fear.

Chapter Fifteen

Spring 1981

Following weeks of ruthless Boot Camp, Reza transferred to Amir's base and applied to compete on the Air Force's wrestling team. In the darkness of day just before morning, Reza ran with strong strides through the base, slowing at the sight of the wrestling training facility. He stopped and watched his white, crisp breath dissolve once again into the darkness. But this time he felt empowered.

"My mats," he huffed. He swung his arms and rolled his neck.

Behind him, a tip of lemon sun peeked over the blackened mountains. It crept into the sky, bringing the inevitable day's light. Reza closed his eyes and allowed his mind to feed on his fears. His country embattled, his town imprisoned and his family struggling against constant peril. With a crushing yell, he banished them all. Before him, the sharp silhouette of the gym and inside, the wrestling mats. Thick, rough, sweat- soaked wrestling mats.

He strapped on the thin red singlet and stretched in the ebbing darkness, waiting for his competition to arrive. By the time the sun hovered directly overhead, Reza had destroyed seven opponents through brutal, humiliating pins. He prowled the gym for more. As the sun set into the early summer sky, Reza completed his dominance. It was he who was feared.

• • • • •

When not wrestling, Reza's official assignment was to drive the pilots from their barracks to the planes. Usually he delivered them in silence as they poured over flight plans and highlighted maps.

Today he drove a pilot who had come to the gym earlier that week to watch the matches.

"I see you have maps there," Reza said.

No response.

"And flight plans, too. Heard those Iraqis are flying French MIGs."

The pilot barely glanced in his direction.

"I wrestle for the Air Force. I think you saw me last week."

"My brother wrestles."

"What weight class? Maybe I've wrestled him."

Silence.

He must not have heard me. "I said, what weight class is your brother?"

"Look, kid, I don't know. I just have him wrestling so he doesn't have to go to the front lines." He returned to his maps.

Fighter planes roared overhead; Reza's voice screeched above their engines. "What the hell's that supposed to mean?"

No answer.

Reza pulled into the pilots' hanger and turned off the jeep. "I didn't mean any disrespect. I'd be on the front lines—if that was my assignment."

The pilot grabbed his flight bag and walked away from the jeep.

Reza gripped the wheel and spat through clenched teeth. *This driving is bullshit! Amir assigned me to a coward's post!* He sped through the base to Amir's office and pushed past the guards at the front. The glass pane in the door rattled as Reza slammed it behind him. Amir looked up from his desk. "What now?"

"I'm going to the front lines!"

"You're staying in your assignment driving pilots," Amir answered and returned to his paperwork. Reza looked hard at his brother. Amir's bony frame hunched over his desk as he squinted at his paperwork. Everything about him seemed pasty to Reza. Even his beard grew thin and looked like dirty clay in the office light.

"I don't care what Baba told you about keeping me safe. I won't live a coward's life!" He stepped up to Amir's desk and leaned into his face. "I won't do it, Amir. I won't."

Amir dropped his pencil, took his glasses off and rubbed his eyes. "You're a driver and a wrestler. And there's talk of you competing at Nationals. You go to the front lines, if you're lucky, you're killed. But most likely you'll be shot and wounded." He looked hard at his brother. "Get it out of your head Reza."

"I can't."

"You will. Bring us pride by beating Army and make the National Team." He returned to his documents. "Don't do anything stupid to jeopardize that."

"Fighting for Iran is stupid? Where'd that come from?"

"From you," Amir said. His eyes still focused on the paperwork.

"These are my people!" Reza yelled.

Amir bolted from his chair. "You're not a devout follower of Islam so you have no right standing alongside those who are!"

Reza bit his lip. He thought of the soldiers standing outside the office. "So, that's my choice? Die in the name of Khomeini's Islam or live like a coward? Is that what this has come to?"

Amir had no answer. He shook his head and let out a deep breath. "And in a few months we have leave to go home, and neither of us is telling Naneh you're on the front lines."

"Telling Naneh? Is that what this about? Or is it because I know they're using Islam to frighten and control people?" Reza punctuated his statement by pounding his fists on the desk.

Amir grabbed Reza by the wrist. He held his brother and stated in a deep, low tone while glancing toward the guards outside his door. "You will not speak such blasphemy in my office."

The two stood locked in defiance, their chests heaving. A guard shifted his boots outside the door and seemed to peer in the window. Amir spoke through clenched teeth, "So you expect me to give you a soldier's pack and put you on the next caravan to the front lines?"

Reza backed off. He lifted the wooden chair and pulsed it over his head. Finally, he sat in it. "I don't know. I just—those pilots. I drive them out, and they don't come back. I feel like I'm hiding." He rubbed his face. "I won't hide anymore."

A ticking of the clock penetrated the room.

"Then," Amir said with a sigh. "I will make you an ambulance driver."

"A what?"

"Ambulance driver, Reza. If you have to get to the lines, then you will drive our ambulance." He resumed reviewing his documents and muttered, "You'll get more than your fill of war."

Several moments passed while Reza scanned the office. For what, he didn't really know. "*Merci.*"

Flipping through another stack of papers, Amir said, "I'll set you up with Kahn. He's been driving almost two years and hasn't been killed yet. He's a little nuts, but you'll be, too, after you see what he's seen." Amir rubbed his face. "There's no going back, Reza. If you want to do this, you can't quit."

Reza nodded and left the office.

August 1981

A little nuts? This guy's completely insane! The ambulance bounced down the baked desert road as Kahn talked in nonstop circles about everything and nothing. Reza wasn't even sure if Kahn realized he was also in the cab. At first Reza responded with the obligatory "yeah" and "uh-huh" but soon understood it made no difference to Kahn.

Kahn, a round little man with a few hairs, fewer teeth and no formal education, considered himself an expert in international politics. He lectured his trapped audience as to the delicate nature of the Iran-Iraq relationship.

"They're like a married couple who sleeps together but never quite gets to the sex part 'cause they keep arguing about who's gonna start out on top and who's gonna start out on the bottom," Kahn said.

"Uh-huh," Reza replied.

"Ya see, there's no real border. The borders between Iran and Iraq don't define anything. They merely mark where two expanding imperial dynasties—the Ottomans and the Persians—ran into each other in the sixteenth century. That's where they should've had the sex and we'd all be one big happy family. But instead, and two centuries later, mind you, they signed some treaty," Kahn said. He pulled a yellow ball of wax from his ear. "No one can keep it hard for two centuries. This treaty split Kurds, Shiites and Arabs along a vague line somewhere in the mountains."

"Oh."

"That's just the foreplay. They should've just gotten to the sex.

But instead, there was a breakup of the Ottoman Empire after World War I and most of the Middle East was divided up like fancy shoes between one-legged hookers."

"What?"

"Then you got World War II. Countries starting to see oil is real important for their tanks and planes, and the English and Americans don't want to see Iran get too cozy with the communists. You get me, Raheem?"

"Reza."

"Who?"

"Me. My name is Reza."

"Yeah, Reza. Right, you're Amir's boy."

"Brother. I'm his brother."

"You look nothing like him, but he's a fine officer. Nice wife, too. Doesn't talk too much. Had me over for dinner. Once. How long have you known him?"

"My brother?"

"That's who I mean. Amir. Heard he did a lot for Khomeini during the Revolution. Damn Shah, well it wasn't all his fault. Iran's history is full of get conquered, build an empire, have a revolt and get conquered again."

The ambulance bumped over the dry desert floor, weaving occasionally around the charred remains of various vehicles and smashed aircraft. Reza wondered how much further until they rescued wounded soldiers and how much more he could take of Kahn.

"This war really started in 1975, when Shah showed up with his hard-on full of oil to the Algiers Agreement. Iraq just bent over and gave up all that oil-rich borderlands along the Shatt al-Arab. And do you know why? Shah agreed to stop supporting Kurdish rebels in Iraq."

"That's a rumor."

"Rumor my hairy ass. By 1979 Saddam Hussein clawed his way to the top of the ruling junta of Iraq and was just waiting to take full advantage of the chaos unleashed by the Revolution." Kahn paused to smash a black bug crawling across the dashboard. "He heard about Khomeini executing all Shah's senior military officers and figured he'd catch Iran on her knees." He wiped a string of drool oozing through the stubble on his chin. "Hussein was just waiting."

"Revolution was supposed to make things better," Reza said.

"And so is sex. Ask any fighting couple. Just jump in the sack for a few hours and no one remembers who's mad at who. But Hussein, he's a tricky bastard. He plotted ways to put the disputed border back in Iraq's favor. His armies officially crossed into Iran last September, but they were here for months before that. Just watching, just waiting."

The ambulance began to slow down. Reza looked out the filmy window. *I never thought I'd be so glad to see a pile of dead bodies in my life.*

Kahn stopped the ambulance and Reza reached for the door handle.

"No, Raheem, don't get out yet."

They stared out the dust-coated windshield. There is no silence like the silence brought to earth by the dead.

"Give them a minute."

"Give who a min—"

"Shhh, our soldiers. Shhh. Give them their final peace. They will tell us when we can get out."

Reza sighed in respectful compliance. And then he looked out the window again. Everything seemed thick, stuck. He counted five soldiers, maybe six. Their twisted, rotting corpses lay stacked by the side of the road.

Reza whispered, "Did they die that way?"

Kahn shook his head. "Their brothers laid them together by the road so we'd find them." Resting in the bodies' shade, a lizard watched the black flies darting about the decomposing wounds.

"Did you hear anything?" Kahn asked.

"No. It's pretty quiet."

"Then you're not listening."

Reza listened again. *I hear some wind, maybe a bird or two and flies.*

"It's time." Kahn reached for the door. "They said it's okay to come out."

Kahn pulled a burlap sack from under his seat. It clanked and swayed with obvious weight. He approached the soldiers, stopped a few feet away and scanned their bodies. Pulling his shirt over his nose, Reza walked directly to the stack. He started to lift the top body and asked. "How do we do this, Kahn? Do we just load 'em in the back? Should I grab the feet and you—?"

"No." Kahn shook his head in frustration. "Their limbs pull off sometimes and make a real mess. No, first we look for their gifts."

"Gifts? They're dead."

"Shhh! Have some respect. They bring us gifts like this." he said pulling a gold ring from a finger.

"Oh, man, are you insane? That's not a gift. That's some dead guy's wedding ring."

Kahn proceeded to crack open their stiff jaws. Snap!

"What the hell are you doing that for? It broke. They don't smell bad enough, you gotta open their mouths and let the—"

"Shhh! Show some respect. They can't help it if they smell. You will, too, when you're dead," he said. "Now, be a good boy. Hold this here head so I can pull out a few gifts."

"You're taking his teeth. Are you mad?"

Kahn looked at Reza and simply raised a single eyebrow. Then he pointed at the soldier's rotting head. Reza looked around—for what, he wasn't quite sure. It just seemed as if he didn't want anyone to see him. *I can't believe I'm doing this.* He gripped the skull; Kahn took his pliers and pulled out the gold teeth. Dropping them into the burlap bag, he smiled slightly at each clink. Finally, they loaded the bodies in the back and covered them with a thick plastic sheet.

The smell of rotting flesh penetrated the cab. Reza pulled his shirt up over his nose to the laugher of Kahn. "That won't stop anything. The dead don't care about your shirt."

Reza released the cloth and squinted into the sunlight. He tried the shirt-over-the-nose idea again and began pondering ways to cover his ears. He closed his eyes. The heat of the desert afternoon and Kahn's incessant babble finally lulled Reza into a dark, unsettling sleep. Just as he fell into dreams of his home, Kahn burst in.

"You don't seem like a soldier. Heard you're a big deal on the mats." Kahn pulled a piece of meat from his teeth and flipped it in the cab. "What are you doing here?"

Reza looked at Kahn in pure puzzlement, unable to read this babbling man. With a tired sigh, Reza recited, "I am an Iranian soldier fighting for the—"

Kahn gave Reza's shoulder a shove. "You don't know what you're fighting for. Just like those poor village families selling their young sons to serve in battle. And," Kahn said, pointing to the empty sky, "half those pilots you drove out were imprisoned after the Revolution. Khomeini had to let them out to fight the Iraqis. That Khomeini's figuring he's got forty-five million to Iraq's fifteen million and he'll just outlast them 'cause we've got more bodies to throw on the battlefield, more boys . . ." Kahn drifted into an unusual silence. He seemed to be listening.

Crash! Boom!

Reza jolted upright and gripped the dashboard in panic. "What the hell was that?"

"Missile," responded Kahn, as if he had just said, "slight breeze."

"Missile! What the—? Missile!"

A second thunderous explosion rocked the ambulance and Reza pivoted his head wildly looking for this missile.

"Can't see them," Kahn said. "You can only feel them when they ride up your ass."

A third and fourth explosion, each louder than the last, and Kahn brought the ambulance to a stop.

"Good, good thinking, Kahn. You're turning around."

"Nope. Just hoisting the white flag. I think it's under your seat. Yep, that's it. Now, get on outside and tie that to the pole sticking up like a whale's hard-on to the top of our truck."

Reza opened his mouth to ask a question, decided it was fruitless, tied the white flag on the whale's hard-on and jumped back in.

"Good and tight? If it falls off, they just might aim at us."

"I think so. Maybe I should check it again."

But Kahn started back down the road and the missiles faded just as quickly as they had arrived.

Across the madness on the desert floor rose hundreds of military tents. Drawing closer, Reza pulled the sounds of war together with the movement of soldiers. Jeeps drove along unmarked roads as the men of war rushed with purpose through their city. A fearsome perimeter of tanks greeted them. Kahn waved to the guard at the entrance and drove directly to the huge hospital tent. Reza couldn't take in one image before jumping to the next.

"There's a war, Reza. Get out and collect your soldiers."

"*Chashm, agha*[1]."

Reza followed Kahn into the hospital tent. Rows of cots stretched out endlessly, twisting with the mangled bodies of moaning soldiers. Smells rank with infected flesh rushed at Reza.

1 Sir

His legs trembled and, before Reza could steady himself, Kahn was helping him to his feet. He had fainted. With a quick smack, Kahn commanded, "Get up soldier!"

Shaking his head, Reza desperately tried to process the suffering. He could only stare.

Kahn walked over to an officer who sat behind a makeshift desk at the far end of the medical tent. Reza watched Kahn exchange a few words, sign a couple of forms and then return with a look of satisfaction.

Pointing to a body lying on a bloody cot, Kahn said, "Lift the end of this one."

Reza looked into the face of a soldier younger than Hassan, his leg missing, his face contorted in raging pulses of pain. "Hey, buddy. We're going to get you home," Reza said.

Kahn also pointed to another one, barely conscious and wrapped in a dirty, blood-soaked blanket. "He won't last the night," Kahn said. "We'll take him, too."

Picking up his end of the stretcher, Reza backed out through the tent and toward the ambulance. The movement made the young soldier groan and Reza thought about what Kahn had said. He wondered if this boy's poor parents sold him to serve in the Iranian army and to bring their family honor.

The doors to the ambulance creaked open and unleashed a wave of air so foul it pierced through Reza's skin. He loaded in the first boy and followed Kahn back to the tent for the second.

As they secured the cot of the second young soldier in the back of the ambulance, the soldier suddenly let out a scream. He grabbed Reza's arm as Reza started to back out. "You can't leave me here! With dead things! What kinda ambulance is this?"

"It's all right, kid," Reza said. He put another sheet on the soldier. "It's a short ride and soon you'll be at the base in a white hospital . . ."

His grip tightened. "No! Don't, don't leave me! They smell and they're creaking and I can't . . ." He broke into hysterics as Kahn climbed into the cab and starting honking the horn.

"Let's go, Raheem."

Reza paused. *Riding with dead guys. Riding with Kahn.*

"I'll be riding back here."

"Well, if a cold, dead finger jams up your ass, don't say I didn't warn you. Corpses get mighty horny," Kahn said.

The young hand dug into Reza's arm.

"Don't worry, Kahn. I got it handled."

"Suit yourself."

• • • • •

The wasteland's sun retired from her day, but it brought no relief. Reza crawled back into the cab after his two passengers passed out, and he had tried to do the same. No luck.

"Cold, dead finger up your ass? Decided to spend a little more time with Ol' Kahn?"

"Yeah, something like that," Reza said. Then he stared out the window.

"You ain't Iranian, ya know. Ya ain't no Arab neither." Kahn took a long look at Reza. "You a Kurd?"

"What?"

"You're from Kermanshah. Millions of Kurds down there. You one of them?"

Reza wasn't sure how to answer this question, so he went with, "Half. On my Naneh's side."

"Half. Half. Ya half a body? Got just one arm and one leg? Half." Kahn snorted and spat out the window. "Kurds got screwed, ya know. They just never got their own lines drawn in the sand. The oldest ethnic group in Iran's part of the Middle East, so old they even started religion. Bet you didn't know Zoroastrian is the root of Islam, Judaism and even Christianity."

"Some people say that."

Khan snorted again. "Kurds got themselves a language. Some even got their own currency, flag, song. Did you hear some people say you Kurds are one of the biggest causes of this whole war?"

"Iraq attacked us," Reza said, surprising himself in his attempt to defend Khomeini.

Gripping the steering wheel, Kahn mumbled. He spit out the window and licked his cracked lips. "Attacked us. Who's us? We say we're Iranian, but that's because the whole damn Pahlavis clan showed up in 1935 and decided to rename everything 'Iran.' Know why?"

"Something to do with sex?" Reza asked.

"Damn right something to do with sex. Shah was putting on pretty clothes for the West. They're dressing us up. "Iran" means "Aryan." They're trying to look fancy so the West wants to come over and spend some money. No, No, you're not Iranian. You're Persian."

This really wasn't a huge revelation to Reza. He'd had these discussions, of an altogether different flavor, with Mr. Mehdian.

"I've heard that. Persians have been around for 2,500 years, had emperors like Achaemenes, Cyrus, Darius and—"

"Imagine the women those guys got? How many wives? Ten. Twenty. Thirty or more. Only stopping for grapes and a quick nap. Yep, Shah shoulda took more lessons from history, from real kings. Paid more attention to his people and less time buying tanks and planes from the West."

Reza couldn't decide who Kahn supported. He felt like he was watching a dog chase its tail. Sleep seemed impossible with the heat and the smells and Kahn's voice scratching through the air. He figured he'd try to give Kahn a new topic. "Shah gave the poor people land, hospitals, schools, and—"

"Women the right to vote," Kahn said. "I liked that. But the Shia clerics who controlled the land and the people, well they didn't take too well to Shah's reforms. And Khomeini, he told them one thing and then told the people another." Kahn shook his head. "Khomeini came in and stole the whole Revolution when we weren't looking."

"I had a teacher at school who said Iran was like a teenager, demanding things she wasn't ready to have." He considered bringing in a sexual metaphor, but had no experience to draw from.

Kahn was impressed, though, seemed to like the idea of Iran being a teenager. He patted his passenger's shoulder. "Teenagers. The horniest damn bastards to ever roam the earth. Yep, I can see that. Shah figured a few visits from Savak, those damn Nazi recycles, would keep everyone in line. Nope. Once teenagers get a taste of more—more anything—they want more of that and more of everything else." He let out a deep, saddened sigh. "Iran and Iraq shoulda just quit bickering and got to the sex part. Then it wouldn't smell so bad in here."

Chapter Sixteen

Irvine, 2010

Every other Saturday, I meet with the woman's writing group and Tuesday nights I meet with my eccentric writing group. It's so cliché, but every word I write has their encouragement, their critique and their wisdom. It's Saturday and I arrive at the coffee shop exhausted and pretty near throwing in the towel.

"I'm in over my head," I begin. "I'm going to tell Reza to find someone else. There's just too much history and culture and politics and head scarves and secret police and wrestling stuff, and I haven't even gotten to the escape yet and now I gotta figure out how to write that which is not even the climax like I thought it would be because then he gets some call from his sisters in Turkey and that's a whole 'nother adventure. How am I going to do this?"

Melissa calmly sips her espresso as Alice adjusts her hat. MaryAnn's always-perfect fingernails simply click together as her hands fold. Elaine and Joyce give a slight sigh.

"It's just too much," I reassert. "And who's going to want to read a book about a bunch of Iranians?"

"Is that what you're writing about?" asks MaryAnn.

"I don't even have a title," I continue to whine. "And I don't know *what* I'm writing about."

"The joy is in the writing, in the journey," MaryAnn reminds me. Her comment is followed by a warm bath of support and a few deserved "snap-out-of-its."

And I breathe. I pass out my pages and we begin the revisions.

• • •

I'm also referred to an Iranian author, Zoe, and we meet for lunch at a local restaurant. I spend the first twenty minutes babbling about Reza, the courage and loyalty of his family, everything I've learned about Iran and how I want to open people's hearts and minds.

"Especially in the schools," I say. "It's the perfect fit for the tenth grade curriculum and if we can break down stereotypes it may help end the misguided prejudice against people from the Middle East." I stop and look at Zoe. I hope I didn't offend her.

"What makes this project so inspiring," she says, her warm hands reaching across the table to touch mine, "is you."

Pictures

Team photo of Iranian Wrestlers. Reza, Ardeshir and two others will defect

Reza in Championship tournament

ID photo of Reza for Iran's National Wrestling Team

Reza's gold medal from the Military World Championship in Venezuela 1982

Nimtaj and Abbas and a mystery child in the background. (1975) in Kermanshah

Reza and Hassan in California 1987

Hassan and Reza 2010

Farid and his wife in Iran

Abbas, Mostafa and Reza. One of the last photos taken before Abbas passed away.

Rasha, Mehri, Farah, Soraya, Pari and Mariam. (1995)

Reza and
Soraya in
her home
in Europe

Reza and Ardeshir playing
around in Ardeshir's home gym.

Reza and his two sons at a
high school tournament

In 2000, students
and staff at Dana
Hills High School,
voted to recognize
Reza Abedi as the
Teacher of the Year

Chapter Seventeen

March 1982

After months of driving in the ambulance, Reza was forced to turn all his attention to wrestling. Determined to show the strength of the Iranian nation, Ayatollah Khomeini demanded that a world-class military wrestling team compete in the upcoming 1982 World Military Wrestling Championship in Venezuela. Reza knew his fate would be determined by earning a place on this team. He needed to defeat every wrestler in his weight class from all branches of the military.

In his green and yellow standard-issue warm-up suit, Reza leaned against the wall just outside the base's training facility, his muscular arms folded across his sculpted chest. His once-playful grin was gone. Instead, his dark eyes searched among the scurry of soldiers and wrestlers for his childhood friend. It was Ardeshir's walk that he noticed first. Like a brown bear crunching through the tall grass, Ardeshir grumbled up the road. Reza waved to his friend.

"Ahh, you did make it," Reza said. "It's nice you still want to get your ass kicked."

They shared a long hug. Although Ardeshir looked menacing with his dark beard claiming territory across his neck and chin, his humor remained. "These Air Force wrestlers can't think you're all that good," he said. "All the generals coming over to see you? Needed to be here to keep you in place."

"The place I'll be in is first," Reza said. "That's the one with the gold."

"Is that so?" Ardeshir replied. His voice became low. "I've seen the guy you're wrestling. He's takedown."

Reza shrugged.

"He's got a weak right knee," Ardeshir said as he pointed to his own right leg. "Shoot it."

Reza shook his head and flexed his biceps. "Don't need to." He looked at Ardeshir, his eyebrows furrowed. "Don't tell me those things."

Ardeshir shrugged. As they stood in silence, a wrestler walked between them.

"Hey, what's with him?" Ardeshir said. "He's got green and yellow streaks all across his back."

Reza turned and saw the young wrestler. "Just painted the mats. Guys get pinned and covered in it." Reza looked around and lowered his voice. "How's being a *Sepahi*?"

Ardeshir made a joking gesture to check Reza's back, but no one at the base came close to being able to pin him, and Ardeshir knew it. Then Ardeshir's face grew dark and he lowered his eyes. "Beirut was bad. My father's now a part of the elite guard for Khomeini. Sometimes I go with him." Ardeshir looked around and leaned into Reza. "Khomeini's intense."

Reza acknowledged the comment in a nod, but a feeling of eyes and ears pouring out from the very walls closed their conversation.

Ardeshir moved to a safer topic. "You and Amir going home next week?"

"A ten-day leave," Reza said. "Amir arranged it."

"Good to have a brother who can make that happen."

"Always good to see the family before—" Reza paused. "Before I leave for Venezuela to compete in the Championship." A forgotten smile braved its way across Reza's lips.

"That sure you're leaving for Worlds?" Ardeshir gave him a shove. The two walked away from the facility in silence for several minutes.

Reza kicked a small rock and looked to the sky. "I need to see what's out there."

"Need to make the team first," Ardeshir said. He pretended to check Reza's back again for paint.

Reza swiped his hand away and the two began to wrestle on the stony surface, grunting, sweating, bleeding and—finally—laughing. A sound that seemed sadly foreign.

• • • • •

Later that afternoon, officials of the highest rankings stood along the perimeter to evaluate potential champion wrestlers. Mounted on the grey gym walls, the exaggerated portraits of Ayatollah Khomeini seemed to steal the stale air and bear down on the sweating men. Amir came in and sat next to Ardeshir on the metal bleachers. He pointed to the doorway where Reza would appear. "He's on the scales in the locker room," Amir said. "He should make weight, but I'm not sure he's prepared for this level of competition."

Ardeshir looked straight ahead. He clasped a fist under his chin and gave a single nod. "He's prepared."

"If he loses this match, he will not be on the National Team."

Turning to Amir, Ardeshir said, "He knows that. And he won't lose."

Several minutes later, dressed in a red singlet, Reza stepped into the center of the mat. The perfect contours of his muscles rippled with sweat, but his breathing stayed steady. He circled his opponent. His sleek movements showed strength and skill, his face locked with purpose.

After the first round, Reza was behind by two points, but he had found a weakness in his opponent and calculated his next move for a sure pin. The second round began and the wrestler had Reza's arm and used his leg to toss Reza to his back. Reza attempted to counter the move and they both crashed down on Reza's shoulder. Wicked streams of pain tore through him. His shoulder was dislocated. A thirty second stall and Reza made it to the end of the second period, but he was behind by six points.

Amir looked at the military dignitaries. He turned to Ardeshir. "Reza's through. Look at his face, he can't go back out."

"He's going back out and he'll pin this guy," Ardeshir said.

"This guy's the real deal," Amir said. "Not some kid from Kermanshah."

"You'd have to pull out Reza's other arm and both his legs before he'll quit in front of these—well, before he'll quit, period." Ardeshir spat into his hands and rubbed them together, whispering, "Shoot that right knee."

Reza did go back out for the third and final period, his shoulder smeared with a potent salve that burned his eyes. In a blind fury, Reza shot his left leg, switched to a double leg and somehow lifted his opponent. Smash! The two landed on the mat with Reza desperately using his legs and one arm to score points.

"He's got him. He's got the pin," Ardeshir said.

Amir nodded.

The referee pulled Reza's arm up for victory, but Reza cried out and grabbed hold with his working arm.

Ardeshir slapped Amir on the back. "Just another kid from Kermanshah." He stood and made his way down the bleachers.

With red, swollen eyes, Reza stumbled toward the blurred image of Ardeshir. Ardeshir reached out, embraced his friend and led him to the locker room.

"I can't see," Reza repeated in mumbles. "It's burning my eyes."

"I got you."

"My shoulder."

"It's still there."

Reza rested on a bench, his back pressed against the wall. Ardeshir handed him a towel and Reza rubbed his face. He opened his eyes and blinked until Ardeshir came into view. "I'm going to Nationals."

"Would have made it easier if you shot the right knee."

Reza grinned. "We're going to Venezuela," he said. But Ardeshir looked away.

• • • • •

The two-day drive took Reza and Amir through the burnt remains of a once thriving, ancient culture. Women scurried along streets in full coverage of solemn black *chadors* or long loose clothing with a tightly secured scarf. No one smiled, let alone laughed. Even the children they passed on the streets peered at them through mask-like faces laced in fear.

As if covered by a suffocating blanket, Reza and Amir spoke very little in the isolated safety of their Jeep. Without realizing why, Reza shot an angry glance at Amir each time they passed an image that reminded him of Ayatollah Khomeini's new Islamic order. Finally Amir spoke.

"It was about the oil," he said, seeming to answer the question Reza wouldn't voice.

"What?"

"The Revolution," Amir said. "Right after World War I, Shah's father signed a contract with the English giving them drilling rights and most of the oil profits."

"That was over forty years ago."

"Listen to me," Amir spat. He gripped the steering wheel and his knuckles went white. "Then World War II made oil more important than gold and the cold war made the West fear what they saw as communists."

"You're making no sense," Reza said. *I don't want to hear your crap excuses for Khomeini.*

"Because you're not listening." Amir rolled down the window and spit. "Parliament elected Mossadegh in 1950. Mossadegh told the damn English that Iran is taking back her oil. He said we'd split profits and use Iranians as high-tech workers." He looked at Reza. "Are you understanding now? Mossadegh had the balls to stand up to those English bastards. Even when they boycotted the oil and tried to do everything to cripple the economy, Mossadegh would not compromise."

"And Shah?"

"That coward. He wasn't even in the country when they took out Mossadegh." Amir looked directly at Reza. "The English and Americans knew Shah would cut them a deal and the oil monies would flow right back into their bank accounts."

"So where's the oil profits under Khomeini?" Reza said. He stared at Amir, daring him to answer.

"Shah sold us to the West."

"That doesn't answer my question."

Amir's fingers twisted on the steering wheel. "Shah had to go."

Reza opened his mouth to repeat his question but realized Amir didn't have answers, just excuses. He thought about Mr. Mehdian. He thought about America.

They finished the trip without speaking. Reza dreamed that Naneh's chai, the firm handshake of Abbas and the bright eyes of his siblings could restore his fading hope.

A dust cloud welcomed the Jeep at sunset. Reza and Amir paused as the car doors' echo faded into an eerie silence. No welcome, no life radiating from their childhood home. Reza glanced at Amir, who scanned the roof and walls for a sign explaining the stillness. Amir walked toward the back alley while Reza turned in a full circle, looking, listening. *Something's wrong.* He pushed open the door and entered his courtyard, as he had done so many times before. The fountain-well, still and quiet, did not celebrate his return.

He took two steps toward the main room, and through the cracked and dirty glass he saw her. She leaned against the wall, her uncovered hair hanging in strings about her shoulders. He rushed toward her and then froze at the sight of her face. The flesh of her cheeks was torn in rips and jazzed claw marks. Two hollow eyes looked at him and for a faint moment, ragged lips formed a smile. "You're home."

"Naneh! Nan—what—what happened?" Reza wrapped his powerful arms around her frail body. Had she not spoken, he would not have recognized her.

Nimtaj's body shook violently as the sobs consumed every fiber in her being. "You're home, home . . ."

"I'm here," Reza said. "Please tell me what's wrong."

Pari and Mariam scurried in from their room and hugged Reza. "You're here!" they squealed. Reza hugged his sisters and kissed their cheeks. "Pari. Oh, little Mariam. Are you okay? Where's Soraya?"

Amir came into the room and stood without purpose. He glanced from Reza to his mother and sisters. Mariam went to him. "Did you bring Hassan home? Did you get him out?" Mariam asked.

Amir crouched down, held her arms and looked into her face.

"Bring Hassan home from where, Mariam? Where is he?" Amir asked, trying to keep an even tone.

Stepping forward with authority, Pari said, "They took him away. They took him in a black truck and Naneh can only see him on Thursdays."

Reza and Amir glanced at each other in paralyzing fear, the reality racing through their minds too awful to voice.

"Naneh, listen to me." Amir turned to his mother who lay sobbing in Reza's arms. "Who took Hassan? Where is he?"

She clawed at the long scabs and gaping wounds in her face until Reza pulled her hands away and held them at her sides. Nimtaj shook with cries.

Reza tried to calm her. "Stop. You're frightening the girls," he whispered. "It's me, Reza. Please, please Naneh. Talk to me."

Her chin dropped to her chest. She could say nothing.

Soraya entered the room, her radiant beauty shaded in grey like a fine silver platter now tarnished. "Reza, you're home. Please help him," she said flatly. Her eyes held no expression.

"Soraya?" Reza said in more of a question.

Amir knelt next to Nimtaj and spoke with measured words. "Naneh, tell us what happened."

Nimtaj took a breath and stared straight ahead. "They took him. You were gone. Here I sat. Here I sat in my home. Minding my household."

She stopped and pulled her arms from Reza's grasp in a vain attempt to claw at her face. "No, Naneh, no. Stop hurting yourself. You have to tell us what happened."

Through eyes like an old mirror, she relived that day. "From the walls. They crawled in from the walls. And dropped from the ceiling. And poured in my windows and poured in my doors. Thick, black boots. And terrible rifles. They just shouted and shouted. And they—they took my baby away—they took . . ." Her sobs overcame her voice.

"Where, Naneh? They took Hassan where?"

"To Dizel Abad Prison."

"No!" Reza shouted. "No, Hassan, no, no . . ." It was Reza's turn to cry. He fell in a heap against the wall and shuddered in sobs. Mariam tried to wipe his tears, but he held up his hand to direct her away. Battling the images of Hassan's nightmare, he could only be his body to breathe. Just breathe. *Oh God, Hassan.*

Amir laid his mother's exhausted body onto her mattress and turned to Soraya. "Where is Baba? When does he come home?"

"Sometimes he sits on the roof," Mariam answered. "Sometimes he sleeps there, too."

That's where they found him. Sitting cross-legged, surrounded by the butts of burned-out cigarettes and staring blindly into the setting sun. He showed only a glimpse of joy in seeing his sons and hugged them as if his strength could somehow reach through and touch Hassan.

They sat on either side of their father and remained for hours. Listening, crying and talking.

Abbas retold the terrible events that led to Hassan's arrest. Hassan spent too much time with his Kurdish cousins and soon found himself guilty of bringing food to starving children. Unfortunately for Hassan, these starving children were Kurds. Ayatollah Khomeini called all Kurds criminals and that made Hassan's act a crime.

"They told me they'd keep him one night," Abbas said. "That was a month ago."

The bitter hot winds circled around the men and mocked their shame. Reza paced across the roof, swinging his arms and gritting his teeth.

"Baba," said Amir. He pulled his father's arm until Abbas's hollow face finally turned to him. "Have you gone to see him?"

"On Thursdays, Nimtaj and sometimes Pari and Soraya travel to the prison and stand in line for hours with hundreds of others." Abbas's voice remained steady, void of any feeling.

"How is he?" Reza whispered, not knowing if he really wanted an answer.

Abbas turned to Reza. "He's not you, Reza. I don't know how much he can take. You know—you know what happens in that prison . . ."

Amir's mind was reeling with questions and no answers. "What does Mostafa say? He knows people. I can make some calls, Baba. I know some people, too, people who would listen to us."

"We've tried all that, Amir! Don't you think we've contacted everyone we know? These are not our people. And every day they take prisoners out and shoot them. And every time Nimtaj goes out there, I'm so afraid she will come back with just the pile of his clothes." Abbas rested his head in his hands and rocked side to side.

In Reza's mind, he saw Hassan sitting next to him in the truck when they drove to the prison for the raid. He heard his screams when had awoken from his nightmare, the nightmare that now he lived, alone. But Abbas had not seen the fierce determination Reza sensed in Hassan, and Reza believed he would survive.

"He's strong," Reza finally said as he sat next to his father. He wanted to touch him, to take his pain, to somehow promise him Hassan would live. But there was nothing he could do. "Who's helping to take care of Naneh and the girls?" Reza said.

Abbas looked harshly at Reza. "Rasha, Mehri and even Farah come when they can. When they can be escorted by their husbands." Abbas shook his head in disgust and disbelief. "I don't know the life we live anymore." Amir looked away. It was not supposed to be this way.

Abbas led the boys down the ladder and they walked back inside as Soraya began to spread the *sofreh.* Reza took a corner and helped her smooth the stained cloth over the rug. The family moved in a functioning silence. Passing platters, clicking spoons and empty swallows of water replaced the sounds Reza ached for—the sounds of his family.

For the next several days, Amir worked feverishly with Mostafa to find a way to free their brother. Deals were harder to make and much more expensive.

Reza spent most of his time with Naneh. In the tradition of mourning, Nimtaj had torn the skin of her cheeks for her son. Reza helped her apply healing herbs to her wounds and held her as she wept.

Thursday.

"I am going with you," Reza said as Nimtaj tightened her chador around her riddled face.

"How can you be seen there? Someone might think you are mixed up with crimes." She opened the door and headed into the courtyard. "It will be too dangerous."

Reza looked out into the blackened morning. His jaw tightened. "I am going."

Nimtaj paused and looked at her son. "It will be too hard."

"Naneh, I will see my *baradar.*"

She pulled his clenched fists into her hands. "You're walking into a nightmare."

"Hassan lives it." Reza said, trying to shake the memory of his brother's screams.

Nimtaj and Reza started down the dark path to the bus depot. They walked in silence and were soon joined by others who also moved in slow, focused steps. Waiting at the bus depot, he felt cloaked by the courage pulsing from these mothers of the prison's children.

The bus pulled up a kilometer short of the prison, without explanation. The driver turned to his cargo. "Get off! *Ajaleh kon!* And don't expect I'll come back for you."

In unison, they moved. They did not speak. They marched the final distance to the menacing grey walls that tore their families apart.

Reza looked up at the prison in disbelief that he now stood before the same place he had once conquered. *I swear on this spot, I will kill them all if anything happens to Hassan.*

Following his mother, Reza found himself back inside those terrible walls. Cages, large cages stuffed with men, some with yellow eyes over grey beards and still others barely of the age to produce a whisker. All pushed and piled together. Their arms reached through the bars, across the chasm to the free on the other side. Nimtaj's voice was lost in the cries of other mothers.

Reza pushed to the front of the frenzied crowd, searching, yelling, shaking. "Hassan! I'm here! Hassan!" Reza wrapped his hands around the cold prison bars and pressed his face through the opening. *Let me see his face! Hassan! Hassan! I am here!*

• • • • •

"Did you see him? Is he okay?" Soraya pulled Reza to the kitchen and peppered him with questions.

Reza only nodded. He held Soraya as she cried. "Please don't leave us, Reza. Please, please . . ." she sobbed. "We need you here. We need you home."

• • • • •

Restrained by a ten-day leave, Reza and Amir forced themselves to return to the base. Amir promised to continue his work with Mostafa and Abbas until Hassan was free.

Nimtaj chanted prayers as she passed her sons under the Koran. She then kissed the book and gave it to Soraya. Farah handed her a glass of water with flower petals gently floating to the top. As the brothers walked from the house, she poured water on the ground behind them the way she had done for all her beloved travelers. The tradition assured her of their safe and imminent return.

Chapter Eighteen

July 1982

With the World Military Wrestling Championship only weeks away, the wrestlers from the Army, Air Force and Navy were sent to complete their training at the main facility in Tehran. Fueled by a toxic mix of anger and desire, Reza's grueling routine included fourteen-hour daily workouts and punishing wrestling drills.

Reza again stayed with his aunt, but his demeanor carried a much more serious air. He had endured too much and ached for the freedom he imagined in Europe. Taking the bus back to her house, he heard whispers of "people" who know of "ways" to get smuggled out of Iran. Ways that cost hundreds of thousands of *toman.*

Entering his aunt's home, he took his usual path for the shower. But tonight her phone conversation froze him.

"He just walked in. I'll tell him. How can I thank you, Mostafa? You've done so much for our—do you want to talk to him? He's standing right here." She handed Reza the yellow receiver. "It's Mostafa."

"Allo. Is Hassan out? . . . Oh, okay. He'll stay strong." Reza squeezed his eyes and rubbed them with his fingers. "So, what's going on? Of course I will . . . yeah, I know that area of Tehran. Why tonight? . . . I see . . . No, I'll go alone . . . I'll be fine . . . yeah, me too. It's better if I just go alone."

Reza watched his aunt pace across her favorite silk rug. *Why does it have to come this?* Fighting the rage to punch a hole in the wall, he took a deep breath. *How did we get to innocent people having to escape from Iran in the middle of the night?*

Khaleh Banou stopped and looked down at her toes brushing across the bright threads. "I'll sell it if I have to. I'll sell everything to get her out of the country before the *Sepah* finds her. If they find her and arrest her . . ."

"You won't need to sell it," Reza said. "Mostafa worked out a better price with the people he knows. I'm going tonight, and your daughter will be in Turkey before sunrise."

"I should've made Helena leave months ago." She lit a cigarette and paced through the room. "Who could know it would get so bad here? In Tehran?"

Reza watched her but he could think of nothing to say.

Aunt Banou crushed out her half-smoked cigarette and sat on the rug next to Reza. She traced a bright gold thread with a shaking finger.

"I didn't know Helena was in such trouble," Reza said.

"Who's not in trouble anymore? Who's not in some photo at some rally? You get dragged into Evin Prison to give names of other random people in those photos and they get dragged in, beaten, and who knows what else."

Reza pushed Hassan's face from his mind. "Nothing's going to happen to her. I'm going to take her tonight and pay Mostafa's friends. She'll be safe this time tomorrow."

"*Inshallah,* Reza. *Inshallah.*"

"If Mostafa says it will be fine, it will be."

She hugged her nephew. "Do you know what this trip to the World Championship means?"

"I hope it means World Championship and a gold medal."

She pressed her lips and shook her head. "No, Reza. It means you'll be out of Iran."

"But we'll be so heavily guarded. I've thought about that, too, but," Reza paused, "*Sepah* are going to escort us everywhere."

She held his face. "Reza, if you return you'll never leave."

"But I'm afraid if I leave I'll never come back."

"Then don't come back."

Fighting tears, he could not find his voice. *How can I leave? They'll kill Hassan. And who knows what else they might do? My family can't pay for my freedom.*

• • • • •

After delivering the smuggler's fee, Reza returned and once again reassured his aunt that Helena was safe.

Sleep tried to comfort Reza, but nightmares of Hassan and thoughts of defecting ripped him from his slumber. *What chance do I have to defect into a country where I know no one and barely know the language? I can't put Naneh through losing another son.* He thought even a suspicion of such an attempt would mean torture and death. But more daunting than this loomed his fear of how his escape could end Hassan's life. Wrestling with his fears, his dreams and his desire, the only thing he knew for sure was that his place on the National Team was a ticket out of Iran. "What would you have me do, Hassan?" whispered Reza into the night.

• • • • •

As expected, Reza dominated his matches and became a leading member of the Iranian National Wrestling Team. Soon they would take the coveted passport picture and prepare to depart from Iran. Each time a teammate mentioned the passport photo, Reza felt his heart twist.

Welcoming another exhausting training session that would drain his tumultuous thoughts, Reza walked into the gym just as the blackened sky entertained the thought of pale yellow.

A coach called him to the side. "Reza, you have a challenge match in three hours for your place on the team."

Reza stared in disbelief. "Is this—is this a joke? Did Ardeshir put you up to this?"

"No joke, Reza. Three hours. Are you fifty-seven kilos?"

"Am I—am I fifty-seven kilos? Maybe fifty-eight or fifty-nine. I've been training, not cutting. How's this possible? I've earned my place on this team!" He looked throughout the empty gym for answers. "No one's come close to me. Who is this wrestler?"

The coach, unwavering in his mission, stated flatly, "He's been in Romania for another National Tournament and he's Ayatollah Khomeini's personal bodyguard." He paused and rescanned the gym he knew to be empty. He leaned into Reza. "He's good, Reza, really good."

Really good? What the hell is going on? Reza shook his head and tried to process what he was being told. "Bodyguard? Khomeini's personal bodyguard? Why does that matter? Who is this guy?"

Ardeshir came up and stood by his side. Reza's face and animated body language gave Ardeshir a chill. "What's going on?"

"Coach said some bodyguard's coming from the Romanian tournament to challenge my place."

Ardeshir turned to the coach. "Who?"

The coach looked around a third time. "Mashadi Aghee."

The two words landed like boulders at Reza's feet. He lost his breath and searched for his voice.

Ardeshir understood Reza's reaction. "Mashadi Aghee," Ardeshir said. "From a few years back? That's not right. Reza's earned his place! He's . . ."

Reza turned and walked blindly across the silent, unforgiving gym. *Shayton's eyes have come back for me.*

Ardeshir looked back to the coach. "This is wrong!"

"Watch your tone, Ardeshir," the coach replied. Then he leaned into Ardeshir and lowered his voice. "Didn't you see Reza in the Nationals a few years back? Mashadi Aghee crushed him like a dead leaf. Reza doesn't stand a chance and he knows it."

"Then you don't know Reza."

• • • • •

Three hours met Reza with brutal force and threw him on the mat against the demon he thought he would never face again. Mashadi Aghee's large arms stuck out in an unnatural position, making him more gargoyle than man. Reza glared into his face and fought the images of his humiliating defeat. *Focus. Focus.* His eyes canvassed the grotesque body, looking, searching, feeling.

In the first few seconds, Mashadi went for a takedown and shot Reza's leg. But Reza was ready for him, got a head snap and pushed his face to the mat. The score was tied after the first period.

Unlike matches of the past, there were no cheers. No pumping fists, no calling out moves. Ardeshir stood in silence, his mighty arms folded, his eyes blackened in a shared rage.

In the second period, Mashadi tried to shoot a double leg with super-human speed, but Reza sprawled. He swung his legs free and spun to square himself to Mashadi. End of second period. Score still tied.

There was no air, no light, no sound. Reza's body turned each feverish cell against the demon who breathed on him. He moved with a rhythm commanded from beyond time. He felt no heart. He felt no soul. Wrestling is as old as mankind. So is fear. And rage.

In the final seconds, Reza snapped Mashidi's head down and he was able to lock up the far side cradle for a pin. He felt slices of tissue give way under his crushing grasp. He stood. Sweat drained from every pore and he glared at the referee. *Raise my hand.*

• • • • •

Hassan stood blindfolded in the overcrowded prison cell. It was barely large enough for ten men, and the guards had recently shoved in twenty more, making it impossible for anyone to do anything but stand. Hassan's bare feet alternated painfully between puddles of urine, feces and blood. A man collapsed and shoved Hassan and others into the cement wall; some men cried out and attracted the attention of the guards. Hassan heard the thump of boots and the dreaded clang of the key. He listened for the sounds of what was to come.

A man with the stench of cigarette smoke yelled into the crowded cage of blindfolded men. "You men and your noises! You need more friends in here?"

Silence.

"I think someone's sleeping." A sound of rubber dragging on the stone floor. "Wake up, you stinking pigs!" A powerful spray of water pounded the prisoners, tearing flesh and cracking bones. The men screamed and cried, and somewhere a man babbled in insane laughter.

Luckily, Hassan's recent push against the wall set men in front of him and protected him from the water. The wet allowed him to slip his blindfold slightly above one eye. Before him lay more than thirty shivering bodies. Some, younger than he, were piled like broken toys in the far corner. Hassan slowly stepped through the human wreckage toward the boys.

• • • • •

Ardeshir looked at Reza and the two simply nodded. Reza's face held no joy, as he walked calmly to the edge of the mat to spit blood. Behind him, he heard the referee call out, "Mashadi Aghee is the *ghahreman*!"

"What?" Reza rushed to the center and roared, "I pinned him. I had him in the cradle . . ."

The referee showed no emotion. "Abedi, you lost."

Reza looked around in disbelief. "I didn't lose!" He turned in desperation to find Mashadi, who had already left the gym. "This is nonsense! I beat him! How can you even say that?"

"Are you questioning the rule of God? I am God's eyes and ears and his Holy One sees all. You lost. Mashadi Aghee will go in your place. It is said to be so." He began walking off the mat.

Ardeshir stood by Reza's side and gently touched his elbow.

Reza understood, but could not simply give up. "Your excellence, I implore you to allow me another match to prove my strength to—to the almighty."

The clenching will in Reza's voice made the referee stop. He turned to the coaches and said, "Tomorrow. Twelve o'clock."

• • • • •

Cruel metal chains wrapped around Hassan's ankles. Hands bound and face blindfolded, the clanking sounds told Hassan the chains were being locked to the ceiling hooks. He felt them tighten and cut into his burning skin.

An unfamiliar voice, shrill and nasty, came from all parts of the room. "I will ask you again. Who did you work for?"

"For no one, sir," Hassan quavered.

Closer now, bringing the smell of rosewater.

"You lie!" The guard spat each word. "You'll tell us who you worked for or you will not see tomorrow!"

Lowering his head, Hassan imagined the chains wrapped around his infected feet. He sighed and recited the sentences he'd shared hundreds of times. "I don't know what you mean. I worked for no one. The children were so hungry, so I brought them bread." He turned toward the voice. "That's all I did."

With an unforgiving pull, the clanking chains yanked Hassan from his chair. He was dragged across the stone floor for a few meters. Then nothing. No sound. No movement.

"Tell me who you worked for." Came a voice looming just above Hassan's head.

"No one sir." He hated the tears that dripped from his face.

Clink. Clink. Clink. From his chained feet, Hassan dangled. The pounding blood in his brain soon erased all thoughts but one: Let me die.

• • • • •

Warm water poured down from the showers and Reza scrubbed his body with rage.

"You're scrubbing your skin off," Ardeshir said.

"I don't care."

"You beat him once. Beat him again."

"Beat him? I'll kill him."

Ardeshir glanced nervously around. "Shhh! You want to get arrested?"

"I want to get to Venezuela."

"These guys are serious." Ardeshir stepped closer to Reza.

Reza turned off the water and stared into his friend's face. "You have no idea how serious I am."

• • • • •

Reza willed twelve o'clock to arrive with a furious flurry of intense workouts. Mashadi Aghee came to the gym five minutes before the match and took his place as if he had already won. Reza crouched in his wrestler's stance and glared into Mashadi's face with one thought: vengeance. Three seconds into the match and Reza struck at Mashadi with the venomous precision of a cobra.

"Take him," Ardeshir whispered from the side of the mat. Only a few matches were occurring that day, and many wrestlers gathered to watch this battle.

His body rippling in the sleek movements of a thoroughbred, Reza moved with unchecked power and precision. He bit his lip until it bled. *I will destroy you.* Mashadi relied on the predictable moves of a beast looking to crush skeletal remains.

Once again Reza pinned Mashadi to the mat.

Once again the referee raised Mashadi Aghee's arm in victory.

Reza leapt to his feet as Ardeshir firmly pulled his friend into the corner of the gym. "Don't do this. Think about your life and—"

"I'm not going to let him take my place! It's my place!"

"Calm down. Take a breath." He looked around. "I can talk to the general and get a third match."

Reza glared at Ardeshir. "Do it." He bolted from the gym.

• • • • •

Hassan's convulsive vomiting slowed, allowing him to crawl from the thick, bloody pool. Alone in the tiny cell, he had no sense of time or space or humanity. He seemed to know only varying degrees of suffering without the bother of asking why. More than three weeks had passed and he knew he had not been granted his mother's weekly visits. The guards enjoyed telling him that no one had come to see him, but he knew such lies were intended to create pain. He rocked in the corner farthest from the door and dreamed of the warmth of Nimtaj's chai. The terrible voice echoed in the vacant chamber and broke into his thoughts. "Abedi, visiting hours. Oh, wait, no one comes to see you." The baritone laughed.

Hassan didn't move. He didn't even look up.

"Unless you know a Nimtaj." The baritone paused to let the subtle cruelty sink in. "Do you know her, Hassan? Little woman with dark hair and dark eyes. Says she's your mother."

Warm tears poured from Hassan, but he couldn't bear to speak.

"Well, she's here. Wanta see her? Wanna say hello? I gotta hear you, Hassan. I can't be sure unless you tell me." The boots turned and began to thud out of the cell. "Never mind then."

Hassan's trembling voice felt desperate in the darkness. "I do, I do want to see her. Please, let me see my Naneh."

Thuds paused. "Who did you work for Hassan? Give me the names and you can see your Naneh." The baritone waited and then added, "She's right outside that door."

Hassan shook. "I didn't work for anybody." He pulled in the foul air and slowly breathed out each word, "I am—telling you—the truth."

The guard sighed and unlocked the cage. "You stupid, stupid kid. Come on, get up. Let's go."

Hassan cautiously rose and approached the door.

"*Zood bosh*! I haven't got all day. Move!"

Hassan stumbled into the next room and blinked painfully to adjust to the humming fluorescent bulbs hovering in the booth.

• • • • •

Reza collapsed in a dark alley somewhere in the streets of Tehran. Daylight yielded to the smothering night before Reza slowed in his crazed run through the tormented city. He pulled his legs into his body, wrapped his arms around his knees and cried. He wept for his country. He wept for his family. He wept for himself. He cried until he had wrung out his soul like a sponge, now fragile and useless. Reduced to nothing more than the vast bareness of the black above him, he willed his being to feel only empty, vacant and alone. Reza fought the desires trying to fill him. He fought to push away the courage given by his mother, the confidence bestowed by his father, the hope shining in the eyes of his sisters and dignity endeared to him from Hassan's dark prison cell. Reza struggled to deny a fate sewn in him when he first stood on his humble flat rooftop and looked out onto the world. A fate to be free.

• • • • •

Nimtaj sat in the dirty booth, her distorted image staring at her from the thick pane of clear plastic. She lifted the black receiver and waited for the guard to bring her son.

Filthy and ragged, Hassan moved as a corpse looking for a final resting place. He stopped when he saw her and dropped into the seat on the other side. He had grown slightly taller and his eyes sparkled as a child's when he saw his mother.

She pressed her hand against the barrier. "Are you well?"

"I am, Naneh."

"You will be home soon. I promise."

"I know."

He pressed his hand to mirror hers. Pleased that her flesh showed signs of healing, he attempted a smile. "You look better."

"Hassan," she said with the steady pulse of maternal power, "you will come home. You will live. You will survive and you will come home. Think that every minute of every day. They can do this to your body, but they cannot touch your soul."

Hassan nodded, but Nimtaj knew she needed to save her son. A guard approached her. "Your time is finished."

Nimtaj looked into Hassan's face. "Son, this prison does not define you. It does not keep you. Give them only your flesh and bones."

"Now, woman. *Zood bosh.*"

Hassan opened his mouth, but he couldn't speak. Nimtaj whispered to him as the guard grabbed her arm to pull her away from her son. "You hold your fate. These are a coward's walls."

A second guard pulled Hassan by his emaciated arm.

Reaching height known only to mothers, Nimtaj's tiny frame filled the room as she faced the guard. "*You* are the prisoner," she said. "When you turn the key on innocent children you entomb your own soul."

The filthy eyes looked away and the guard gave Hassan a final push through the door.

"No one is free! Your wicked ways imprison us all!" She cried out as the guard dragged her from the room.

• • • • •

A damp morning chilled Reza to consciousness. The beady eyes of an alley rat brought Mashadi Aghee back into his mind. He closed his eyes—to remember. He's eight and lying against the side of his house, holding his swollen foot; he's in the snow, gathering his books; he's standing in Mr. Mehdian's empty office; he's carrying Hassan's bleeding body from the prison; he's nursing his mother's torn flesh. As the scattered images blazed inside him, one seared his soul that he could not erase: he's lying pinned under Mashadi Aghee. Clenching his fists and squeezing his eyes, he fought to banish it. Fought to erase the memory from his life. From the shadowy corners of his mind, he sees himself on the bus. He remembers his brother's words. "I know you'll beat him next time, Rez."

Reza wiped the tears from his face and leaned toward the alley rat. "I will defeat you." He began to evolve into spastic yells as he crawled on all fours toward the vile creature. "I will crush your body. I will take you and I will throw you. And snap your spine!" The rat stared, took an uncertain step back and ran into a darkened hole. Reza rose.

He walked back through the morning streets of Tehran and already felt like a foreigner. Dirty, hungry and drained to the point of total exhaustion, Reza randomly bumped into people as he staggered into what he thought was the gym.

Looking up from his workout, Ardeshir shook his head as he watched Reza fumble across a mat, looking for someone—anyone. Coach Barzegar approached Reza, put his arm around his shoulders and walked him to the back corner. Ardeshir looked around to see if anyone else had noticed and followed them.

Reza nodded as Coach Barzegar mumbled and pointed toward his left knee. Ardeshir came and stood next to Reza. Silently, the two wrestlers exchanged hugs. They looked to Coach Barzegar, who again tapped his left knee and walked away.

Ardeshir glared at Reza. "Shoot it," he whispered.

Reza's eyes burned red.

• • • • •

All the wrestlers for the Iranian National Team had their passports completed and were ready to depart for Madrid, the first stop on the way to Venezuela, in less than twenty-four hours. Mashadi Aghee furiously protested the third match, but the doubt lingering about him forced the issue.

Dusk ripped the sunlight from the sky, but the oppressive heat refused to leave the gym. Mashadi Aghee grunted as he took the mat and prepared his stance against Reza. Reza took two solid steps to the middle and eyed Mashadi's left leg. Ardeshir followed Reza's glare and nodded. "Take it," he muttered.

On Reza's first move, he shot the left knee. He tore at the precious cartilage like a lion ripping the neck of his prey.

In a few violent seconds, Reza's beast lay defeated.

Ardeshir ran to Reza, but Reza had perched himself on Mashadi Aghee's back, his red eyes burning, his whispers calling through clenched teeth, "Who will be next? Who will challenge me next? Who?"

Ardeshir lifted Reza and pulled him from the carnage, speaking quietly into his ear. "It's over. You won."

Chapter Nineteen

2010

It's all over the news. I cringe as politics, ignorance and fear consume every conversation. They want to build a mosque at Ground Zero. They are Muslims. And Muslims must be terrorists.

My extended family thinks I should abandon the project for my own safety. "Maybe," they say, "you should wait a few years."

I turn to my blog and write.

> "Instead of deterring me, I find I'm even more passionately committed to finding a way to bring this story to light. Imagine, if someone read this book and rethought the chain: Iranian--must be a Muslim---Muslim---must be a terrorist.
>
> I think we can agree that not every Priest is a pedophile, not every Jew is cheap, not every Christian is a hypocrite, that some white men can jump and some black men can't.
>
> Can an American *only* be defined by birthright? skin color? language? religion? A piece of paper? Or should we define each other by the core values a person incorporates into his or her life? Values of family, freedom, honor, dignity, respect, tolerance, loyalty. You know the list.

Reza held these values so dear, that he risked his life to be free. He faces death—not just to come to America, but to be an American.

And what is Reza's American dream? Riches? No. Fame? No. His dream was to earn a college degree and to become a teacher. In his words, "to become the best possible person I could be."

Should I wait to tell share his journey? Or do we need to hear now more than ever before?"

• • •

The books that surround me speak. They speak with the light they shed from *Uncle Tom's Cabin* and the voice they gave to migrant workers. They speak with inspirational stories and with words that moved nations. I look at their straight spines and wonder. Did anyone tell you to wait?

Part II

Chapter Twenty

August 1982

For the second time in his life, Reza Abedi boarded a plane. He wore the team's uniform: a crisp white jacket, deep green pants and his first tie. Reza strutted down the aisle and plunked down next to Ardeshir. They smiled briefly.

Ardeshir and Reza spoke little. Reza shifted continually in the seat and Ardeshir kept his gaze out the window. As the plane began to descend, Reza leaned over to him. "Try to yawn," he said. "It helps your ears."

"Forget my ears," Ardeshir said. "I need to puke."

"I've got nothing to throw up." He looked around. "It's stupid we can't eat the airplane food because it's not prepared by a Muslim chef."

"You've got to make weight anyway." Ardeshir tried to yawn. "You'll eat soon."

• • • • •

The plane landed at Madrid International Airport and the Iranian wrestling team disembarked into an unfamiliar world. Bright colors. Sounds of people laughing and talking loudly. Women in short skirts, silky blouses and flowing hair. Seeing the citizens walking freely and smiling without shame, Reza thought back to painful images of Iran. But, sadder still, he longed for the happier memories from his childhood.

The twenty-member, bearded wrestling team, half a dozen coaches, four *Sepahi* and the mullah walked through the Madrid terminal pelted by fearful stares and dirty looks. Reza noticed a woman pull her child closer as they approached. He wondered if the sight of the blindfolded American hostages, fresh in the minds of onlookers, stirred anxieties at the sight of the fearsome Iranian wrestling team. Slowing to make his way to the back of the procession, he hoped to absorb a few sights.

"*Salam,*" came a low voice from a man sitting on a stool in front of a newspaper stand. Reza turned and saw a middle-aged man take a drag from his cigarette and nod. From his looks and accent, Reza figured he was Iranian. Reza returned the nod.

Ardeshir had also slowed his walk and now kept stride next to Reza. "What are you doing?"

"Looking for something to eat."

Ardeshir turned to look at the man in front of the newspapers. "What did he say to you?"

"He said, '*salam,*'" Reza said. His voice hit a higher pitch. "Do you have a problem with that? Should I report him to *Sepahi* so they can hang him as a traitor?"

Ardeshir shook his head.

The team's last meal, a full twenty-four hours ago, began to gnaw at the sculpted athletes. The mullah stopped the procession and announced that in five minutes it would be time to bow their bodies for prayer. He commanded the wrestlers to go to the restroom for the ceremonial wash in preparation.

"As if we haven't freaked out these people enough," Reza said to Ardeshir.

Ardeshir tried to grin. "He's just trying to," he said, "be true to Islam."

Reza wrinkled his face and rolled his eyes. "We're in an airport." Shaking his head, Reza headed toward the restroom. He walked in on the mullah in the midst of his ceremonial wash. Reza looked into the mirror and met the mullah's eyes. They were dark, clouded and foul. His bulbous nose dripped with the water running off his forehead.

"Brother, it is good you've come in to cleanse before prayer," the mullah said, not taking his eyes from Reza's.

Reza nodded.

With no way to exit, Reza approached the sink. He started to take off his shoes and socks to wash his big toes, as is the tradition, when the mullah stopped at the restroom door.

He turned to Reza. "Brother," he said, "open this door. I cannot touch the unclean handle whereas you have not yet cleansed."

Reza looked up in disbelief.

"*Chashm.*" Reza walked to the door, pulled the unclean handle and made an exaggerated motion to give the mullah plenty of space to exit.

Quickly returning his sock and shoe to his foot, Reza unceremoniously washed his hands and walked out. In the middle of the terminal, he joined his team. Facing Mecca, they bowed their bodies onto the prayer rugs and chanted Islamic prayers.

His attention drifted. A young woman in a very short skirt sat precariously close to the team and slightly spread her legs. Reza felt hot, red blood rush to his face and barely uttered another word of prayer.

They boarded the plane for the final destination, Venezuela. The stewardess pushed the cart down the aisle and Reza recognized the shiny red Coke cans. She took out a can opener and popped open the top, releasing the spray of fizz. After pouring the liquid into a glass of ice, she handed it to a passenger across the aisle. Right then, Reza decided to make his list. In his mind, he kept an inventory of all the things he would enjoy when he was free. The first being a Coke.

The team landed in Venezuela and drove past the posh hotel in which teams from every other nation would stay. Their van pulled into a heavily secured compound surrounded by a chain-link fence and with Venezuelan MPs posted at the entrance.

Stepping out of the van, Reza looked up at the barred windows in the cement building. He grabbed his bag and followed the team up the four flights of stairs.

"When do you think we'll eat?" Ardeshir asked Reza as they ascended up the final flight in the grey stairwell.

"It better be soon," Reza replied. Hunger ripped into his belly.

The wrestlers entered the unremarkable room lined with two rows of metal-framed bunks. Reza tossed his duffle bag onto a top bunk and sat on the edge. Ardeshir dropped his bag on the bottom and joined Reza. Neither spoke.

The coach entered and announced, "Our Muslim chef will prepare our *halal*[1] meal. Do not eat their unclean food."

Shaking his head, Reza headed toward the bathroom. He closed the door and pressed his body against it. After taking a

1 Food prepared in accordance to Islamic Law

few slow breaths, he washed his face in the sink and looked at his image in the mirror. He thought about Hassan.

Reza joined Ardeshir and the two walked down the stairs. "I'm going to eat you in a minute," Reza said.

"Relax, Reza. They just want us to have the best." But Ardeshir could not meet his eye.

Even in the cafeteria, Reza felt the stares from the international wrestlers. He walked through the large hall and spied leftover food on a tray near the restroom. Pretending to go the men's room, Reza grabbed handfuls of food off the tray and shoved them into his mouth. Ardeshir scolded his friend but did not report him.

• • • • •

The World Military Wrestling Tournament opened in a glorious ceremony featuring bands and balloons, cheering crowds and colorful flags. Each team marched proudly behind the beautiful young lady carrying their country's flag—every team except Iran's. The mullah insisted that a woman not proceed in front of the team holding the Iranian flag, so fellow Air Force wrestler Saam trudged dutifully carrying the red, white and green flag of Iran.

"He looks ridiculous," Reza said to Ardeshir as they began to assemble for the team photo.

"It has to be this way, I guess," Ardeshir said. He cleared his throat. "Have you seen the guys in your weight class?"

"Only the American looks decent. The rest are soft," Reza said. "How about you?"

"They're nothing," Ardeshir said. "I'm gold."

"I heard coach say they're doing the first three days of Free Style and then the Greco-Roman. At least we'll be eating soon."

Ardeshir patted his solid stomach, and turned his shoulders toward the photographer for the team photo. "Smile!"

• • • • •

The Iranian wrestling team remained closely guarded the first day. Whisked away after the ceremony, they once again had to wait for the specially prepared meal. Following the meal, they went to shower in rusted, grey stalls at the end of their fourth-floor barracks.

Reza stood under the cold spray of water.

Saam, the teammate just one weight class above Reza, came into the shower. Although his chiseled body spoke to his champion caliber, his facial features resembled a young boy's. With droopy eyes, autumn streaks in his hair and lips more rounded than flat, his one great advantage on the mats was his element of surprise. The strength of a man disguised as a child.

"Ready for tomorrow?" Saam said as he turned on the next shower.

"Of course. You?"

"*Baleh,* just another match," Saam said. He looked around. "Sometimes, however, it seems like there should be something, you know, better out there . . ."

The steam obscured Saam's face, but Reza searched until he met his eyes. *What are you saying?* Even though the next two stalls were empty, Reza turned on their water full blast. With the additional noise of pounding water, he turned to Saam. "Better," Reza whispered. "Are you thinking of finding somewhere better?"

Saam looked around the showers and leaned toward Reza. "I am."

Reza nodded. "Me, too."

Behind them, Ardeshir's voice came echoing through the sticky air. "What the hell are these on for and no one in them? Showering with ghosts or what?"

Saam took a step to the side.

"Just had them on waiting for you," Reza said.

"Damn right you did. Always wanting to be next to my naked, beautiful body. Can't blame you." He peered through the steam. "Hey, Saam, you looked mighty pretty today holding our flag. Did you get to wear them nice panties, too?"

"Go to your grave."

Reza turned off the shower, dried himself and lay on his bunk. He stared at the blank ceiling. *Maybe Mostafa already got Hassan out. Maybe they're heading for Turkey right now.* He tried to smile, but he heard Soraya's final words as she sobbed into his chest. *"Please don't leave us, Reza. Please, please. We need you here. We need you at home."*

• • • • •

Reza watched Saam closely over the next couple of days. Saam knew English well and Reza spotted him more than once talking to the American wrestlers, coaches and some men in regular clothes. The conversations were always fast, in corners or crowded areas, and if Reza had not been directly following Saam, he would have missed them. *He's finding a way to defect. He's not going back.*

Three brutal days of competition sucked the rest of Reza's energy. These were the best wrestlers in the world who had come to claim a gold medal. Wrestlers whose strength and skill surpassed human limits in the vicious attacks they waged on thick, unforgiving mats.

Ardeshir's weight class featured a three-time Spanish champion, whose mangled ear stuck in mismatched chunks against his head. He possessed animal-like quickness. For the gold medal round, Reza worked his way to the front of the section reserved for wrestlers and called to his childhood friend, "Run the mountain, Ardeshir!"

Ardeshir circled his opponent but quickly found himself behind on points. Reza raised his fist and shouted to him, when Saam touched his arm. "Don't turn around. Just keep cheering. Cheer loud."

"Sprawl! Use your legs!" Reza shouted.

In the crowd of yelling wrestlers, Saam pressed himself against Reza's back. "If you want to defect, it will happen on the last night."

"Get 'em, Ardeshir! Move!"

"You can only bring one pair of clothes, nothing else. *Hichi.*"

"Get up, Ardeshir! Now, pounce!"

"You will throw those clothes out the window at a time I will tell you."

"That's it! Shoot the leg. Go for the pin!" Reza yelled.

"We'll escape with the shift change of the *Sepah,*" Saam said. Then he paused, gave a few cheers of his own and returned to Reza. "It is the Americans who will help us."

"That's good," he whispered. *The Americans.* "Don't let him turn you!" Reza yelled.

"Wearing only your underwear, meet in the dark alley outside the compound."

"Hold him, Ardeshir! Keep his body on the mat!"

"Tell no one."

Saam was gone. The referee raised Ardeshir's arm in victory. Champion.

August 10, 1982

Wearing their gold medals, the Iranian wrestlers stood proudly on the winners' platform. Ardeshir leaned over to Reza. "My gold's shinier than yours."

"I'm sure it is."

"What's the matter with you?" Ardeshir asked. "You're the World Champion and you look like you're going to your own funeral. Lighten up."

Reza faked a smile and fingered his gold. "You're right. First place is good."

"That's more like it," Ardeshir smiled. "Girls love gold."

Finding his real smile, Reza shook his head at his friend. "*Baleh,* they do." He looked across the gym. "What's your mullah making a scene about over there?"

"Where?"

"Over there. He's pointing at us and then at the Americans. Did he just—did he just point at me?"

"You've been acting so strange lately," Ardeshir said. "No, he didn't point at you. But he's angry about something."

The Iranian wrestlers now stood awkwardly on the platform waiting to be joined by the other gold medal wrestlers for the group photo. Due to the mullah's demand that the Iranians not stand near the Americans, the photo was taken separately. The newspapers printed the photo with the two teams pasted together by a jagged line.

• • • • •

Three days of Greco competition followed. Freestyle wrestlers from the other teams could choose to stay or enjoy the sights of Caracas. The Iranian wrestlers were required to stay in the gym to watch the competition. Each had to check with a *Sepah* every two hours. To be late would be a certain court-martial.

Reza checked in with the *Sepah* and stated he would be watching the Greco matches. He arrived at the crowded gym with the intention of disappearing into the crowd to collect his thoughts. Lost from Ardeshir and dressed in his single pair of street clothes, Reza blended into the stands.

Not too long after, a young man sat next to Reza, smiled and nodded. Noting the spray of his dark chest chair, gold-link necklace and shimmering black pants, Reza decided this man wasn't a wrestler.

The man smiled at Reza. Reza returned the smile and studied the features of his face. *He wants something from me.*

The man pointed to himself. "Emilio."

With the same gesture, "Reza."

"English?"

"Little," Reza answered.

Emilio put his arm around Reza's shoulder. "A good looking guy like you should see the town. The girls will come flocking to us both," Emilio said. Reza nodded.

Emilio began pointing to the prettiest girls in the gym. He then pointed to himself and to Reza. And then to the door.

Reza narrowed his eyes and studied Emilio's face. *He wants me to leave with him to attract girls.* Reza looked at the *Sepahi,* who seemed engaged in the matches. *I do have two hours.* Reza held up two fingers, saying. "Two. Two."

Emilio slapped him on the back. "Two, of course. One for me and one for you."

Not two girls, two hours you idiot. Reza held up a two and pointed to the clock on the wall. "Two," he repeated.

Emilio looked at the clock. "Oh yes, curfew. Sure, I'll have you back by 2:00 a.m."

Reza misunderstood, nodded and followed him to a guard Emilio knew by a side exit. Soon the two men pulled up in front of a local disco bar. Taking in the sights, Reza drew in a deep breath. *Just for a couple of hours.* And he stepped into another world. His soul sucked in the pulsing music, devoured the spicy food and danced with the exploding lights. He talked with women who leaned in to show off their cleavage and rubbed their tight butts against his thigh. Emilio seemed to enjoy watching Reza as much as he enjoyed himself, but as the bartender announced last call, Emilio pointed his new friend in the direction of the door.

Walking into the dark night, Reza froze. *What time is it?*

"Sorry we've stayed so long," Emilio said, seeming to acknowledge the fear crisscrossing Reza's face. "It's just about midnight. You looked like you were having too much fun."

Reza's movements became erratic and he paced along the side of the car.

"Just get in. I know the MPs at the barracks. They'll let us in."

I'm dead. I'm dead and I've killed Saam, too. I'll be locked up. To-night. Shot, killed, hung, court-martialed. I'll be . . .

Emilio grabbed Reza's arms. "It's okay. I know people. Just get in the car." He opened the door and pointed for Reza to get in. They drove back to the barracks.

Emilio pressed the necessary bribe into the hand of the Venezuelan MP, who then allowed them back into the compound. He parked the car and Reza touched the handle.

"Can you get into your barracks?" Emilio asked, pointing at the barracks door.

Reza nodded, slowly got out and showed Emilio his ID card.

Emilio smiled and drove off.

Reza approached the barracks. *Please don't let them hear me. I'll be locked up. Court-martialed.* He looked up the shadowed flight of cement stairs. *They'll kill me. Right here. Tonight.* His shoe touched the first step. *I shouldn't have come back.* He shuddered in the darkness collapsing on him. *But how could I escape without help?* In a fog, Reza's trembling legs moved up the first three flights of grey in the vacant stairwell. He forced air in and out of his lungs and rounded the corner for the final hallway. Stopping. Listening. Praying. *Breathe. Breathe. Please let the Sepah be gone or asleep or . . .*

Burning like ice on his fingers, the knob twisted and the door squeaked open. He squeezed his eyes. *No more sounds.* He took two steps and closed it behind him. Just as he turned, an AK-47 pushed against his gut.

"Stop right there!"

"*Chashm, agha.*"

"I should shoot you," the *Sepahi* hissed. "Traitor."

Silence.

He raised the barrel to Reza's face and tapped on the trigger. "Report to the mullah at 0600."

Their eyes locked. "Yes, sir," Reza said. He felt a sweat bead form on his forehead. Standing straight, he let it trickle along his temple.

The guard's finger twitched on the trigger and Reza caught a flicker in his eye. Glancing down, the *Sepahi* motioned with the gun for Reza to walk.

He moved down the silent aisle of sleeping men and slid onto his mattress. In the suffocating darkness, Reza winced at the rattling of his metal bunk. *Stay calm.* He clutched his gold medal hidden under the pillow. *They're going to kill me at 6:00 a.m.*

In silence, Ardeshir clasped his hand tight over Reza's mouth and pressed his lips next to Reza's ear. Reza felt hot breath.

"Don't make a sound," Ardeshir said.

Reza nodded.

"They're going to shoot you."

Another nod.

"And arrest me."

"You? Why you?"

"SHHH!"

The sound of boots shifted at the door. A step, a second step. Then the settling of a body in the chair. A click as the rifle rested against the wall.

The dark silence held their heavy breathing. Ardeshir lifted his head to look for movement in the room lit by a single beam of moonlight. "They've been grilling me all night." He stopped to listen. "You're dead and you've dragged me into it."

Reza looked at his friend and mouthed each word with the slightest breath, "I'm—not—going—home." Ardeshir lifted his head and stared.

Reza squeezed his eyes and rubbed his face with his fingertips. Then he pulled Ardeshir's ear next to his mouth. When his lips touched the edge, Ardeshir tried to draw back, but Reza held him, his breath sounding out each word. "Come—with—me."

Ardeshir pulled away. "No."

Reza whispered the words again. "Come with me."

The sound of heavy boots started down the aisle and froze the childhood friends. The footsteps passed in the darkness and paused at Ardeshir's empty bunk. Continuing in an uninterrupted pattern, the boots headed down the stairs and sealed the boys' fate.

"We're dead," Reza whispered.

"They can't kill us here," Ardeshir said. "Too messy."

Reza hoisted himself up onto his elbow. "Come with me."

"I can't. My family—I—just can't."

"You want to go back to being a killer for Khomeini?" Reza's whispering voice shook. "Living with rage and fear? I can't do it." He looked at Ardeshir. "And neither can you."

Ardeshir rolled onto his back. Under the single stream of moonlight, Reza saw tears roll down his friend's face. *I'm so sorry, Ardeshir. But we have to find a life.*

• • • • •

Looking into the rising sun, Reza wondered how many men before him welcomed a new day as their last. He reported to the mullah in the stark barracks at the end of the fourth floor.

"And I will ask you one more time, what was your errand last night?" said the mullah. "Who are you working with?" He paced in front of Reza, fingering his prayer beads.

Reza stood with strength and purpose. Flanked by two armed guards, he stared ahead. Rage ravaged his body. *You filthy, sick coward hiding in your black robe.*

"I left with a local to see the sights," Reza said. "I lost track of time."

The mullah stopped his pacing and seemed to look at Reza for the first time. Reza's eyes scoured every pore on the mullah's face. Above the bulbous nose, two rodent eyes peered through puffy flesh and squinted into Reza's fixed gaze. The mullah approached and brought his twisted face within an inch of Reza's. "Lost track of time? You expect me to believe you just forgot to look at a clock? Your disobedience is unacceptable." He seemed to look for any sign indicating fear.

Reza's teeth ground together and every muscle in his body tightened until his very breath stopped. *You are nothing.* "I mean no disobedience," he said. "I lost track of time."

"Should I be concerned about your allegiance to Iran? To Ayatollah Khomeini? To our almighty Allah?" The mullah stepped away and turned his back.

You know nothing of loyalty. My Naneh prays every day with a pure heart, and my Baba lives a life of honor. You're filth, not fit to be shoes on their feet. Reza forced his teeth to unclench and looked at the cement floor. "No, *agha.* My allegiance to my country is true."

The mullah continued to the door. He turned half his body to Reza. "You will be dealt with at the appropriate time." He looked at the *Sepah.* "Take him."

Reza's eyes blazed into the back of the Mullah's skull. *Coward.*

• • • • •

The Iranian wrestlers walked through the closing ceremonies of the World Military Wrestling Championship. Again, Saam held the Iranian flag. He looked more than ridiculous to Reza. He looked positively wrong. Pictures and parties followed, but for Reza, Ardeshir, Saam and a fourth defecting wrestler, Ramin, this late night held the promise of either a new life or a horrific death.

After all the other wrestlers had showered, Saam went to the stalls. Reza looked at Ardeshir. Ardeshir closed his eyes and gave a single nod. They followed Saam into the showers.

Saam scrubbed his body and did not acknowledge either of them. Shifting from side to side, Ardeshir looked at Reza and clenched his fists. He started rapidly shaking his head. Touching Ardeshir's elbow, Reza whispered, "You're okay."

Reza moved closer to Saam and tried to make eye contact. Saam just kept scrubbing. Steam filled the stalls. Ardeshir scrubbed. More steam billowed. Saam finally looked around. He glanced first at Reza and then at Ardeshir. Ardeshir's huge hands held his head, and only his elbows poked out through the fog. "He's okay," Reza whispered.

Saam drew a 1 in the steam on the wall and pointed to himself and then a 2 and motioned toward Ramin. Ramin, one of the few wrestlers who could match Ardeshir in both size and strength, held up two fingers. His dark eyes burned through the steam at Reza and Ardeshir. The two fingers tightened into a fist and he walked out, wet still dripping down his mammoth arms and chest.

Reza moved closer to Saam. "First and second," Saam murmured. "You must watch."

Saam then drew a 3 for Reza and looked at Ardeshir. Reza nodded his head. Saam drew a 4. Ardeshir stared but gave no indication he understood. Saam shot a look at Reza. "I got him. He's fine," Reza whispered. *Come on, Ardeshir, finish the fight.*

• • • • •

Night can be so still, so motionless that even death seems restless. Thick, sticky air pressed upon the chests of the strongest wrestlers in the world. They lay there helpless and shivering. Fear crushed sense from their minds and reduced them to animals preparing to gnaw their limbs from steel traps.

Shortly before 2:00 a.m., Reza rose. He walked into the bathroom and closed the door. He wrapped his hands around the cold bars and pressed his face against the opening. In the moonlight, he remembered Hassan. Crushed in the cage between the other prisoners, Hassan's ragged gaze locked with Reza's. He began shouting, but Reza couldn't hear him above the mothers' cries. Reza stretched his arm to get closer, closer to somehow touch Hassan. Hassan's arm, too, reached with one outstretched finger pointing to their mother, repeating, "Go! Leave now! Go!"

Reza squeezed the iron bars and rested his forehead against

their cold. *Oh, God, Hassan, will you ever forgive me?* He let go. He pulled the clothes he had hidden behind the toilet and wrapped them around his gold medal. He popped open the window and dropped the clothes through the bars. *Naneh, please understand.* Vomit crept into his throat as time crushed every sensation he'd ever felt. Willing his legs to move, he walked across the silent barracks. *I have to breathe. I have to look calm.*

In only his boxers, he approached the guard at the door. "I need a drink."

"No way, Abedi," the *Sepahi* replied.

"Come on. I'm thirsty."

"Toilet's got water." The *Sepahi* shifted his entire body to block the door. Behind Reza, the *Sepah* could see Ardeshir's figure move toward the bathroom.

"Seriously, where am I going in my underwear? Five minutes. Just need a drink," Reza said. *Keep breathing. Stop shaking.*

The guard leaned on the doorway and looked Reza up and down. "Turn around. Show me your hands." Reza complied. "Why's Ardeshir in the bathroom?"

Reza's throat closed around his voice; he struggled to sound annoyed. "Look, I don't know. Maybe he has to pee. I just need a drink of water."

"You have five minutes, Abedi."

Reza walked calmly down the first flight of stairs and then raced down the final three. He grabbed his clothes and felt for his medal. Then he looked up. No sign of Ardeshir.

Spotting the Americans' van, Reza tucked everything under his arm. With a quick glance, he bent at the waist and tiptoed to the van. The Americans directed him to lie facedown in the back with Saam and Ramin on either side.

The night pulsed with his crashing heartbeat. In the front, the two American wrestlers shifted constantly, looking out the window toward the compound. The one in the driver's seat turned toward the back. "Where's the fourth?"

Saam looked at Reza. "Ardeshir's getting us killed."

Reza lifted his chin to the driver. "He's coming. Just give him five more minutes."

"We don't have five," the American whispered. "He's got two."

Saam pressed his face to Reza's. "Ardeshir screwed us. He got scared and turned us in."

"He wouldn't do that. He's coming. He—probably got stuck with the *Sepah.*"

Saam shook his head. "He's turned us in."

The Americans turned to the wrestlers. "Shhh! Someone's coming."

Hot tears rolled down Reza's cheeks. *Please, please be Ardeshir.* Fast, heavy footsteps approached. *Running. He's not supposed to be running. Why is he running? It can't be Ardeshir.*

The van door slid open. Someone jumped inside. With the lights off, the van sped out of the compound. Ardeshir squeezed Reza's hand.

Chapter Twenty-One

August 12, 1982

Little Mariam stood in front of the family, holding her "Reza's #1" sign and pointing at each plane that touched down at Tehran's airport. "Is Reza on that one, Naneh?"

Nimtaj leaned over to her youngest. "I hope so, *azizam.* Just remember to hold very still and no loud talking."

"I know, Naneh." Turning to her oldest sister, she asked, "Do you think he's on this one, Rasha?"

Rasha and Mehri and now Soraya, Farah and Pari wore their dark, encasing *chadors,* carefully tucking in every strand of hair and erasing any hint of makeup. Soraya's natural features gave her face a look of enhanced beauty, and Nimtaj always insisted she stand in the very back.

"Maybe, Mariam. Just hold your sign high so he will see us when he gets off the plane," Rasha said, as she balanced her youngest child on her hip. She looked back at her brother. "Mostafa, any idea?"

Mostafa simply stroked his chin and raised an eyebrow. He moved next to Abbas, gave his father a rare grin and patted his back. "Reza made us proud today, Haj' Abbas. He comes home a *ghahreman.*"

Abbas, who wore his best suit and seemed to look six feet tall, suppressed a smile and continued to rock back and forth on his heels.

Mostafa watched the movement of the *Sepah,* seeming to make note of faces and rank. He had gathered his family to the left of the other waiting families; the left was nearest the exit.

Despite the growing excitement of each landing plane, the absence of Hassan hung over the family. Everyone felt it. No one said it: "If anyone should be here to greet Reza, it should be Hassan."

Finally the plane touched down. The huge metal doors swung open and the first wrestler walked down the roped aisle. "Something's wrong," Mostafa whispered.

* * * * *

The American van sped through the streets. Struggling with directions, Spanish street signs and constant looks to see if they were being followed, the American wrestlers began to argue. Reza noted their high-pitched tones and exaggerated gestures, as the van turned left, then right, then made a U-turn.

"They're lost!" Ardeshir said. "We're dead."

"Shhh!" Saam scolded. "Their lives are at risk, too. They'll get us there."

"Where?" Reza asked, realizing for the first time he didn't know where he was going.

"The safe house," Saam said.

Ardeshir was about to protest when Reza spoke before him. "The Americans will not let us down."

A few hours later, the van bumped down a dirt road. It came to a stop and the driver turned to his teammate in the passenger seat. "This is it." Reza heard a crack in his voice, as if he were about to cry. Then he saw the two hug and Reza felt a lump in his throat. He wished he knew English better. He wished he could say a proper thank you and express how much he admired their courage—how much it meant for him to be free.

They slid open the door and the four defecting Iranians stepped outside.

"Welcome to freedom!" the American driver said.

"Your courage made this possible," said Saam. "We will forever be thankful to you." Reza hugged them and said, *"pahlavan."* They looked confused.

"Hero," Reza said.

The American wrestlers nodded, climbed back into the van and drove away.

The four walked through the backyard of the small house somewhere in a wooded area. The screen door was torn and there were no lights on. Reza tried to peer into a dirty window, but the shutters blocked his view. They hesitated. Finally, Saam tapped on the door, which was covered with green, peeling paint. They waited.

Just as they began to step away, the door flew open. A woman's arm, wrapped in a red velvet robe, waved them in. Reza went first and Saam went last. They walked into a dark kitchen. When the light flipped on, Ardeshir bolted for the door. Saam blocked him with his body and the two began to struggle. "What the hell's the matter with you?" Saam said.

"He's the Iranian ambassador! We've been set up! He's . . ."

The ambassador walked over and placed his hand on Ardeshir's arm. "I am the ambassador. But no, you have not been set up."

Ardeshir shook his head as if trying to clear a bad dream. "Ambassador, you can't help us. They'll kill you."

The ambassador lit a cigarette and sat at his polished kitchen table. He motioned for the others to do the same. "That is true."

Reza sat in a heap in a chair too big for his body and stared at Ardeshir. He knew Ardeshir's position made it possible that Ardeshir had guarded the ambassador in Iran during a meeting with the Ayatollah Khomeini. Reza leaned forward in his chair and rested his head in his hands. *There's no way the Americans set us up. Just no way.*

The ambassador's wife, a native Venezuelan, brought the men tea and homemade rolls, but only Ramin reached for one. After Reza saw he didn't die from the first bite, he also took a piece.

"Come on, men. My wife makes the best. Please, do not insult her cooking. Eat up."

Saam took a drink of tea. "*Merci*, sir. We're just a bit on edge to eat. Please share with us how this is going to work."

The ambassador took a long drag from his cigarette and looked at Ardeshir. "Your friend here, from the Revolutionary Guard, he is very right. Nothing short of death for a defector will satisfy your Ayatollah Khomeini. A very public, very brutal death."

Reza started choking on his roll. One smack from Ramin and the chewed slimy wad landed square in the middle of the table. "I'm sorry, sir. I'll clean that up," Reza said. He looked around for a napkin.

"No need," the ambassador said as his wife scooped up the glistening mass. "So, let's get to how this is going to work. Tomorrow night, I will send you with a letter in Spanish to a friend of mine at the police station. He will determine your safest place and arrange for an official translator to plead your cause for political asylum. And, from there, you will get your visas and get on with your lives."

Reza reached for another roll. *That sounds easy enough.*

Ardeshir rubbed his thick, black beard. "That's it?"

The ambassador rose from his chair. "That's it."

"What's in this for you?" Ardeshir asked.

"For me? For me? I guess that is a fair question given your background where there is always an expectation for something in exchange. Well, I, too, will defect and live out my life with my beautiful Venezuelan wife and kids and have no more ties to that madman. Good night, gentlemen."

• • • • •

Mariam's high-pitched voice called out, "Reza! Reza!" as each grave wrestler trudged off the plane.

Nimtaj grabbed her hand. "Shhh, Mariam. Just hold your sign."

Returning from a brief conversation with a coach, Mostafa began to herd his family toward the exit. Abbas wouldn't move. "Baba, come. We must go."

"No, I want to see my son."

"Baba, you will. Just not now. We need to get the girls home."

The last wrestler had walked down the aisle and the huge metal doors slammed closed behind him. Mariam began to cry. "They forgot Reza."

Nimtaj's eyes met Mostafa's. He bowed his head. She covered her mouth with her hand. "Not another son," she whispered. She pulled Farah, Soraya and Pari in front of her to move them toward the exit. "What happened?" they whispered. "Where's Reza?"

"Shhh. Just walk. Farah, hold Mariam."

Mostafa grabbed Soraya's arm. "Go home and take down every picture of Reza, every award or anything that has his name." He shot a nervous glance toward the *Sepah.* "And all the banners with Reza's name in Kermanshah. Every one must come down."

Soraya recoiled. "No, I will not deny my brother. We don't even know what happened."

"He defected. And I'm not worried about him. It's Hassan. I have a deal. I'm so close, but now . . ."

"But now," Soraya trembled, "now they'll kill him? Oh, Reza, what have you done?"

They looked up just in time to see the Revolutionary Guard leading Abbas down the darkened corridor, their hands twisting the sleeves of his best suit.

• • • • •

Word reached the safe house that Iran sent a top-level team, disguised as OPEC representatives, to Venezuela to search for the wrestlers. The four were brought to a prison cell for security reasons.

Ardeshir grabbed the cell bars and shook them with all his strength. A guard came to the cell and spoke to Reza. "He all right? I can take you to the staff room."

Reza stood next to his friend. "No, we're good. *Merci.*"

The guard nodded. "No problem. Good translator comes tomorrow and you'll get your visas."

"Ya sure?" Ardeshir barked.

The guard looked at Reza. "Tomorrow."

Reza pulled Ardeshir's fingers off the bars. "Thanks."

Ardeshir sat on the edge of the cot with his head heavy in his hands. "This is all messed up. We've been in this damn cell six days now."

The cell offered two bunk beds and a square table with too-small wooden chairs. The wrestlers' bodies, used to grueling workouts and at their peak of World Champion physical excellence, suffered in the cage.

Saam continued his pacing. "It's complicated. No one figured it'd make international news. We're safe here and tomorrow we have our political asylum. It's just taking a little longer than we thought."

"Well," Ardeshir said as he stood up to face Saam, "it's taking too long, period."

Reza stood between Ardeshir and Saam and pressed his hands against their bodies. "Sit down," he said. "Both of you." Ardeshir waited for Saam to move and then he sat. Reza sat next to him. Neither spoke.

• • • • •

The short, stout man wore an old brown suit and had more hair in his ears than on his head. His face carried a permanent look of being annoyed and he cleared his throat so often that Reza wanted to flush it out with a hose. Each wrestler took a turn to tell his story until the translator simply held up his hand and then motioned for the next one to begin. He picked imaginary lint from his pants and rarely asked questions.

"I don't like the way this is going," Reza said to Ardeshir, who nodded in agreement.

The Jewish translator retold the stories he heard from the wrestlers in Farsi to the Venezuelan government officials in Spanish. In the end, the wrestlers were given a six-month visa for religious—not political—asylum.

They returned to their cells to wait for the paperwork to be processed and tried to unravel this decision. Ardeshir's voice bounced off the cement walls. "What the hell is religious asylum? The ambassador said political asylum! I knew this couldn't work, I knew—"

"Hey! It wasn't my idea to bring you!" Saam yelled. "I'm sure they'll have a huge welcome party for you in Tehran! I'll drive you to the airport myself!"

This time Ramin stood between the two as Reza lay down on his bunk. He paid no attention to the others and looked over to Saam. "What's this mean?"

Saam sighed. "It means we have six months in Venezuela. During that time, we can apply to the embassies of the different nations for help and admission to their country. We'll have an apartment to stay in, but that's it. We'll have to find jobs and ways to pay for food and anything else we need."

Reza's voice floated calmly from his bunk. "How are we going to find jobs? No money, no Spanish, six-month visas. We're Iranians, we're—"

"We're dead men. That's what we are!" Ardeshir resumed his pacing. "Venezuela is ass-kissing Iran because of OPEC. The UN won't let them send us back, but that's it. We're being left to twist in the wind until the *Sepahi* finds us and takes us back to Tehran."

The Venezuelan official approached the cell and shook hands with the wrestlers. He radiated genuine joy as he presented their six-month visas. They were dropped off at the apartment the Iranian ambassador had arranged for them. Free men.

September, 1982. Thursday.

Soraya, Pari and Nimtaj, carefully covered in *chador*, took the crowded bus ride to the prison. With almost trance-like movements, the women departed the bus and took their places in line. No one pushed or shoved. And no one spoke. Inch by inch, they moved forward. Once at the front, they were ushered into a waiting room with rows of booths separated by thick plates of dirty plastic.

"Why did the line stop?" Pari whispered to Soraya.

Soraya craned her neck. "It is the mother two in front of us. The guard cannot find her son."

Nimtaj gently closed her eyes. Soraya and Pari gripped her hands and became silent. They would not look into each other's faces for there the truth would be written. Once Reza defected, no one was safe.

Holding a small pile of blood-stained clothes, a guard approached the mother waiting ahead of them. She looked at the bundle. She cried out to the dead. Her fists pounded on the guard's chest as she damned everyone. Dropping the clothes, he dragged her toward the door. In a moment, she was gone. As her cries echoed in the remaining mothers' hearts, the small corpse of clothes lay untouchable. Another guard came and took it away.

Pari's hands were sweating and trembling. Soraya struggled so hard to stop her tears, the room began to spin. Only Nimtaj did not waver. She kept her head high and her eyes fixed on the row of booths.

It was their turn. "Hassan Abedi," Nimtaj said.

The guard looked at his clipboard. He flipped a page. And then another. He tapped on the paper. Turning to another page, he paused.

Lifting her face to look directly into his, Nimtaj repeated, "Hassan Abedi."

With a grunt, he returned to the crinkled papers.

Pari squeezed her mother's hand and Soraya closed her eyes. In the awful silence, they waited.

Without looking up, the guard pointed. "Third."

The girls scurried ahead of their mother and pressed their palms against the shield. Hassan's hand met theirs and he smiled. His eyes went to his mother and he nodded the "I'm okay, Naneh" he gave every time she came.

Soraya reached for the phone and Hassan picked up his end. The news that they had come to share suddenly seemed frightening. What if he hears it as his death sentence? What if he curses and hates his brother?

Nimtaj lifted the phone. "My son," she said. "You are well?"

"I'm strong, Naneh, yes," he said. But his gaze followed Soraya and Pari, who looked away.

"Naneh," he said. "What's going on?"

"Reza," she said. Then she gave the phone to Soraya.

"Oh, no," Hassan said. "Did he lose in the championship?"

The phone trembled in Soraya's hand. Her lips parted but with no sound.

"What?" Hassan said.

"He's—" Soraya looked into Hassan's wary eyes. "He's not coming home."

Hassan's face crisscrossed with questions. "Not coming?"

"He escaped," she said. Tears spilled down her cheeks. "Ardeshir, too."

Hassan covered his face with his hands. He shook.

"Hassan?" Soraya whispered.

He clenched his fists and smiled, a great joy unlocked from his soul. "My brother is free. My brother is free."

November, 1982

The warm rain streamed from the leaking roof and formed a puddle next to Ardeshir on the lumpy couch. By digging through dumpsters, the wrestlers had assembled some furnishings, clothing and often their meals. They were recruited to wrestle for the Venezuelan wrestling team and worked out in preparation for the upcoming Pan Am tournament. But, as the Pan Ams drew near, so did the reality that it would be too risky to compete.

Ardeshir sat staring at another article written about the three defecting Iranian wrestlers before he dropped it onto the pile of newspapers and walked around the empty apartment. It was quiet except for the sound of the forever rain. He went to the window and lightly placed his hand on his gold medal, which lay on the window's shelf. The gold medal reflected the grey sky. Rubbing his freshly shaven face, he looked in the direction he thought to be Mecca and mumbled. He looked at the phone and moved toward it. He turned his back as he lifted the receiver and pretended to push the buttons.

"Baba," he said to no one. "I'm the world champion, Baba. And I'm a free man."

Hearing footsteps come up the stairs, he dropped the phone back into the cradle and resumed his place on the couch. Quickly he picked up the newspaper.

The articles had drawn attention to the wrestlers, and folks donated food or invited them over for a homemade dinner. One such family consisted of two sisters, older and heavier than the wrestlers. Tonight, these sisters invited only Reza and Saam over for dinner.

Reza returned to the apartment like a man who had fallen off the end of the earth and wasn't sure if the world would ever be right-side up again. Ardeshir looked up and cocked his head. "You all right? I thought you had dinner at Dori's."

"I did."

"Where's Saam?"

"He's still," Reza said, "stuck there." His face was flushed and vacant.

"Stuck there? Why's he—Rezzza—" Ardeshir broke into a huge smile. "Did you get laid?"

Reza looked away. "I don't want to talk about it."

Ardeshir broke into crazy laughter. "You did! You got nailed by Dori! Wow, she must have world champion moves to pin you down. Good thing she didn't have to make weight, she's probably got you by ten kilos. She's probably—"

"Thanks. Thanks for the play by play." Reza sat on the wet couch next to his friend. "It wasn't all that—well, I thought . . ."

Ardeshir put his arm around Reza. "It gets better. Pretty soon you'll be able to make all three periods."

Reza just shook his head. "Where's Ramin?" he asked.

"Huntin' for food. And this is getting old. I got thrown off the bus again today."

"Hang on from the back. They don't see you there."

"I'll try to remember that."

Looking at the phone, Reza took a deep breath. He blew the air out slowly and turned to his friend. "Saam did say—well, he can help us make a call home tomorrow."

Ardeshir lifted his face to the ceiling and spoke to the dripping sky. "I can't call home, Reza. You know that."

"Just to say you're okay. Just to say—"

"To say what? That I've disgraced my family so that I could—eat steak bones from trash cans!" The anger in his final words punctuated the frustration they all felt.

Reza let the silence heal the room. Then he started each word slowly. "I know. I'm sick of it, too. But, it's got to get better. We still have some of the money given to us by the American Embassy."

"For the information I sold to them about being in the guard. But we still have no visas. We still don't have—a life." Ardeshir paced about the room.

"Tomorrow we're going to the Canadian and French embassies. Germany's the next day. Someone's going to let us in." The words fell empty and even Reza wasn't sure if he was trying to convince Ardeshir or himself. He stood up from the couch but realized he had nowhere to go. He sat back down again onto the squish of the damp cushion.

"And if they don't?" Ardeshir said. "Then what? Are you going to do Dori every night for a meal? You're going to wait in the alleys for the waiters to dump the trash at eleven?"

Reza sighed. "Let's just work on calling home and then we'll figure out the rest."

Ardeshir went into the kitchen. He opened the cupboards he knew to be empty and slammed them shut. He was about to begin another tirade when Saam and Ramin came up the steps.

Saam looked at Reza and both men shook their heads. "We need another plan for food," Saam said. And they all laughed. They laughed until their sides ached and their lungs burned. They laughed until their eyes swelled with tears. They laughed until their exhausted bodies collapsed on the floor. They laughed until they cried.

• • • • •

The following morning Saam struggled for hours on the phone with operators of different nationalities. Sometimes in English, sometimes Farsi, sometimes splintered Spanish. The broken, desperate conversations always ended with Saam slamming the receiver. "They can all screw me!" Saam cried out. "They can all . . ." He broke down in frustrated sobs and Ardeshir sat by his side. He looked at Reza, who furiously rubbed his face with his hands. They had no money; they couldn't place a call.

"You have to find that man you met," Ramin said. He lifted

the telephone receiver and motioned with it to punctuate each word. "If he knew how to get you in and out of the compound that night, he'll know how to place a phone call."

"Okay," Reza said. "I'll try to find him."

• • • • •

That evening, Reza worked his way to the nightclub Emilio had brought him to weeks before. He waited in the darkened doorway until Emilio walked out. Emilio's face broke into a huge smile. "My friend, Reza. You sneaky bastard! I read about you. One night with Emilio and you don't want to go home, eh?"

"Something like that." Reza watched a few girls walk out of the night club, then motioned for Emilio to walk away from the entrance. "My friends and I are having some trouble."

"Oh, your Spanish has gotten better. Come, Reza. I'll drive you to my favorite bar and you can tell me all about it," Emilio said.

"No bar. I just need some help making a phone call," Reza said. "And I thought you might know someone to help us."

They approached the car and Emilio motioned for Reza to get in. He sped down the darkened streets while Reza recounted the last several difficult weeks.

"I wish you had come to me earlier, my friend. I can help you. I know people. Some good people and some not-so-good people. It's all the same. But I have phone people who will help you and your friends call home. Here," he said, driving with one hand and writing with the other, "you dial this number. You ask for Juarez, tell him Emilio said to help you and it will be done."

"Thank you so much." Reza folded the paper and tucked it into his pocket. "This means a lot."

Emilio waved his hand. "It's nothing. Now, food. Jobs. I know people who need men of muscle to, you know, help work some deals out. It pays well. We'll talk."

"Sure, Emilio, we'll talk," Reza said. "You can let me off here."

"Nonsense. First we drink, then I drive you home."

• • • • •

Reza called the number and made the arrangements with Juarez, who suggested they call friends of friends, not directly to their homes.

Handing the phone to Saam, Reza said, "You should call first." Saam talked to a cousin and set up a time for his family to come to that house in two days. Saam hung up the phone and turned to his two friends, who sputtered, "What did he say? Is everyone okay? Did they question our families?"

Saam cleared his throat. "He said they're okay, as far as he knows. There were rumors we were killed trying to escape but he thinks no one believes them. That's all he knows."

Ramin made the call next, made his plan for a future call and relayed the same rumors. He handed the phone to Ardeshir. "No, Reza should go next," Ardeshir said. "He's needs to know about—about Hassan."

Reza held the receiver. His hand shook. "No, go ahead Ardeshir."

Ardeshir put his hand on Reza's shoulder. "Dial." Reza's hands trembled so violently that Ardeshir had to press the numbers. They called Farid's house. On the third ring, a voice said, "Allo?"

Reza couldn't speak.

The voice again. "Allo? Is anyone there?"

Reza creaked into the phone, "Farid?"

"He's not home. Call back."

"No! Wait! It's me, Reza."

Silence.

"It's me. I'm okay."

A deeper voice. "Reza? Is it—you?"

"Farid! I'm so glad to hear—how are you? How's my family? What have you heard?"

"Your family is all right. They brought them to the station every day, asking questions, your mother, sisters, me, everybody. But, nobody knew anything."

There was a silence. Reza heard Farid draw in a deep breath.

"Farid, tell me!" Reza said. "Is it Hassan?"

"Haj' Abbas had to find a new job. But Mostafa took care of that. And then your Naneh, she . . ."

"She what?" Reza paced with the phone.

"She had a heart attack, Reza," Farid said. "Two actually."

"But, she's—she's . . ."

"Yes, she's alive. I think they are talking of moving from Kermanshah. The war is so bad there. Bombs drop every day. It's so hard and she worries so."

The air still hung with one word: Hassan.

"Farid is—is Hassan—is he . . ."

"He's still there. Mostafa's been working with people. Mehri saw my mother in the market place and she said he's almost out." Farid let out a long breath. "They will be so happy to hear you're safe. Where are you?"

"Hassan's almost out," Reza repeated so Ardeshir would hear.

Farid heard the tremble in Reza's voice, so he continued. "Maybe even in a few days. He has a hearing and Mostafa's supposed to have all the legal fees lined up. So, where are you?"

"A few days, that's so, so good to hear." He took a deep breath. "It's kinda messy, but things should be getting untangled in the next month. Hey, can you get my family to your house at this time in two days? I could call back."

"Yeah, Reza, of course. I'll do it. I'll get everybody. I won't even tell them. I'll hand them the phone and surprise them."

"Don't do that. It's too much for Naneh. Just tell everyone I'm safe. Tell them tonight, if you can. And tell them I'll call back at this time in two days."

Reza pressed the receiver to his chest. *Naneh, I'm safe.*

"*Inshallah,*" Farid said.

Reza tried to respond, but he could only hand the receiver to Ardeshir and wipe the tears flowing uncontrollably down his face. Ardeshir said a few words to Farid and hung up the phone.

Two faces looked to Reza with questions they were too afraid to know the answers to. Reza sat on the floor and leaned against the soggy wall. "Naneh had two heart attacks," he said. Without warning, he punched a hole in the wall with his fist. Just before he could punch a second, Ardeshir grabbed his arms. He brought Reza to the ground and lay on his twisting body until he felt Reza's breathing become steady.

"You can't blame yourself for her heart attack," Ramin said. "Kermanshah's being bombed every day. Who can survive that? They need to leave."

"They won't," Reza said. "I know Naneh will never leave until Hassan is free."

It was Ardeshir's turn to dial. Reza summoned the strength to stand next to his friend. He could hear the echo of the ring. After the fourth ring, a baritone voice barked into the phone, "Allo."

"Baba, it's me, Ardeshir. I'm safe and I—"

"I have no son named Ardeshir."

Dial tone.

• • • • •

This time the Abedi family gathered at Rasha's house. The last two phone calls at Farid's filled the home with joy, laughter and then suspicion, so they changed locations. The first time Reza heard his mother's voice, he couldn't speak. Two precious minutes passed before he could find his breath to say, "Naneh, I'm free."

The family placed the yellow phone in the center of the rug. They sat poised in a circle, willing it to ring. To be Reza. Finally it cooperated and rang.

A hand reached for the phone. "Allo, Reza?"

"Allo. Who's this?"

"You don't recognize my voice? It's because I have a beard now."

Reza could barely breathe the word, "Haaassssannnn?"

"Yeah, Rez, it's me. I'm out three days now."

Reza looked at Ardeshir. "He's out. Hassan's out." *Thank you, God. Thank you.*

Hassan continued, "I'm out. Are you talking to Ardeshir? Tell him he's still ugly."

"I do," Reza said laughingly. "Every day. So, can you go back to school? Are you . . ."

Hassan's voice lowered. "No, I have to leave Kermanshah. Tomorrow, I think. Mostafa's guys, they're coming in the middle of the night and taking me out."

"Out? Out where?"

"I don't know where. It's one of those Mostafa things. And we can't tell Naneh. She's—she's been through too much. All I know—it's not Iran. But I'm getting out." Hassan choked back tears. "You—you got out, Rez. I'm—I'm right behind you."

Reza pushed the receiver into his chest and fought the flood of sobs. He pressed the phone to his lips once more. "I'm—it's so good to hear your voice. I know you're going to be—you're . . ." Reza handed the phone to Ardeshir and paced around the room.

Ardeshir took a deep breath. "Hassan, you okay?"

Hysterical sobs answered his question and the phone passed to Mostafa. "He's going to be fine. We've got to go."

"I know. Stay strong."

Ardeshir hugged Reza with the embrace of a bear. Feeling Ardeshir's power dissolving all his fears, Reza allowed himself to collapse into Ardeshir.

"He's out! He's out! That crazy little monkey is free!" Ardeshir said as he held his friend.

Smiling through his tears, Reza could only ache. He ached for Baba's firm handshake, the laughter of his sisters and the soft lines in his mother's face. He ached to climb the cliffs of Kermanshah and to lie under the sprinkled soft moon dust of his night's sky. He ached to be home.

"He's safe," Ardeshir repeated as he gave Reza a final embrace.

The friends looked to each other and their eyes locked. Reza reached for the phone and handed it to Ardeshir. "Dial."

"No, I'm—it's not a good time. I'm . . ."

Reza waited for Ardeshir to finish the sentence, but he only looked to the floor.

"They just needed to get over the shock of it all," Reza said. "They needed time."

With insistence, he shook his head. "I'll wait for Saam and Ramin to get back."

"Why? They could be gone for hours."

Ardeshir stared at the phone. "I can't."

"Make the call," Reza said.

"I need to do this alone."

Ardeshir held the phone and Reza left the room. Ardeshir's thick finger poked each number and then paused. Squeezing his eyes shut, he hit the final button.

"Allo, it's me, Ardeshir."

Dial tone.

He held the receiver, frozen. Reza returned to the room. "Not home?"

"Yeah, no answer."

"Well, let's get dinner and we'll try when we get back." Reza pulled a few bills from his pocket. "My treat."

Ardeshir's long face told a different story. "No, go without me. I got something to do."

"No, you don't. Come on. Thursday is steak night at the cafe."

"I'll meet you there."

"Be there in one hour," Reza said. "I'm going for a run."

Ardeshir walked to the window. "It's pouring rain. Again."

"It'll be just as wet outside as in here. Come on, run with me. We'll find a cliff of kings somewhere."

"We better find something," Ardeshir mumbled. "No, just—I'll just meet ya there."

Reza bolted out the door. He ran into the warm Venezuelan downpour, tore off his shirt, spread his arms and welcomed the beautiful, beautiful rain. He ran down the streets, up the alleys, through the parks. He yelled and cried and smiled and wept. *He's out. He's out. He's out.* Reza collapsed on an empty bench. Chest heaving, he closed his eyes and rested his head in his hands. *Hassan's free.*

Walking to the café, Reza's entire being beat with the rhythm of life. He had lost track of time, but figured it was about an hour. The rain had slowed to a drip, and a few patrons sat at the tables. No sign of Ardeshir. Reza waited.

Another hour passed and Reza went home. The apartment was empty.

Ring. Ring. Ring.

Reza hesitated. The phone never rang unless someone expected a call.

He answered, "Allo?"

"Reza! Where the hell have you been?" Saam said.

"To dinner. I was supposed to meet Ardeshir at the—"

"Ardeshir 's here. With us. It doesn't look good, Reza. You better get down here."

"Where are you? What do you mean it doesn't—"

"I'm at the hospital, Reza. Ardeshir tried—he tried to kill himself. I came home, he was on the floor, he . . ."

• • • • •

Reza walked into the hospital, inquired about Ardeshir and was directed to the peasant ward in the basement. He hustled down the stairs and entered the long dark corridor lined with fifty beds. Ardeshir's bed was at the end of the row. Seeing Reza, Saam and Ramin left Ardeshir's bedside and walked silently to him.

"How is he?" Reza asked, stopping a few beds away.

"Doc said he'll come through. Took enough pills to kill a horse, but not an Ardeshir," Ramin said as he looked back toward the bed.

Reza started toward Ardeshir and Saam caught his arm. "Reza, straighten him out. We've got three weeks left on this visa. We don't need this now."

"Back off. He has no one. His mother won't even talk to him."

"Just straighten him out," Saam repeated.

Ardeshir's empty face stared up at the grey ceiling. Reza pulled a rickety stool to the bedside. Ardeshir's mighty arms hung like a cadaver's over the steel-framed bed. A clear tube tapped into his nose, and two more leading from his arm completed the fragile picture. Reza didn't know how to start, what to say. He allowed the medical beeping to fill their space, hoping Ardeshir would at least turn his head. Finally, Reza rocked side to side to make more noise on his stool. Still nothing.

"Hey, Ardeshir—I know this has been—tough—on everyone—and I—well, I—guess I sort—well, I know this wasn't all your idea—but I really think—"

He studied Ardeshir's face. Nothing. He fumbled through more apologies, more explanations, more promises for the future. Still nothing.

"All right. This is bullshit. You're lying there, feeling sorry for your big self and—and I'll just pull all that shit out of your face and we'll go right here, right now."

Ardeshir turned his head toward his friend. He raised a single eyebrow.

"You heard me, dumb ass. I had a big steak all set aside for you—and you don't show up—and now we're here—and—"

"And what?" Ardeshir's voice wicked and angry.

"And . . ." Reza leaned closer to Ardeshir. "And you are a *pahlavan.*" Reza reached into his pocket and then took Ardeshir's hand. He pressed Ardeshir's gold medal into his clammy palm, and whispered, "That's how you live. And that's how you'll die."

One by one, Ardeshir's fingers closed around his gold medal.

Chapter Twenty-Two

Laguna Niguel, 2010

It's been over a year since we started this project. And this entire time, I have not actually seen Reza's gold medal.

Tonight Reza and I are looking through his box of photos, which span from yesterday to his childhood. "Maybe we should sort them into two boxes," I suggest. "Iran and America."

"Whatever you want to do," he says, holding a photo. "Wow. Look at all my hair."

I smile and start to sort. "Reza," I say, not looking at him. "Ya know, if you came in second place at the Worlds, that's still amazing."

He looks sideways at me. "No, I was first. Gold. First place."

"I just wish we could find that medal."

"I have it here somewhere," he says. Again. He actually opens kitchen cupboard doors, as if he would find it next to the boxes of cereal.

His ten-year-old son slips off the couch and goes into his room. Wearing his blue PJ sweats and white T-shirt, just like his dad, he comes back with a shoe box. Reza and I exchange glances. His son slowly lifts the lid. With a smile, he takes out his treasures. Two Hot Wheels. One Lego man. And all of daddy's medals. Including the Gold.

"So, you stole my medal," Reza says with a smile.

"You told me to keep it safe," his son replies. "So I did."

"I'm very glad you did," I say. "Very glad."

I hold his gold medal and try to imagine. To imagine the fear. To imagine the anguish. I wrap my fingers around his medal and struggle to feel his torment. Could he let Hassan's death pay for his freedom?

"It's really nice," I say to Reza, immediately feeling stupid. I hand the medal to him. I expect tears or smiles. Just any range of intense emotions.

Giving it a rub with his fingers, he says, "We should put it in a case. Some of the letters are fading." He sets the medal on the counter and walks away.

This man never needed a medal to call himself a champion.

Chapter Twenty-Three

Kermanshah, 1983

In tiny gold frames, two photographs sat on Nimtaj's windowsill. Two smiling faces frozen in black and white moments of happiness, of wholeness. A time when children bounded up the walk from school and filled the home with laughter. When her family sat together and shared the day's events while passing steaming platters of golden rice and seasoned kabobs. And when the day finished, the night found these children staring into the ancient sparkling sky, sending their dreams through darkness to be captured by the moon.

Nimtaj's hands lifted Reza and Hassan every morning. She kissed their pictures trapped in these tiny gold frames. And she cried.

• • • • •

The four wrestlers sat in the four dry places of their apartment. Two in the corners, one in the middle and one on the side by the kitchen.

Reza continued to argue for an extension on their visas, but Ramin countered it was impossible.

"Just focus on our real options," Saam said. "Staying here. No. No visa, no jobs, no money, no university. We've got to get out of Venezuela."

"But," Reza said, "we've gone to every embassy. No one is letting us in because that Jewish translator made it religious, not political. So we're stuck. I can talk to Emilio again."

"We didn't risk all this to become his thugs. We need a way to get to a country where we can have a life," Saam said. He stood up and paced in thick steps across the apartment.

Ardeshir also stood. "There's one embassy we haven't gone to. And they'd buy us a plane ticket outta here."

"Oh yeah, who's that?" Saam asked

"Iran."

Groans to a chorus of "You're still crazy, that's a death sentence, there's no way I'm getting on a plane to Iran, they'd kill us the second—"

Ardeshir motioned with his hands to quiet down. "Now, I know how these things work. Hear me out. We go to the embassy. We talk to the new ambassador. We say we were young, stupid kids. We want to go back and bring honor to the country. Believe me, I know all the shit they want to hear. They buy us tickets, we get our paperwork, we get on the plane and we're out of Venezuela."

"And we land in Iran and they shoot us," Saam finished.

Reza also stood. "No, we don't land in Iran. We have to pass through the Madrid International Airport first. There's no direct flight. Remember?"

Saam rocked back and forth in a ball. "There's no way we can pull that off. We'll be so heavily guarded."

"Not really," Ardeshir continued. "They'd just be stationed in the terminal, waiting for us. They can detain us, if they catch us, but they can't shoot us."

Saam walked over to Ardeshir and looked closely at his face. "Are you still crazy?"

"What do you think?" Ardeshir answered.

"I think—I think this plan has about a five percent chance of actually working." Saam looked out the window into the eternal rain. "But it's the only chance we've got."

"I'm not going," Ramin said. His voice deep and laced with purpose. "I met a girl, a nice girl."

Three faces looked at him.

"Her family," he continued, not able to look at them, "they are taking me in. I'm staying here."

Reza walked over and hugged his friend. "I wish you the best."

The next day, three defecting Iranian wrestlers walked into the Iranian Embassy.

February 1983

"*Allah-o-akbar*[1]!" the Iranian ambassador said as he greeted each of the wrestlers who walked into the embassy with their packed duffle bags.

"God is great," the wrestlers mumbled.

The ambassador handed them each a one-way plane ticket to Iran. Reza couldn't look at it; he unzipped his duffle and put his ticket next to his Spanish translation dictionary. *Damn. If they see this, they'll know I'm not going to Iran.* He looked around. The ambassador didn't seem to notice but there wasn't any place to hide it either. He put his duffle on his shoulder and followed the others to the van waiting outside to take them to the airport.

Only Ardeshir seemed to be at ease. The more Reza considered this plan, the more he thought it couldn't possibly work. Saam had to be right. There would be Revolutionary Guards stationed everywhere. Most would probably be in plain clothes. He remembered his mother's cries on the final phone call. "No, Reza. You can't come back. The TVs speak of your return but I know what they will do to you. Don't come home."

The ambassador's van pulled up to the airport. The wrestlers sat perfectly still even after the van door slid open.

"Go with the grace of God," the ambassador said.

If only I believed that would help.

In a corner of the crowded airport, Ardeshir tried to whisper the plan one more time. "When it lands in Madrid, we scatter," Ardeshir said.

Reza raised an eyebrow at his friend.

"And then what?" Saam asked again. "What if they—" His voice trailed off to be locked in the dungeon of what ifs.

"Get to a bathroom or closet or doorway," Ardeshir said. "Stay alert. Don't stop moving. Keep your feet."

"It's not a damn match," Saam said.

"Yes it is," Reza answered.

• • • • •

The plane had an unexpected landing in the Canary Islands. The airline had to process the paperwork of each passenger. Reza was the first to present his passport. "Here. This is me, Reza Abedi, and I'm heading to Iran."

"I can't read this. It's all in Farsi and it's not a proper docu-

1 God is Great!

ment. What is all this?" the immigration officer asked.

"It's just a temporary visa to get us to Iran. That's all I—that's all we have."

"There's more?"

"There's three of us," Reza said, pointing toward his friends.

"It says here you were painters for the Iranian Embassy," she said as she looked at the three world-champion athletes. "You don't look like painters. I have to make some calls."

The three had separate seats and Reza found himself next to a young Spanish man. Reza took in the man's calm face, relaxed demeanor and steady breathing. Still, taking a chance, Reza pulled the newspaper article about the defecting wrestlers from his pocket. Carefully, he unfolded it.

"Hi," Reza said. "Did you read this?"

"Yes, interesting," the Spanish man replied.

Reza cleared his throat. "I think they were brave for trying to escape."

"Yes, very brave."

"Would you help them if you could?" Reza asked. His fingers trembled. He put the newspaper back in his pocket.

"Yes—yes, I think I would," he said. He pulled a magazine from the seat pouch and began to flip through it.

Reza glanced around the crowded plane at the twisted faces of annoyed passengers. The only movement came from the small flurry of officials coming in and out of the front of the plane. They whispered, shrugged their shoulders and shook their heads.

Reza leaned into the man. "I am one of those wrestlers."

The man flipped to another page. "I know."

Biting the end of his knuckle, Reza studied the man's face and then looked out the window. Planes lined up to take their place in the sky. He turned back to the passenger and made his voice very low. "We need help. Can you start to demand the plane take off? Start to complain and—and see if you can get us off the ground," Reza said. He licked his dry lips. "We have to get to Madrid."

The man nodded. "Let's give it some more time, then I will complain."

"Thanks." Reza folded his hands in his lap. It was the only way to keep them still.

Another hour passed and no one could give the airline official a clear answer. The paperwork was processed so quickly and unofficially, it didn't meet anyone's regulations. The Spanish man looked at Reza and winked. Then he started making loud complaints about the delay and soon the other passengers joined in. They left the wrestlers on the plane and continued to Madrid.

Reza leaned his head against the seat and blew out a long breath. His stomach churned and he felt the burn of vomit creep up his throat. Fearing he might puke, he got up and went down the aisle toward the bathroom. The stewardess's cart was parked next to the bathroom and Reza spotted the gleam of the sharp-tipped metal can opener. He grabbed it and put it in his pocket. *I'll slit my wrists if they catch me.* He rubbed the sharp edge with his fingers.

The landing gear screeched across the runway. Reza's sweaty hands couldn't keep a grip on the can opener. His breath came in short, airless gasps as the door cranked open. He looked at his legs. They wouldn't move.

• • • • •

"It is better here, Naneh," Pari said. "Quiet, no bombs and planes. You can rest and get well, but you have to eat." Pari lifted the spoon holding soft rice and pressed it to her mother's lips. "Please, you can't get well unless you eat."

In constant motion, Soraya scurried about the small rented house in the village of Abyek. She straightened pillows and cleaned pots, folded linens and swept the floor. Mariam would alternate between helping Soraya and sitting with Nimtaj, but she always sang her mother's prayers, soft and low.

"Let her rest," Soraya said. "And you should rest, too."

"I can't," Pari said. "Not until she eats."

Nimtaj parted her lips and Pari quickly scooped in two mouthfuls.

"Rest," her mother whispered.

Soraya rolled out the cotton mattresses. "Pari, you and Mariam sleep while I stay up with Naneh."

"No, no," Nimtaj said, her voice struggling to sound strong. "You must all rest."

"But someone must stay with you," Pari said. "What if you need help?"

"Nonsense," Nimtaj said. "I will sleep, too. Together we rest."

The sisters exchanged glances, but it looked like Nimtaj had already begun to drift into a peaceful sleep. They each lay down, closed their eyes and were soon lost in their dreams.

Not wanting to wake them, Nimtaj rose and wobbled toward the basement stairs that led to the bathroom. At the second stair, her legs gave way and the girls awoke to the terrible crash of flesh and bone.

"Oh, my God! Naneh!" They carried her body back to her mattress, wiped the blood and felt for broken bones. A gash above her eye needed stitches.

"When will Baba be home?" Mariam asked again.

"We don't know," Soraya said. "Just go get more clean rags from the kitchen."

"I brought all we have," she said.

Pari gathered an armful of the bloodied cloths. "Rinse these and bring them back clean."

Between moans and prayers, Nimtaj tried to order her girls to stop fussing over her.

"Don't say these things," Soraya said. "You should have woken us to help you."

Pari's tears dripped off her chin to mix with Nimtaj's blood. She took the clean rags from Mariam and carefully cleaned every inch of her mother. After pressing rags to her head for several hours, the bleeding stopped.

"One of us must always stay awake with her," Soraya said. "Mariam, you stay awake for the first hour and then me and then Pari."

Pari started to protest, but Soraya answered, "You need the rest. Please. And this way you will be with her to see the morning."

After several hours, Soraya gently shook Pari's shoulder. "It's your turn."

"How is she?" Pari whispered.

"She rests and then mumbles for Reza and Hassan, and then she sleeps again."

Pari nodded and went to sit with her mother. She gently brushed back the few grey hairs stuck in the dried blood along the gash. Moonlight caressed the creases in Nimtaj's face. With a light finger, Pari traced the web of life from her mother's forehead, across her cheeks and down her arms until she reached her hands. The hands that lifted babies, cooked countless meals and brought baskets of food to all her daughters' gymnastic tournaments. Hands that gave the food to her own children and to those whose mothers did not. Hands that eternally ached to hold her sons.

Nimtaj's chest began to rise and fall in spastic and uneven movements. Pari's fingers pressed gently by her mother's heart. "Naneh," she whispered.

With a flicker, Nimtaj opened her eyes and in them Pari saw life. Bright and beautiful and bold. Then Nimtaj's eyelids closed and her breast lifted in one last final breath.

"Naneh. Naneh. No, Naneh." Pari moved from one side of her mother to the other. She took a cloth and wiped her forehead. "Please, please keep breathing."

To the still ocean beneath a starless sky, her body succumbed.

"Soraya, come quick!" Pari said with her ear pressed to Nimtaj's chest. "Please, Naneh, please don't leave us."

"Naneh." Soraya said as she bolted to her mother's side. She looked into the face and did not see her mother. Death lay in her place.

* * * * *

"Get up. I got your back," the Spanish man said.

"All right," Reza mumbled and forced a slightly louder, "gracias."

Saam had passed through the airplane's doorway; Ardeshir was two passengers behind him. Reza threw his duffle bag over his shoulder, shoved his hands deep into his pockets and took his place to exit down the aisle. As soon as Reza hit the gangway, he drove through the crowds and ducked into the nearest men's room. Hunched over the last porcelain sink in the long row, Saam splashed cold water on his face.

"Where's Ardeshir?" Reza whispered to Saam.

Two men in dark suits came into the bathroom. Saam and Reza froze. Reza gripped his can opener, but the men just unzipped and peed.

Still no sign of Ardeshir.

Saam's hands trembled as he tried to dry his face. "Now what?"

Reza's turn to puke. He stumbled into the narrow stall and knelt on the tile. Holding his gut with one hand and trying to steady himself on the wall with the other, he bent over the cold, grey toilet. In a single, violent heave, last night's dinner spewed into the water. Pieces chunked on the side and the smell caused a second round of spasms. He reached to flush and a hand caught his fingers. "You pregnant?" Ardeshir said leaning over his friend.

"Screw you," Reza replied as he went to the sink.

"Saam, watch the door." Ardeshir gathered them into the far corner. "Four guards on the upper level dressed like dignitaries and at least two more at the terminal. I think the Canary Islands stop threw them, but we've got to work fast. Reza, go see that guy about ten meters to the left selling newspapers in Farsi."

"The man from last time?"

Ardeshir nodded. "Go see what he knows."

Saam held Reza's arm and looked at Ardeshir. "How do you know he's not also disguised?"

"I know," Ardeshir answered.

Reza looked hard at his friend. "He's to the left?" Reza asked, looking at the toilet and feeling another wave of nausea traveling through him.

"*Baleh!* Right outside to the left! *Zood bosh*! *Sepahi* gonna figure we're in here!" Ardeshir said.

Reza walked out of the bathroom and kept his head down. The can opener slipped through his fingers. As if moving underwater, he pushed his feet to the left, seeing only shoes in his field of vision. Inching toward the newsstand, he scanned the Farsi headlines. Words bounced off the pages: "Ayatollah Khomeini brings shame to Iran." "Students rally to protest regime." "Khomeini violates human rights."

Just out of his field of vision, Reza could feel the shadowy eyes of the newspaper man taking in his distressed state. *Breathe. Breathe.* Reza took a step toward the man sitting on the stool, smoking and casually reading a magazine. In the single glance that would determine his fate, Reza took in the brown leather shoes with worn soles, pants that weren't quite long enough and a dull shirt with two stains. He could trust this man with his life.

Reza picked up a paper and walked to the man sitting on the stool. Standing tall and sure, he lifted the folded newspaper and pointed directly to the headline denouncing Khomeini.

"How many *toman*?" Reza asked, looking into the weathered face.

The man eyed Reza. "For you, I have a deal."

From the second floor of the terminal, Reza saw four Iranian men in black trench coats head toward the escalator and push through the crowd of people. *They've spotted me.*

The paper shook in Reza's hand. "Please, sir. Me—me and my friends. We need your help. We're the wrestlers from Iran. We escaped at the Worlds six months ago."

The four black trench coats wove through the crowded line to get to the escalator.

"I know," said the newspaperman, taking a slow drag.

"But those men there, in the trench coats, coming down the escalator, they're from the Iranian Embassy and they're coming for us and we—"

He nodded. "Where are the others?"

"In that bathroom, there, by the door." Sweat trickled down Reza's temple and he gripped the newspaper with both hands, but still it shook.

"You must calm down, *doost-e man*," said the Iranian and he slipped off the stool and crushed out his cigarette. "Go to your friends and bring them to that door with no sign. I will meet you there."

The four trench coats got off the escalator. Reza couldn't move.

Slapping down his magazine, the newspaper man said, "*Zood bosh*! Get your friends. You must go now!"

Reza poked his head into the men's room. It was empty.

"Ardeshir! Saam! Where—"

A stall door opened and the two stepped out. "We think they came in here."

"No," Reza said. "They're still on the escalator. Grab everything and follow me."

"Where?" Saam said.

"Just walk behind me," Reza hissed in frustration.

The three wrestlers stepped outside the airport's bathroom. Crowds of people passed by them but the newspaper man was nowhere to be seen.

Ardeshir grabbed Reza's arm. "Where is he?"

Reza stood paralyzed.

Giving him a shake, Ardeshir said "What did he tell you?"

From behind them, a voice. "Follow me."

They turned to see the newspaper man standing with another man with a large scar cut into his cheek. "*Ajaleh kon!*" The scarred man said as he led them toward the door with no sign.

They followed him to a large, black car. Reza got in. Ardeshir slid in next to him and turned to Saam. Behind them, Ardeshir saw the guards heading toward the car. "Get in!"

The newspaper man ran to the driver's side, slammed his door shut and sped out of the employees parking garage. He looked into his rear-view mirror more than he looked through the windshield and the three wrestlers craned their necks in every direction. Looking for what, they weren't really sure.

After several minutes, Reza leaned forward. "*Merci.*"

The man nodded. "You're safe now. They couldn't follow us."

Reza leaned back and closed his eyes. As the roar of airplanes faded, he felt daggers rip at his heart. *Why do I wish I were on that plane?* Throbbing thoughts pounded stakes into his skull. *I should have just gotten on board. Maybe they wouldn't have killed us. Maybe they'd give us a chance.* His stomach churned thick black waters. *I could have hugged my sisters and then pressed my gold metal into Baba's palm. I could hold my Naneh and tell her I'm all right.* Ardeshir's huge paw reached over and wiped tears from Reza's cheeks.

Reza felt his face. *Am I crying?* He looked at Ardeshir and did not hide his pain.

"Maybe we should have gone home," Reza said.

"We don't have one anymore."

Chapter Twenty-Four

Spring 1983

In exchange for the help and safety, the three wrestlers agreed to do an international news conference to expose the tragic events happening in post-revolution Iran. They were first taken to shop for new clothes and a fine suit just for the conference.

Ardeshir smiled at himself in the tailor's full-length mirror. "Damn, I'm handsome."

"Oh, yeah, and smart," Saam countered. "Just try not to say anything too stupid tomorrow. These people are counting on us. We can't let them down."

"My experience," Ardeshir said as he smoothed his lapel, "will give them more information than you can even fit in your walnut brain."

Walking into the fitting room, Reza gathered the tail end of their constant bickering. He couldn't help but grin at his childhood friend sizing himself up in the mirror. Reza held the packages of his clothes and tucked his nose into the bag one more time to breathe in the scent of new. He called to Ardeshir. "Okay, handsome and smart, take that off and let's go. The driver's waiting and I want to get my thoughts together before this conference."

Ardeshir went into the changing room. First, he sang. Then he shouted over the door. "Think all you want! The cameras will only be looking at me!"

"Just put your clothes on and let's go," Reza replied. *I wonder if Farid will be able to see this. Maybe I could try to call him, have him help me out with what to say.*

The dressing room door burst open. "Damn, I'm still handsome."

* * * * *

The driver took them to their new apartment. Their mouths fell open as they looked wide-eyed at the clean walls, the nice furniture and the kitchen stocked with food.

Saam spoke first. "Now this is a place to live." He turned to the driver. "*Merci.*"

The driver nodded. "Of course. You're comrades and we'll take care of you. At the bottom of the stairs will be a twenty-four-hour guard, and there are numbers by the phone for anything you need. Please, get comfortable and I'll be back tomorrow to pick you up at 8:00 a.m. Get a good rest."

They ran their fingers over the furniture. Ardeshir kept opening the stocked kitchen cupboards, even the ones he had looked into many times already.

Saam came from the back rooms. "There's one for each of us. And the beds are soft and on a frame." No one spoke. "Okay, well, I'm going to the first room on the left and hang up my clothes."

Walking to the kitchen, Reza smiled at Ardeshir and then sat heavily in the chair. He reached into his pocket and put the can opener on the table. A mist of tears replaced his smile.

"What's that for?" Ardeshir asked.

Reza only shook his head. Ardeshir took the can opener and threw it in the trash.

* * * * *

The wrestlers slid into the cab and the driver took them through the streets of Madrid. He spoke in excited short sentences, alternating between pointing out landmarks and thanking the wrestlers for exposing Khomeini's brutal regime. Reza noted Ardeshir's fingers pull into fists as his jaw cemented in rage. Ardeshir leaned over to Reza. "Shut him up or I'm snapping his neck like a turkey bone."

"We're almost there," Reza said. "Just relax."

"You don't even know where we're going," Ardeshir said.

Reza shrugged and looked out the window. The driver babbled on.

When they pulled up in front of the Plaza Espana Hotel, the driver jumped out and embraced each wrestler. Reza stayed close to Ardeshir, who seemed a thousand miles away. They followed the driver through the back entrance and stood just outside the large pressroom. A babble of international language and clicking of camera equipment came from inside the room. Ardeshir walked several paces behind the group.

Saam stopped and turned to Ardeshir. "We need to do this."

"I know."

"Especially you," Saam said. "The world needs to know what you've seen."

"I'm here," Ardeshir spat.

Reza turned around and walked toward Ardeshir, who held up his hand and shook his head. "I'm fine," he said to Reza. "Just give me a minute."

Reza nodded and waited by the door. Cutting through the noise of the pressroom, he heard the strained breathing of Ardeshir. He hesitated. He wanted to go to his friend and tell him his father would understand. By telling the world the truth, maybe they could help save thousands of lives. Ardeshir placed his arm around Reza. "Good thing I'm handsome." He swallowed hard.

"*Baleh,*" Reza said. "Good thing."

Cameras clicked away as the wrestlers entered. Saam walked in first, with Reza and Ardeshir following behind. Saam fielded most of the questions about the Revolution, the war with Iraq, the issues many Iranians had with Shah and now with Khomeini. Reza answered a couple of questions. Ardeshir remained silent.

"What's next for Iran?" a reporter asked.

"It's hard to say," Saam replied. "The people need to send the message to Ayatollah Khomeini that the Revolution was not to make Iran an Islamic Nation."

"Many say he stole the Revolution," Reza added, remembering his conversations with Kahn. "And The Iraq War is a slaughter." He thought of the young man in the back of his ambulance. "Some of Iran's soldiers are barely older than boys."

"There's so much to know," Saam said. "So much."

A deep voice froze the room. "He's going to kill them all," Ardeshir said. "He won't stop until every one of them is dead. Families dead. Husbands, brothers, sons, wives, sisters, daughters." He looked directly into the silent room of reporters. "He'll eliminate them all."

Reza turned to Ardeshir and saw a face that was not Ardeshir's. He saw a face carved on a mountain side, speaking for the souls who will become the damned. Several seconds passed and not a person moved.

A reporter directly in front of Ardeshir cautiously raised his hand. "Can you expand a little bit?"

Ardeshir looked through him. "Thousands are being murdered as we sit here."

The room began to buzz again, cameras clicked and pens scribbled across pads. Questions flew. "How do you know? Who will be murdered? Do you have proof? Is it by direct order of the Ayatollah Khomeini?"

Reza and Ardeshir locked eyes. Reza nodded.

"The hanging judge," Ardeshir said. "Ayatollah Sadeq Khalkhali will have everyone from Shah's government eliminated."

"You mean killed?" asked a reporter.

"I mean murdered." Ardeshir sat up a little straighter. "They have lists. Names and addresses."

"And Khomeini approves of this?"

Reza leaned into his microphone. "Khomeini said that legal procedures are nothing more than a reflection of the Western sickness."

"Can you tell us what happened to Ayatollah Kazem Shariatmadari?" asked a reporter. "I believe he was a voice for the people?"

"His demotion and house arrest prove no one is safe under Khomeini," Ardeshir answered. "No one."

"Do you know who else is being targeted?"

"Yes, "Ardeshir said. "I do."

The room fell into a fierce silence.

"Thousands of brave men and women of the National Front[1], *Fedayins*[2], Kurds[3], *Tudeh*[4] and—" he paused. The driver and many men around the room shifted their feet and bowed their heads. "And all members of the *Mojahedin*[5] will be hunted like animals and murdered."

Reza folded his hands and touched them to his forehead.

1 Political party: democratic and secular; founded by Mohammad Mossadegh in early 1950s

2 Political party: largest socialist party in Iran

3 Middle Eastern Ethnic group

4 Political party: Communist party formed in Iran in 1941

5 According the 1992 US State Dept Report regarding the Mujahidin, the Mujahidin supported actions to overthrow Shah, and post-revolution, the overthrow of Ayatollah Khomeini's regime. Some factions of the Mujahidin were involved in violent acts in these overthrow attempts and have therein been defined as a terrorist organization. Reza's involvement with Mujahidin ended in 1982.

Tell them, Ardeshir. Tell them everything. Before he could look at Ardeshir, he felt his words.

"Thousands! Thousands of men who dared to dream for freedom. For honor!" Ardeshir pounded his fist on the table and then stood up. His naked voice thundered. "The streets of Iran are being stained with their blood!"

• • • • •

"It is unfortunate, Mr. Abedi," the *Sepahi* said as he pulled a fresh pack of cigarettes from his desk drawer, "that your son cannot seem to find his way onto an Iranian airplane."

Stale smoke, sweating men and a faint trace of rosewater mixed with the smells of the fresh coat of white paint. On three of the stark walls in the tiny room hung a too-large portrait of Ayatollah Khomeini. His pitiless eyes pierced into Abbas's soul.

Abbas pulled his hands from the dark wood desk, leaving his steaming imprint of fingers. "*Agha,* I am sure there is a reason."

"Of course there is a reason. He is a vile traitor!" Venom spat from the crooked, yellow teeth. "And we have grave concerns about the rest of your children."

Leaning back in the chair, Abbas tried again to reason. "Sir, my oldest son is a high-ranking officer in the Air Force. He is a . . ." His voice trailed off.

The officer produced a manila folder from a stack on his desk. He opened the top cover and lit a fresh cigarette. "*Baleh,* let's look at this little family of yours." He produced a pile of typed pages. "Amir's a fine officer in our Air Force and it has been noted."

Abbas nodded, wiped sweat from his forehead and leaned slightly forward.

Taking a long drag, the man continued. "But then we seem to run into problems. Some very significant problems." His cloud of smoke blew against Abbas's face.

"I'm sure they are just . . ." Abbas reached out to touch a photograph, but the officer pointed at him with his cigarette. "Sit back," the officer said.

"*Chashm,* sir."

"Now, Farah and her husband live here, as do Rasha and her husband. But, Mehri's family has just moved from Iran."

Abbas squirmed. "Her husband had business. I'm sure they plan to return as soon as the transactions are—completed."

"You seem so sure. I hope you are right. And then we have Mostafa. Interesting fellow. I believe he is in this building as we speak."

Abbas pulled his lips in tight and held his breath.

"I will call and see if we can find him." He lifted the sticky receiver, spat out several commands and dropped the phone back into the cradle. "Seems he may be busy."

Looking into the portrait hanging above the *Sepahi*, Abbas muttered and narrowed his eyes. The *Sepahi* paused but did not acknowledge what he saw.

Instead, he continued. "Which brings us to Reza. A world-champion wrestler. I actually saw him myself at the base. A gifted, tenacious young man. He should've been raised to bring pride to his country." The officer stood, exposing his large belly wrapped in a dull, green uniform. "Not to humiliate us!"

The door behind them opened and Mostafa landed with a thud on the cement floor. Abbas reached for him but Mostafa waved him off. He rose to one knee and limped to the second wooden chair in front of the desk. His blood-crusted hands rested on his legs.

The officer sat and smirked. "You must be Mostafa. Thank you for joining us. I was just getting to know your family."

As Mostafa spoke, blood trickled from his swollen jaw. "Always a pleasure to meet with the *Sepah*."

The officer snorted and crushed his cigarette into the overflowing ashtray. "As I was explaining to your father, there are significant concerns about the loyalty of your family to our Ayatollah Khomeini." He waved his hand to indicate the pictures surrounding them. "So, let me get to the point." Leaning forward and looking directly at Abbas, he asked, "Where's Reza and where's Hassan?"

With the bruised and swollen face, Mostafa looked to his father and shook his head. He turned to the officer. "My father is a simple man. He will not know."

Lighting a new cigarette, the *Sepahi* smiled. "Perhaps you can enlighten us."

Mostafa gave a slight laugh. "As you can see, I've been enlightening your friends for several hours." His cough produced a bloody mucus that trailed down his chin. "Their whereabouts is unknown to us."

The officer took a long puff and returned to the papers in front of him. "I see. Well, that leaves a few daughters that can still be taught to respect the laws of Ayatollah Khomeini."

Abbas and Mostafa looked at each other.

The officer shuffled through documents, sorted photographs, moved more papers. "Ah, here. We have Soraya, Pari and little Mariam at seven. Mariam is probably still a bit too young for marriage, but I can see beautiful children coming from your other daughters. First, we must find the right husbands. Husbands who will teach their children to love and respect Iran." More shuffling of papers and pictures. "*Baleh,* Soraya. I've noted a friend I have known for years, whose wife just passed away. Tragic but it may just work out well for your family." His thick finger traced the outline of her face while a smile crossed his lips.

Abbas reflected the white of the walls caging him. Reaching a broken hand forward to touch the photographs, Mostafa stuttered, "I'm sure we can work things out."

The officer pulled them away under his dirty fingernails. "Mostafa," he chuckled, "surely you did not think we could simply forget your family's insult to our great nation. We must be sure it does not happen again, and with the right husbands it will not. I will ensure they have the right husbands."

The opening of the door seemed to surprise the officer. He bolted from his desk and saluted at attention. The Elite Unit officer motioned for him to sit and move to the right. He never looked at Abbas or Mostafa. Walking behind the desk, the officer bent his left arm behind his highly decorated uniform and spread the papers and photos with his other.

He looked at the officer. "Are we discussing suitable husbands?"

"*Chashm,* sir."

He looked at Abbas. "Are these your daughters?"

"*Baleh, baleh,* sir," he said with a shaking voice. "These are my little girls."

Without looking up, "Do you know where Reza and Ardeshir are?" the officer asked.

Mostafa answered, "No, *agha.* We do not."

The Elite Unit officer gathered all the papers and photos into the file. He looked to his subordinate. "I will take it from here."

The *Sepahi* shut the door behind him, leaving an empty echo in the room.

The Elite Unit officer looked to Abbas and Mostafa. "We've never met. But you know my son."

Abbas looked hard at the facial features and breathed the word, "Ardeshir."

The Elite Guard continued, "You have six months to get your family out. After that, I cannot help you." He tucked the folder under his arm and headed toward the door.

Mostafa shifted in his chair and wiped the blood from his chin. "Sir, it is with great appreciation we thank you for your help. As you know, it is increasingly difficult and expensive to make these things happen and with our resources recently depleted under similar circumstances . . ."

Ardeshir's father paused at the door but did not look back. "Six months, Mostafa. Not a day more."

• • • • •

Reza walked into their apartment just in time for dinner. Ardeshir jumped from his seat, grabbed Reza around the waist and spun him in a giant circle. "Did you hear?"

"No. Hear what? What's the news?"

Ardeshir dropped his friend and took a deep breath. "Ok, the five months here, they've been, well, let's just say great!"

Reza raised his eyebrows. "Okay, we'll say great. And three of the wrestlers I'm coaching could compete in the—"

"Yeah, yeah. That's interesting. But think beautiful girls. Think about this." Ardeshir drew the figure of a woman with his hands.

"You finally got a date?" Reza chuckled.

Ardeshir looked serious and took a step back. "I did. As a matter of fact, I have a date."

"Stop the riddles and tell me what the hell is going on."

Ardeshir nodded. "I have a date with the American Embassy. They said they're letting in a lot more Iranians starting next month for political asylum. That's me and you. We're going to be surrounded by all the beautiful blue-eyed babes—"

"Seriously? And you have an appointment tomorrow? Who do I call? How can I get—"

Ardeshir smiled. "And I made one for you, too. But, if you want to stay . . ."

Reza sat on the couch. He let his arms fall to the side and his head rest on the cushion. "It's been good here. I know Spanish a lot better than English, but the universities in America are the best. I could go full-time."

"You could," Ardeshir said. "I've even looked into programs

where we could wrestle for a university and it helps us pay for the college."

"Really?"

Ardeshir sat next to Reza. "*Baleh.*" The two stared straight ahead.

• • • • •

Saam had his appointment at the American Embassy first. He came out of the interview offices and into the crowded waiting room with a huge grin. The room of folding chairs held excited immigrants, who buzzed about the opportunities awaiting them.

Reza and Ardeshir stood. "Well?"

"Canada," Saam said. "And then maybe the U.S., but first Canada."

Soon after he left, Reza's name was called. He took a huge breath, smoothed his shirt and walked down the hallway.

Reza walked into the office, his paperwork in order, and he met a large man behind thick glasses. His office smelled of fine Italian leather, although Reza only saw old furniture and piles of paper. *Mr. Mehdian would have loved this office. I wish somehow I could let him know where I am, where I'm going.*

The man asked a few questions, mostly about wrestling, and pounded paper after paper with a huge stamp. Reza interrupted, "Excuse me, sir. Am I—are you approving me for America?"

"Canada, son. It's on the same side of the ocean," he answered, without looking up from his stamping.

"I know that, sir. I was told that America's letting in a lot of—Iranians."

"They are." Stamp, stamp. "You're not one of them."

Reza shifted on his folding chair. "Sir, if you could look into that a bit. My friend and I, well, we were thinking of the Southern California state."

"Why's that?" Stamp.

Reza hesitated, "Uh, we've seen pictures of a lot of pretty girls. They all live in the Southern California state."

He looked up from his stamping. Removing his thick glasses, he rubbed his face. "Pretty girls. We don't have pretty girls in Madrid?"

"I didn't mean that, sir. My friend and I, we've been through a lot and, well, my first priority is of course to go to the university and get a degree."

The large man chuckled. "Are you one of the wrestlers who did the press conference a couple of months back?"

"Yes sir," said Reza. "There's three of us."

Leaning back in the torn leather chair, the man replaced his glasses and smiled. "Took a lot of guts to do that press conference. Okay, kid. I'll find a way to get you to the Southern California state."

When Reza came out of the office, Ardeshir was still in his meeting.

Reza danced through the streets all the way to his apartment. Saam had already called home. Reza's recent calls home had been short and a bit bizarre, no one really wanting to say much, but Reza understood the difficulty his situation had presented to his family. Still, this exciting news was too good not to share.

He tried his sister Rasha. No answer. Mehri. No answer. Dare he call home? Maybe just a short call. Again no answer. *Have to try Farid.* Several rings until his aunt answered, "Allo."

"Allo! It's me and I have—"

"Speak quickly."

"Okay, I've tried to call my family, but they've—"

"*Zood bosh.*"

"Aunt, I think I'm going to America soon. Please tell my family and tell them I will call them—"

"No, don't call them. Don't call here. I will tell them you are still safe."

"What's the matter? Has something happened to my family?"

"No, not yet. Do you remember your uncle in Paris?"

"Of course."

"Here, write down his number and call him when you get to America."

"Yeah, okay. I've got a pen."

Reza wrote down the number and hung up. Saam looked at him with a raised eyebrow. "Everything all right?"

"I don't know." Reza tucked the number into his pocket. "I wish I could talk to Mostafa."

Saam nodded. "Hey, did you talk to Ardeshir?"

"He was already in and being interviewed when I came out. He should be home by now." Reza looked at the clock. "Let's start the celebration and he'll be here soon."

The warm spring air gave way to a damp Madrid evening as they worked together in the kitchen to create a special feast.

Reza pulled out a bottle of dark Spanish wine. "The perfect way to toast to our freedom."

Saam chuckled. "The unclean drink of infidels!"

Just as they sat at the table, heavy footsteps pounded up the stairs. The door flung open. "I'm screwed!" Ardeshir called into the apartment. Swinging an empty bottle of wine, he looked with wild eyes around the apartment, as if searching for someone hidden. At first, Reza hoped he was joking, but Ardeshir's face showed no sign of laughter.

Saam poured wine into the third glass. "Come, sit, drink. Let's figure this out."

"Didn't you hear me? I'm screwed! They won't let me in!" Ardeshir slammed the door and sat at the table. In one gulp, he drained the glass and motioned for a refill.

Reza knew this could be a long night. "Who won't let you in? Southern California? That takes some talking. I had to work the guy a little bit myself, but—"

Draining his second glass and reaching for a refill, Ardeshir yelled, "The whole damn country! The whole United States of America is afraid to let Ardeshir in." He drained his glass and motioned for the next. Saam popped a new cork. Ardeshir waited for him to pour. "Apparently my paperwork shows Rev gaurdd duuuuuty and I'm a damn assassin for the man with the big, big turban."

Reza removed Ardeshir's wine glass, so he grabbed the bottle. "Ah, *baleh.* Let's take a looky looky at you. Ah, says here you be a *Sepahi,* ooooh myyyyy, that sounds important!" Swig from bottle. "Ohh, a family business, I see. Daddy, too. Big strong daddy and his favorite son, Ardeshir." He took a last, long swig, wiped the red, dripping wine and bellowed, "You might be just toooo dangeroussss."

Ardeshir slept face-first on the kitchen table. Saam made sure there were no pill bottles of any kind in reach. The next day, Reza went to the American Embassy but without an appointment. He was turned away before he could even get near an office.

After days of pleading, Reza convinced Ardeshir to try one more time. "We've come so far. Just make an appointment so you can go in there and talk to them."

• • • • •

Ardeshir fidgeted as the woman with red hair puffed on top of her head reviewed his file. The gold chain of her pointed glasses glinted from the single bulb in the office. She continually sighed and looked at the same papers over and over, as if hoping they would change. She finally looked up. "I'm so sorry. There are rules, procedures. They're put into place by people who seem to think they know what is best and I—I just have to follow them."

Ardeshir rested his head in his hands, rubbing the fresh shave of his face. He looked up. "I know. And I wish I could talk to those people and tell them that I'm not like that. That's why I left Iran. I've cooperated with everyone since we first came here and gave them all the information I know. I spent days talking to the American CIA. Why would I do that if I was still loyal to the Revolutionary Guard?" He looked to his feet and mumbled, "To Khomeini."

"I see," she sighed. "Well, that's not really noted in here. Do you remember who you talked to?"

Ardeshir straightened his back and smiled. "They don't give you their names."

"Well, let me send your file upstairs and I'll ask if . . ."

"Upstairs? Again? My file's been upstairs three times now. That's what I thought we were talking about today. My friend leaves for the Southern California state in two days. My other friend is already in Canada. If I'm such a danger, why leave me in Madrid?"

The red-haired lady scooped his papers and tucked them into his file with a huff. "Well, I don't know. Just wait here. I will take them upstairs myself and ask about this CIA thing."

An agonizing hour later, she came back. Ardeshir sat stone-still in the chair. He couldn't look at her.

"Ardeshir," she said. She reached for his enormous hand and patted it like a small child's. "You will join your friend in the Southern California state."

Grasping her hand with both of his, he touched it to his forehead. "Thank you."

• • • • •

The door opened to the tiny Southern California apartment and they stepped inside. They fell on the floor, gripping their guts and laughing hysterically. Reza and Ardeshir just tried to pick up two Southern California beach beauties with the English they practiced so hard on the plane. "You like us men?" Their first try didn't go so well.

Chapter Twenty-Five

"The students are going to ask why you wanted to come to America," I say to Reza as we drive to our Author-in-Schools presentation.

He looks at me sideways and then grins. "To meet girls."

"These kids are twelve," I say. "Think of another answer."

"Okay, to meet college girls," he says.

"That's not where I was going with that."

He laughs. I don't.

"Well, should I tell them I didn't even know American money when I came here?" he says. "People would pull up to the gas station and hand me this wad of bills and say words. And I'd just bob my head and smile and push buttons."

"Good," I say. "More of those stories."

"I watched TV to learn better English. Should I say that?"

"I guess, but they are going to want to know why you risked everything to work at a gas station, meet girls and watch TV."

We pull into the middle school parking lot and I want to go over our presentation, but since Reza was running late—again—there's little time. He knows I'm annoyed.

"It's hard to explain these things to people who've always lived here," he says. "I just wanted to go to a university and be a teacher."

I hand Reza his note cards and pop open my laptop.

He flips through the cards and mumbles to himself. I rush through the Powerpoint, trying to commit the notes to memory. Then I close the lid and look at my friend. I remember it's his life we're putting on stage and each time we do he has to relive some very painful memories.

"They're going to love you," I say. "You are inspiring and brave and kind and smart and tenacious and noble and—"

"Good looking."

I chuckle. "Yes, with that smile and bright eyes, it's a wonder you're not a model."

He grins into the rearview mirror and checks his teeth. "I want to tell them about the story of the mouthwash. I think they'll laugh."

"Great idea! It would be a good way to illustrate the many differences between our cultures. From the food to the traditions, clothes, school, eating on the floor and, geez, we could talk for hours."

He's holding the card where he learns about his mother and I reach over to touch his arm. "You're doing a good thing today."

"Americans are not too different from Iranians," he says. "You just have funny accents."

Chapter Twenty-Six

Summer 1983

Reza pulled on his college wrestling team sweatshirt to take off the 4:00 a.m. chill. Each time he put it on, he rubbed his hand over the tight, white English letters. At the community college, Reza and Ardeshir dominated on the wrestling team but they worked harder in the classes. At the end of this semester, they hoped to be accepted on a wrestling scholarship to the four-year university, Cal State Fullerton. When not in class, at the library or at wrestling practice, he and Ardeshir alternated working the graveyard shift at the local gas station.

Looking through the bulletproof glass of his attendant's booth, Reza checked for headlights of possible customers. All clear. Pulling the trick quarter from his pocket, he twisted it with the fishing line and spun it in the pay phone. By pulling on the line, he could make an expensive overseas call with just one quarter. Still no answer at his home in Kermanshah.

A customer pulled into his gas station, asked for "twenty on ten" and handed Reza a wad of bills. Still struggling with general conversations, he smiled, nodded and carefully pushed the correct buttons.

Last month, his conversations with Mostafa came from a Pakistani prison's payphone. Hassan had been arrested crossing the border and locked into a cell of filth that Reza couldn't bear to imagine. Although Mostafa assured Reza he worked out a price for Hassan's release, Reza felt sick until he had heard Hassan's voice from Mehri's home in Belgium. That was two weeks ago. Now, he wanted to hear that voice again.

Three rings. "Allo"

"Hassan! I miss you!" Reza shouted into the phone. "It's so good to hear you!"

Hassan bounced from foot to foot, a habit he kept from his time in prison. "Rez! I've got great news. Mostafa got the student visa for me to come live with you. I fly into LAX next week."

"He what?" Reza spun the quarter, terrified he'd lose the call.

"I'm coming next week," Hassan said. "And he almost has everyone else out, too!"

Reza glanced to see oncoming headlights. "Everyone? Hassan, stop and slowly tell me everything."

"Well, I guess Amir and Farah are staying in Iran but . . ."

Honk! Honk! "One minute sir," Reza yelled.

"He's worked out a price to get everyone to Mehri's."

"When?"

Honk! Honk!

"I don't know. Mostafa's going to call you when he gets back with the details. But Reza, I'm going to come and live with you!"

Reza held the phone in one hand and rubbed his face with the other. "You're going to love it here. When is Mostafa coming back?"

"You know Mostafa. Nobody knows."

Honk! Honk! A voice bellowed out of the station wagon. "Hey! Who works here?"

"Make him call me right away."

"I'll be there next week. Next week, Rez!"

Reza held the receiver to his chest and hugged it with both arms. He tried to speak without tears, "It's going to be great."

Honk! Honk! "I need some service!" the station wagon driver yelled.

• • • • •

Ardeshir and Reza arrived the next week at LAX three hours early. On his twentieth trip to check the air flight information, Ardeshir grabbed Reza's arm. "Stop. He's coming."

"I don't like airports," Reza said. "I just want him to get here so we can go."

"And if you keep checking the flight board, it makes the planes go faster?"

Reza continued to pace. "What if the paperwork wasn't right and he got sent back to Pakistan?"

"What if the queen had balls? She'd be king," Ardeshir replied.

Despite his nerves, Reza smiled. Ardeshir pulled Reza into a chair, where he continued to shift in his seat until Ardeshir smacked him on top of the head with a folded newspaper. "I knew I should've left you in the car."

Time pressed weights onto every fiber of Reza's being. When the plane finally pulled into the gate, Reza couldn't move. Ardeshir had to hoist up his friend. "He's here, Reza."

Reza swallowed hard and knew he would be unable to speak.

The doors cracked open and Reza had to steady himself against Ardeshir. Faceless people filed off and Reza feared that maybe Hassan had changed so much he missed him.

Ardeshir grinned. "No, there's a lot more people coming. Just rela—oh, there he is! Hassan! Hassan! Get over here, you rat!"

Hassan had changed. Taller, thicker and with a mustache. But still the same smile Reza remembered every night in his dreams. It felt so good to hold his brother.

• • • • •

The July heat sparkled and danced across the Pacific Ocean. Hassan and Ardeshir pushed their feet into the warm sand. Ardeshir continued to walk toward the breaking waves, but Hassan just stopped. Ardeshir turned around. "You need to say "hang ten" and run into the surf."

"That's the stupidest thing I ever heard," Hassan said. He pushed the sand around with his foot, trying to make a small cave.

"I'm telling you, it's what all the Californians do." Ardeshir took some deep knee bends and twisted at the waist. "Works with the girls every time."

A couple of shapely bikini-clad young women walked through the ocean's white wash a few feet in front of Ardeshir. They turned toward him and giggled. He smiled and waved. "Hanging ten with a surf's up."

The girls continued to walk and laugh.

"Stand there if you want to," Ardeshir said. "I'm cooling off."

"When's Reza getting back?" Hassan asked as he cautiously walked toward Ardeshir.

"Late," Ardeshir said. "Didn't he tell you he's meeting with the tutor to prepare him for the entrance exam?"

"He said one of the coaches was helping him."

sloshball game featured burley wrestlers, a beer keg at second base and special guests from three sorority houses.

Ardeshir pointed, but not to Hassan. "Look, those are called dolphin shorts. They come in stripes and solids and they are the most beautiful things I've ever seen."

Reza grinned. "I like the stripes."

"And you've been home studying and missing all this!" Ardeshir chided, smacking his friend upside the head.

"Finals next week. But this is a good break."

A teammate ran to the bench. "Abedi, you're up!"

Reza turned in slight panic. "Up?"

Handing a bat to Reza, the teammate continued, "Yeah, up! Get up to the plate."

Reza still looked baffled and Ardeshir began laughing. Reza took the bat, figured out which end to use and stood at home plate. Somewhere, Journey's "Don't Stop Believing" blasted from a boom box. The players in the infield had a mitt in one hand and a red plastic cup in the other. The pitcher, with her ponytail in a blue scrunchie, leaned across the mound showing her cleavage as she tossed the ball. The ball went past Reza. He didn't move; he didn't take his eyes off the pitcher. A roar of good-natured laughter broke out and a sorority girl bounced out of the dugout to help Reza. Reza turned to Ardeshir and shouted, "Dolphin shorts!" to more laughter.

This time Reza hunched over his new partner and together they hit the ball. Except Reza ran to third base. Halfway to first, the dolphin shorts turned around to see Reza standing at third and looking genuinely confused. She walked over, held his hand and led him to first base, to everyone's applause.

When the next batter hit the ball, Reza scooped up his partner, ran to second and poured beer over them both. The next batter hit a foul tip, but Reza again scooped up his girl and this time didn't stop until they hit home plate. Spinning her around so the beer splashed from her red cup, he declared, "We're safe!"

The college kids from both benches gave Reza a standing ovation.

He returned with his signature grin and sat beside Ardeshir. "Great game, this softball."

"You're an idiot," Ardeshir said with laughter.

"Maybe, but I think she likes me."

Ardeshir smiled at his friend. "She's not drunk enough yet."

Stretching his arms to the bright blue sky, Reza took in a beautiful breath and turned to his friend. "I don't care. I love this country. I love this stupid game with its stupid bats and stupid little balls. I love this sky. I love this Abba Zabba wrapper stuck to my leg. And I love knowing I will still kick your ass every day of the week."

"Easy, big guy. All this love is making me horny."

• • • • •

The three returned to their apartment in a fine mood. Ardeshir dropped on the bed and Hassan lay next to him. Within two minutes they were fast asleep. Reza pulled notebooks from his backpack and spread them across the table. Sitting down with a sharpened pencil, he bent over his work.

The phone rang.

He looked at the clock. It would be too late for anyone from Belgium to call. Maybe it's dolphin shorts.

He answered, "Al—hello."

"Reza? Oh, thank God. We need your help."

"Soraya? Soray— What's wrong? Why are you crying?"

"Reza, they've taken everything. We have no money, no way to buy food, no way to . . ." Soraya cried.

Reza sat on the floor and leaned against the wall. "Where are you? Where's Baba? Mostafa?"

"Istanbul. Mostafa got us to Istanbul and they were supposed to take us all the way through Germany, but then Baba found these people who he thought needed help." She sobbed. "Oh, God, Reza, they stole everything!" More sobbing. "We can't go back there. We can't live here without paperwork."

"Listen to me. Calm down. Where's Baba?"

"He's not well, Reza. Since Naneh passed, he just sleeps."

"Where's Mostafa?"

Soraya took a deep breath. "Mostafa's out trying to find smugglers, but without money I don't know what we'll have to do to get through the borders." She paused. "Reza, it's not good to be girls here without money."

Reza dropped the phone and rubbed his face. He took a deep breath and picked up the receiver. "Okay, don't worry. I'm—" He paused, squeezing his eyes and rolling his head back. "I'm going to come get you."

She sobbed for several seconds, unable to speak. "Mostafa told us not to call you," she whispered. "That it would be too dangerous for you. They might even be watching us for you."

Reza stood and paced as far as the cord would go. "Calm down. No one will catch me. Who has your address?"

"Mehri," she said, sniffing. "She knows where we are. She's the only one."

Hassan had woken up and Ardeshir came out from the bedroom.

"Listen, you're going to be okay. I'm taking you to Mehri's. Just, stay together. Tell Mostafa not to do anything until I get there. Do you understand?"

"*Baleh,* Reza."

Reza hung up the phone and slammed his fist through the wall. Ardeshir grabbed his arms and held his flailing body. When Reza's voice and breathing became normal, Ardeshir released his friend and sat beside him on the floor.

Reza retold the conversation and Hassan blurted, "I'm going too."

Reza shook his head. "Stay here."

"At least I have a visa," Hassan said. "You have nothing and can't even board a plane."

"I'll find a way to get the paperwork," Reza said. "Someone on the team will know how."

Ardeshir stood and paced the room. "I heard José talking at practice about visas and friends who need paperwork. With my student loan money for next semester, we could—"

"José Martinez, the heavyweight?" Reza asked. "You heard him talking about paperwork?" He looked at the clock. "Wouldn't he be at practice now?"

Ardeshir nodded. "He would be but, Reza, he was just talking about getting people over the border to get a job. This is something totally different."

Reza rubbed his face and paced. "Not totally. I can speak enough Spanish. Dark hair, dark eyes, brown skin," he said. "I'll sound Mexican, look Mexican and—"

"That can't work," Hassan said. But Reza had already walked out the door.

• • • • •

Returning hours later, Reza seemed encouraged by his conversation with José. In three days, Reza would have a valid American visa with his picture and the name "José Martinez."

"Maybe here you'll pass for Mexican but no way in Turkey," Ardeshir said. "They'll smell you're an Iranian the second you step off the plane. And what if you have to speak in English? You're faking a Mexican accent. No way."

"I'm going to get them. Baba can't take care of them and you know what happens to girls with no money." Reza stopped and leaned into Ardeshir. "They get sold."

"Mostafa would never let that happen."

"They're in Turkey! What's Mostafa know in Turkey?"

Ardeshir looked at Reza. "Maybe I should go. If they're looking for you, they won't be expecting me."

Reza shook his head. "I know, but I've got to go."

"The mountains in Turkey are too hard for Baba," Hassan said. His face whispered of memories he tried to banish. "And the girls. In the snow. Even if they make it to Vienna, you can't go from Austria into Germany without—"

"Why are you telling me this? I know this! I know. I'll figure out a plan on the plane."

• • • • •

Ardeshir and Hassan pulled up to the terminal and Reza got out. He looked into the car window. "I hate airports."

Ardeshir smiled. "Have a great trip, José. Call us."

Speaking only Spanish, Reza made his way through the terminal and boarded the final plane for his flight to Belgium.

"Would you like a Coke?" the stewardess asked.

"Si," Reza answered with a grin. He sipped the sugary drink but he never really enjoyed it. He just enjoyed being able to say "yes."

With his ears popping and his stomach churning, Reza rubbed his sweaty palms together and tried to focus on the joy he would feel when he would hug Mehri. And soon, all his sisters.

He landed in Belgium and walked with wobbly legs off the plane. Two steps onto the gangway and a little girl hugged his legs. "Uncle Reza!" she said. He lifted her up in a giant hug as Mehri and her husband ran over to join the embrace.

They talked, laughed and cried long into the night. Reza saw Nimtaj in the eyes of his nieces and the nurturing gestures of his sister. The family sat before a traditional meal and Reza savored every bite.

"Do they not feed you in America?" his little niece asked.

"Not like this," Reza said as he took another helping.

"Is that why you are still short?" his nephew asked.

"Short!" Reza said with a smile. "I will show you short!" He took his nephew and spun him in a circle.

With that, his nephew wanted to know more about his gold medal and kept asking to squeeze his muscles. A genuine love filled every cell in Reza's body and he wished he didn't have to sleep. But the time change and exhaustion of the trip pulled him into a deep slumber and he passed out on the floor. Mehri tucked a pillow under his head and covered him with a blanket. Just like Nimtaj would have done.

• • • • •

The morning reminded them of Reza's purpose. Mehri's husband, Habbib, sat Reza down at the table. "Here are all the families' passports. You can sell them. Use the money to hire smugglers. It will be enough for safe passage."

Reza gathered the stack and flipped through them. "*Merci.* Will you be okay without—"

"*Baleh.* We're not going anywhere. In a few weeks, we can go to the embassy and say we've lost the passports and they will make us new ones. But—" He waited until he had Reza's eye. "They will search your luggage. If they find these, you're a smuggler and you'll go to Turkish prison."

Reza tried to grin. "Now I wish I didn't watch *Midnight Express.*"

"And they will pat you down at the airport. In Istanbul, they know Iranian from Arab from—what are you? Spaniard?" Habbib asked.

"I'm a Mexican from the U.S."

"Not in Turkey. In Turkey you're a runaway Iranian with a false passport. Again, they will pat you down and, if they find the passports, you're a smuggler and they will take you to their prison. If you even get that far. If they haven't seen you're not a U.S. Mexican."

Mehri walked in and froze at Reza's pale face. "Habbib, what are you telling him?"

Habbib looked directly at Reza. "The truth."

• • • • •

Habbib pulled in front of the terminal and gave Reza some last words of advice. Although a fresh layer of snow covered the ground, Reza sweated from every pore. He turned to thank Habbib, but no words would come through.

Habbib kissed him on alternating cheeks. "Go get your family."

• • • • •

The plane landed in Turkey.

Reza's fingers slipped off the buckle. The stewardess reached over to help him. "No!" He yelled and then fumbled in Spanish. "Sorry, I—I got it. Just stuck."

She walked down the aisle and said something to another stewardess. *She knows.*

Reza's body moved with underwater motions. Every face that looked at him seemed to say, "You're not José. You're going to prison."

Willing his body to move, he went down the ramp. He focused on just the next breath. *Breathe. Breathe.*

The Turkish guard looked at Reza's passport, at his face, back at his passport.

"Martinez?"

"Si."

"Step over here. Arms crossed over your head. Legs spread."

The passports felt like two-by-fours. Every guard seemed to whisper to the next as they looked at him. *They are just waiting. Playing me.*

"Martinez."

Reza didn't move.

"Martinez!"

"Oh, sí!"

The guard looked at his passport again. "Are you Martinez or are you not Martinez?"

A short breath, "Si, senor. Si, Martinez."

He handed Reza his passport and pointed to a wall. "Wait there."

Nodding, Reza moved toward the wall. As the guard picked up the phone, a large woman came to ask him directions. When he looked back at the wall, Reza was gone.

Reza pulled his head out of the toilet and flushed the vomit. Splashing cold water in his face, Reza regrouped to exit the airport. He imagined hundreds of Turkish guards swarming the corridors for the Iranian Martinez.

Almost blind with fear, he pushed through the crowds and did not look up until he could no longer hear the noises of the airport. He squeezed his eyes closed and slowly pushed his face up into the falling snow. *Thank you, Naneh.*

Chapter Twenty-Seven

December 1983

All day Reza knocked on doors inquiring about the smudged address in his pocket. Using every scrap of language and hand signal he could invent, he asked and asked and asked. Each face darkened when he said, "Old man traveling with three young girls." "Oh, no," they would say. "That's not safe here."

At the end of a dirty alley, he saw the back of a young girl, her dark hair covered in a brown scarf, her movements like Nimtaj's. Reza ran to the figure calling her name. "Soraya! Soraya!"

The little girl turned around; it wasn't Soraya but she ran to him with all her might. She jumped into Reza's arms. "Reza! You came!"

Reza held her, hugged her, kissed her. "Mariam! You've grown taller! I didn't recognize my baby sister! Oh, God, you're beautiful!"

He set her down and knelt before her to take in every inch of her face. She reached to his cheeks and brushed his tears away.

"Where's everyone else?" Reza asked.

Mariam took his hand and led him down the street and up a narrow staircase. She turned the handle and burst through the door. "Told you I'd find him!"

Soraya and Pari came running to Reza. He reached his arms out and held his family.

• • • • •

The morning brought a fresh storm of renewed energy. Mostafa, Abbas and Reza piled all the money and passports into the center of the floor. Mostafa gave the final total. "That should be enough, if we find the right people."

Reza looked at his brother. "How do we do that? Who are the right people?"

"It's not easy anymore, Reza. I've found a certain alley in town where these people gather. We're sending the worst possible cargo."

"Cargo?"

"Teenage girls. They have more value to some kinds of people than anything we have here." He motioned to the pile.

Abbas waved his hand and said with a cough, "I will not let that happen."

"Mostafa, aren't you going with them?" Reza asked.

Mostafa took a deep breath. "No. My wife—you have not met her—is in Iran and she is pregnant with our first child."

Reza's eyes bugged out. "Wife? Pregnant? Child? Well, I'm happy for you Mostafa, I guess."

Mostafa smiled. "Thanks, I guess. She won't be able to travel for some time, even after the baby, so I must go back to Iran as soon as this is taken care of."

Reza flipped through the pile on the table again, as if hoping something would be different this time. He looked at his brother. "Then I should go through the mountains," he said.

"No," Mostafa answered. "We can't risk it. You'll fly back to Belgium and wait at Mehri's for Baba to call. Then you pick them up in Germany and take them bac°k to Mehri's."

"The checkpoints from Germany to Belgium shouldn't be a problem, but what if they don't make it there?" Reza said. "What if they get stuck in Austria? What if . . ."

"Reza!" Baba said. "This is the best plan if Mostafa says it is. Soon as we're on our way through Turkey, you'll fly back to Mehri's and wait for us to call. There are no other options."

"*Chashm*, Baba. I'll wait for your call." He looked at Mostafa. "Let's go find our smugglers."

• • • • •

Black water oozed down the crease in the broken sidewalk. Crusty grey snow formed jagged piles on the burned cars and sewage lining the alley. Limping through trash, mangy dogs pulled on pieces of rotting flesh stuck to old bones. Smells brought Reza back into the ambulance with Kahn.

Mostafa knew enough Turkish and moved like a reaper from thug to thug. Reza followed, trying to avoid the shifty eyes and nasty yellow grins. He twisted his hands together and clenched his teeth. *I will not leave my sisters with any of these people. There has to be another way.*

Without warning, five blackened fingernails rested on Reza's shoulder. He spun around and shot into a wrestler's stance.

The man spoke. "Ah, I thought it was you. How's America, Abedi?"

Mostafa stood next to Reza. "We don't know any Abedi."

"Bullshit. I wrestled myself in the home country. Your brother here, he wrestled in Worlds and then didn't come home from Venezuela." The man pulled a package of hand-rolled cigarettes and offered them to the brothers. "Smoke?"

"No."

Standing next to Mostafa, Reza kept his eyes locked on this man. He scanned his body and studied his expression.

The smuggler struck a match. "I never forget a face."

"And I never forget a favor," Mostafa said. "Since you are in this alley, you must be able to help people in our situation."

The man nodded and blew smoke into the dirty air. "I know people. People who travel by night and rest by day. Are these the people you need?"

"We are sending our sisters," Mostafa paused. "Our younger sisters."

The bright orange tip of the man's cigarette cut into the night as he took a long, slow drag. "I see. That will cost more to keep them—safe."

"I'm going with them," Reza said. He stomped his feet in the filthy snow and turned to Mostafa. "Baba can't protect them. And you know what happens to girls—"

Mostafa held up his hand to Reza and looked at the smuggler. "Tell us about these people, this passage."

"These people, they do what they are paid to do. You need to get to Belgium? That is many days. We would start tomorrow night and sleep each day in a house known by my people to be safe. One day in Bulgaria, one in Romania, one in Hungary, then to Austria, Germany, Holland and to Belgium." He smashed his cigarette. "My people are the best at what they do."

Reza grabbed the smuggler by the arm. "What do they do? Do they sell people or do they smuggle them?"

Gently pulling Reza back, Mostafa said, "You know the price to guarantee safe passage?"

"Of course," the smuggler said. "I only negotiate safe passage. And Reza, your brother's right. It's too dangerous for you. Your safety, I could not guarantee. Tell your sisters to dress plain, with thick clothes and keep their eyes down and they will be safe."

Mostafa and the smuggler talked in low tones with many gestures. Lighting his third cigarette, the smuggler nodded, shook Mostafa's hand and then kissed him three times on the cheek. Reza winced. He joined them and looked hard at the man who had just kissed his brother. "My sisters will be safe. Because I will find you if they are not."

The smuggler nodded and walked into the night.

• • • • •

When Mostafa and Reza returned to the apartment, Soraya opened the door. "It's Mariam."

Now what?

Worry and sadness leapt from her eyes. She stammered, "The tall dresser. It fell on her foot. We think it's broken and Baba took her to the hospital."

"Is she okay?" Reza asked.

Soraya looked down. "She is, but we had to use some of the money. I'm sorry. I should have been watching her. I—I—"

Reza took Soraya and hugged her. "We're almost there."

• • • • •

The phone rang in the Southern California apartment and Ardeshir grabbed it. "Hello!"

"Allo," Reza said. "Are you still ugly?"

"I'll never be as ugly as you." He laughed. "When are you coming home?"

"Soon," Reza answered. "I'm just waiting here at Mehri's for them to call me."

Swatting Hassan away from the phone, Ardeshir continued. "How did you get them out of Turkey?"

"Money. Smugglers," Reza sighed. "I don't like it. And Baba doesn't look well. He coughs and looks—looks sad all the time."

"But they're going to be safe?" Ardeshir asked, giving Hassan a wink.

"Once they get through the mountains and through Austria, it should be over."

"They'll make it."

"*Inshallah.* How's Hassan?"

Ardeshir looked at Hassan. "He doesn't like dolphin shorts. Here, talk some sense into him."

Hassan grabbed the phone. "How's everyone? Do they look strong?"

Reza struggled to speak without tears. "They look great."

Hassan tried to respond, but he handed the phone to Ardeshir and started to weep.

"Hassan," Reza said. "Are you—"

"He's in one of his crying spells. He'll be okay."

"Please, please watch him."

"Reza, I got it here. Take care of your family."

I wish I could. I wish they were all right here with me. Reza took a deep breath. "I have to go."

"Hey, be careful, *doost-e man.*"

Reza rubbed his eyes with his fingertips.

"You there, Reza?"

"Barely," he replied.

Ardeshir lowered his voice. "Stay strong."

• • • • •

Two days became four. Four days became six. And still no word. Reza and Mehri paced and paced. They took round-the-clock shifts sitting next to the phone. Each time the phone rang, hearts stopped and they bolted for the receiver.

At 4:00 a.m., it rang. Soraya's voice. "Please, please," she coughed. "Please tell Reza to come get us."

"Where are you?" Mehri said. "Are you together? Is everyone okay?"

Reza and Habbib rushed into the room.

Soraya wept and Abbas took the phone. "We're somewhere different. They took us into the mountains and pointed. 'Go that way,' they said.'" He fell into a coughing fit. "And now, Pari is too sick to walk and Soraya had to carry Mariam because she's so weak, and—" Coughing finished his sentence.

"Baba, please, can you tell us anything about where you are?" Mehri asked.

He called to Soraya. "Come and say these words."

Soraya took the phone and read the address.

Mehri's face flooded with tears as she wrote it onto her notepad. With a look of anguish, she turned to Reza. He cocked his head. *What's wrong? Something went wrong.*

"He'll be there before nightfall," Mehri said, struggling to keep a steady voice. "God will be with you." She hung up.

Reza headed for the door and Mehri grabbed his arm. "They didn't make it. They're in Vienna."

He froze. "Didn't make it? In Vienna? Why didn't—how can I—" He stumbled through his words. *In Austria! I should have gone! I knew it!*

"Just sit a minute," Habbib said. "Before you go rushing off in the car, we have to piece this together."

"I know I can get from here to Vienna with my American visa," Reza said, still facing the door. "And I can just put them in the car and hope we don't get stopped at an Austrian checkpoint."

"And if you do," Habbib interrupted, "drive through alone and have them walk through with the crowds. They have a better chance of blending in and then you can meet them after the checkpoint."

Nodding, Reza asked, "What about a road from Austria into Germany without a checkpoint? How can I find that?"

"Find a smuggler," Habbib answered. "But I don't think you'll need one. You'll just need some luck through the checkpoints."

Reza took the sack full of supplies Mehri had ready at the door and jumped into the car. He sped into the night to rescue his family from Vienna.

• • • • •

At sunset, Reza pulled up to the address that Mehri had scribbled. He pounded on the shabby motel door.

"Baba! Soraya!"

Abbas opened the door and embraced Reza. Only Soraya rushed over; Mariam and Pari lay asleep on the floor.

"We're going. Right now," Reza said. "Baba, where's your bags?"

Abbas looked blankly at his son. "We have two. That's all I could carry."

"Fine. Pick up Mariam." Reza knelt next to his sister. "Pari, can you walk?" She didn't respond. Reza scooped up her hot flesh, carried her to the car and laid her on the back seat. Soraya sat next to her and Abbas set Mariam on her lap.

Reza sped down the icy roads. The girls slept in the back, but Abbas stared through the crusted windshield. "You need to rest, Baba. You should close your eyes."

He spoke without moving. “No.”

“We have the checkpoint to go through, so you need to rest now.”

Abbas shook his head. “When we are in Germany, I will rest.”

Reza pulled into a gas station for a final fill-up. He came around to the passenger window. “Baba, I need you to give me all your passports and anything that has your name. Everyone needs to be clean.”

“Clean?”

“Clean. No names, no pictures in case we get stopped.”

Abbas dug through his pockets and handed Reza all the paperwork. Reza parked behind the gas station. Quickly he pulled off the back speakers and stuffed the documents under the fiberglass.

“What are you doing?” a sleepy voiced asked.

“Shhh, go back to sleep. Just being careful.”

• • • • •

They pulled into the line of cars at the border checkpoint. Reza saw German officers pointing flashlights into every car in the line. He pulled over and turned to Abbas. “You'll have to walk the girls through,” he said. “Blend in with the crowds. I will drive alone, park just past the checkpoint and meet you.”

Abbas nodded. They woke up the girls, but Soraya protested. “Pari and Mariam can't walk. Just leave them in the car.”

“We can't. They are checking cars but not the people walking.”

Soraya started to speak when Abbas said, “Listen to Reza. Everybody out. Faces down, blend in.” He lifted Pari into his arms. Mariam hobbled with the help of Soraya.

After passing through the checkpoint, Reza pulled over and waited. He closed his eyes for a few minutes of rest. *Please let them through.* He awoke to screaming sirens and banging on his windshield. “Get out!”

“What? I'm doing nothing wrong. I can't rest?” Reza said.

“Get out!”

Reza found himself facedown on the frozen hood, unable to keep up with the German policeman's questions.

“Open the trunk.”

“Why? I haven't done anything.”

Placing his hand on his gun, the officer said, “Open.”

The policeman pulled out bras and blouses and turned to Reza. “You're a smuggler.”

• • • • •

In the holding cell, with about twenty others who were also brought in from the border checkpoint, Reza waited for his paperwork to be processed. One by one, each person was interviewed. Some were released and some were led away in handcuffs. Although Reza wove every lie and story he could imagine, the border officer wasn't convinced.

"I don't care what your visa says, you don't look Mexican," the German officer said. "You sound and smell like an Iranian."

"You can't hold me on how I smell," Reza said. But he remained alone in the holding cell. He squatted in the corner, pulled up his knees and rocked from side to side. *Please let my family be safe. Please, Naneh, protect them.*

He awoke a few hours later to the sound of many languages, each protesting their arrest.

Bolting to the bars, he wrapped his fingers around them and listened for the voices of his family. But he saw them first. Abbas coughed and staggered under the weight of Pari, with Soraya helping Mariam just behind him.

Reza went to the back of the small cell and tried to catch Abbas's attention. *They can't show they know me.* When Abbas saw Reza, Reza turned his back and shook his head. In Farsi, Abbas quickly told the girls not to acknowledge Reza. Abbas laid Pari on the single bench and Soraya leaned Mariam next to her.

The questioning followed. Again people were either led away in handcuffs or sent to the next holding cell to be moved to the camp the following morning. When the cell door opened, Abbas grabbed the guard's hand and held it to Pari's forehead. "If she does not get medicine, she will die."

The guard took his hand away. "In the morning you will go to the processing camp. And there will be a doctor."

Abbas yelled, "No! Morning is too late!" He choked on his coughs. "You have physicians here! Call one!"

"It is 2:00 a.m.," the guard replied. "And no doctors."

Abbas roared through cement cells. "She will not last until morning! Hear how she breathes! She will not last the hour!"

Reza stood to tell the guards the truth, but Soraya walked directly in front of the guard. "You must call a doctor for my sister."

Hearing the commotion, a sergeant came from his office down the hallway. "Call a doctor, for God's sake," he said. "And then send them on the first bus to the camp."

• • • • •

Reza sat on the bench alone in his cell with his head resting in his hands. The guard peered through the bars. "Day after next is Monday. When the embassy opens, we will find out who you really are, José Martinez."

Saturday afternoon brought a shift change. This guard looked like he enjoyed food above all else. He unpacked a bag of bratwurst hotdogs, wiped mustard from his face and sat heavily in his chair. With one hand he flipped through Reza's file and fed himself with the other. "What're you doing here?"

"Don't know." Reza walked to the bars and held them. "I was just sleeping in my car and here I am."

"No charges?"

"Nope. My passport came back clean."

The guard took another huge bite and spoke with bits of meat spraying from his mouth. "Clean's good. Less paperwork to go to the camp."

The aroma of the bratwurst tore into Reza's gut as he picked at the stew left for him on the tray. "What happens at the camp?"

"Officially or unofficially?"

"Both," Reza said, trying to hide the panic in his voice.

The guard took a huge bite and nearly choked. "Officially, they lock you up in the quarantine area for about ten days." He slurped his coffee. "They sort you out, figure what country you're supposed to go to and send you back there. Or they move you to the other side, where you just wait with the other refugees."

"And unofficially?"

"Let's just say this: I wouldn't want to be a girl there. I mean, there's some order, food, cots and basic medicine."

"No guards?"

"It's no prison, if that's what you mean. More like a refugee camp, but they keep you locked up pretty tight those first ten days." He finished his bratwurst and squirted mustard on the second. "Are you military? You look pretty fit."

"I'm a wrestler."

"Thought so. I wrestled myself." He looked at his waist. "Heavyweight. Should have made the National team."

"You look like it," Reza said.

"Any chance you know Dave Shultz?"

"Oh, yeah," Reza answered. "Know him well."

The guard slowly chewed his hotdog. "And your visa came back clean? Well, hell, I'm not dealing with your paperwork." The guard set down his hot dog and unlocked the door. "Goodbye."

"Thanks. Can I get my visa?"

The guard handed Reza his visa and pointed to the door. Reza stepped outside and into a snowstorm. He walked around the station. He went back inside. "Where'd you put the car?"

The guard swallowed the last bite of bratwurst. "Uphill. That way," he said, pointing a chubby finger to the left.

Uphill. Reza arrived at the car lot. His face was red from snow burns, and pieces of frost stuck to the tips of his black hair. He blew on his hands and painfully unbent his fingers to twist the door handle into the single-room office. A sleepy-eyed guard looked up. "Don't drip your snow in here. It puddles."

Reza stomped his feet, shaking snow onto the floor. "I'm here for my car. Give me the keys and I'm gone."

The guard sighed and rubbed the back of his neck. "I'll check your car. If it's clean, you can have it. Follow me."

Not wanting to take his gloves off in the snow, the guard handed the keys to Reza to open the car.

The guard searched the car and paused at the girls' clothes. "What's this?"

Reza hesitated. "Sisters. They borrow the car sometimes."

The wind kicked up a fresh snow flurry and the guard covered his face with his gloves. "Just go," he said.

• • • • •

Ardeshir knocked on the door of the professor's office. "Sir, may I speak to you?"

"Yes. Come in."

"Thank you, sir. My friend, Reza Abedi. He's in your exercise physiology class."

The professor motioned for Ardeshir to sit down in the single chair. "Yes, hard-working student. Always staying after to ask questions. I haven't seen him. Is everything okay?"

Ardeshir sat and swallowed. "He's a—his family. It's complicated. But he talked to all of his professors before he left, except you."

"Where is he? What's the matter?"

"I can't really say." Ardeshir squirmed in the chair. "But you should know that getting a degree from the university has been Reza's dream since—probably since he was born."

The professor chuckled. "You've known him that long?"

"Almost," Ardeshir said. "Since we were eight. We grew up together in Iran."

The professor leaned in and looked with genuine concern. "That's a tough place to grow up."

"Wasn't always but, yeah, it got difficult recently," Ardeshir answered. He redirected to his mission. "But Reza would've never left before finals unless—unless his family really needed him."

"I see," the professor said as he flipped through a grade book. "He's never missed an assignment. He's scored well on all but one test. When did you say he's coming back?"

"Sir, I'm not sure."

"But, he does plan to return and finish his studies?"

"Reza'll crawl through glass to earn his degree."

"Well, I hope it doesn't come to that." He closed his grade book. "Please have Reza see me when he gets back."

• • • • •

Five days. Driving along every road he could find, marked and unmarked, Reza could not find a safe passage to get his family out of the processing camp in Vienna and into Germany without passing through a border checkpoint. Roads that didn't go through a checkpoint ended at the raging, ice-laden Salzach River. Surviving on stolen cheese and bread, he slept in his car and turned off the engine to save gas. On the fourth night, he rented a room in a motel. He left without paying the bill.

That morning, he stumbled into a dimly lit gas station. With a blank stare, he went to the booth to pay for gas. *I've got to find a road today. There's just got to be a way . . .*

"Good morning," said the gas station attendant. "Are you from this area?"

Taken by surprise, Reza looked up into the friendly face about his age. "No, no I'm not."

"I thought so. Are you visiting family or on vacation?"

"Neither."

Another patron approached and exchanged friendly conversation with the attendant. Reza finished pumping the gas and slowly screwed on the cap. *I wonder if this guy would know about roads.* A cascade of fresh snow began to fall and Reza dreaded another frozen night in his car. Blowing bits of ice off the surrounding trees, a gale of wind burned his ears. He tried to pull up his collar as he walked up to the window.

"Hey," Reza started, "are you from around here?"

"Lived here my whole life," the attendant replied.

"And so you know about—roads?"

The attendant nodded, came out from his booth and reached his hand out to Reza. "Sure do. Is there a particular road you're looking for?"

"You could say that."

The attendant shrugged. "Can't help ya if you don't tell me what you're looking for."

For a moment, Reza studied his face as he would an opponent's on the mat. Trying to read his thoughts, predict his next move, look for a weakness. With a firm voice, Reza said, "I need a road that won't be on the map."

Rubbing his gloved hands together, the attendant replied, "I know of people who know such roads. I get off work in two hours. Come back then."

Two hours beat on Reza's chest like the hooves of a wild beast. He thought of his sisters and how cold and scared they must be. He thought of Baba and how he counted on Reza to come through for them. He thought of the chance he was taking with this gas station attendant, a chance fate had forced on him.

• • • • •

"Ah, you're exactly on time. Two hours," the attendant said as he locked the booth and put on his coat. "When is the last time you had a hot meal, my friend?"

Reza couldn't remember. "Thank you, I just need a—"

"A road. I know." He started walking to his car. "Then follow me."

"To the road?"

He unlocked his car. Holding his hand on the ice-covered door, he turned to Reza. "Maybe you're not hungry," he said with a smile, "but my grandma made hot stew tonight and I'm stopping there first."

Hot stew. Grandma's hot stew.

• • • • •

After his third bowl, Reza thanked his new friend, Ivan, once again. And once again, Ivan simply waved him off. "It's nothing. Some days you help people; some days I help people. I could see you're a good guy."

"My family, we always—shared food in the bad times," Reza said, nodding.

"And who hasn't come across a bad time?" Ivan said. "When you're full, we'll meet a friend of mine who'll help you with your errand."

Scraping the sides of his bowl with his spoon, Reza thanked Ivan's grandma again. She replied with a smile and went to fill his bowl a fourth time.

"No, thank you," Reza said. "It's wonderful, but I'm actually full."

• • • • •

Sliding and skidding down the icy roads, Ivan drove into a dingy neighborhood. Hungry dogs lurched at Reza when he got out of the car. "Back!" He gave a sideways glance at Ivan, who seemed unaware of the mangy beasts as he headed into an alley. Reza looked around. Ivan faded into a doorway and Reza followed him.

They stepped into a shadowy one-bedroom flat. Several people slouched on the dirty sofa while two more pulled white powder into their red, flaring nostrils. Against the grimy walls, four automatic weapons hung from rusty hooks. A thin man rose, shut and locked the door behind Reza.

"Come, sit." Ivan waved to Reza, who stood motionless in front of the locked door. "You're safe here. Just sit."

Safe here?

From down the hall, an enormous man with eyes too small for his face and hands too large for his body greeted Ivan with a hearty hug. "My friend! It's been too long!"

"Yes, too long!" Ivan again looked at Reza. "I've a friend who needs your help."

The brute approached Reza, who still hadn't moved, and reached out his thick fingers that ended in black fingernails. "Welcome. Come, sit."

"I'll stand," Reza replied.

"Reza, come sit. We can help you," Ivan said as he sat at a small, splintered table at the far end of the room. He then mumbled to the brute, who nodded and went back down the hall. Suddenly, a skeletal figure of a woman leaped from the couch and sprinted toward Reza. "You want fun?" she asked, craning her thin neck to his face. "I can make fun."

"No, I don't want fun," Reza replied. He stepped around the girl and sat next to Ivan.

"It'll be fine," Ivan said as he lit a cigarette. "My friend'll have the road you need."

Moments later, Reza pored over maps of paths along icy rivers and trails through wooded areas near the camp. He made notes on the back of a paper plate and strained to commit every landmark to memory. His mind reeled. *We can't get lost in these woods. I've got to memorize every turn.* Ivan's large friend pointed out pitfalls, like the German guard towers and the ridge wide enough for only one man to cross at a time.

"Course, this last storm could've covered some of the markings," the man said. "You'll know you're safe in Germany when you see the train station." Sitting in the chair, he folded his arms and sized up Reza. "I don't suppose you'd like an opportunity to earn money on your trip?"

"No!" Reza snapped. Then he softened his tone. "No, thank you. I appreciate your help. Just looking to move my family."

Ivan gave a brief scenario of Reza's situation as Reza continued to study the maps. The large man added some important details about the camp, the roads and told Reza he should look for someone outside the camp first to get specific information before going inside. "Sunday's visiting day," he said. "The most coming and going's on Sunday and that's the best chance to get them out unnoticed."

"What's today?" Reza asked, suddenly aware he had no sense of time.

"Friday," Ivan said. "And tomorrow's a work day for me, so we should head back home."

Nodding, Reza took a last focused look at the maps and made final notes on the plate.

Although Ivan insisted Reza stay the night on his grandma's couch, Reza slept little. His mind raced up and down the icy trails, trying to will his broken family across the narrow rock ridge and under the guard towers.

Reza thanked Ivan and his grandma, devoured a hot breakfast and headed to the camp.

• • • • •

Just after dawn, Reza parked next to the clump of three huge trees and tried to scout out the promised path. Fuzzy morning light bounced off the gentle piles of snow lining the blue ice of the river. In the silence, peace bathed the trail, inspiring Reza to drop to his knees. He closed his eyes and whispered, "Please, Naneh, please help me take us across this path."

He spent hours that morning studying the guards, the gates and the general movement of the camp. Noticing a man who seemed to be doing the same along the far perimeter, Reza took a chance and approached him when he drifted back into the woods.

"Are you a resident here?" Reza asked.

The man raised a furry eyebrow. "Who are you looking for?"

"My father and three sisters," Reza answered with a tired sigh.

"You don't want sisters here. There's one shower. It's not good."

"Where are they? How do I get to them?" Reza grabbed the man's collar.

The man pulled away. "Let go of me!"

"Sorry," Reza mumbled, releasing him. "I haven't been well. I'm—can you help me?"

"*Baleh*," said the man. "Where are you from?"

"Kermanshah," Reza said. The word sounding sadly foreign to him.

"Qom," said the Iranian. "We can help each other."

Reza reached to the man and exchanged the traditional two kisses. "I have maps," Reza said.

"Don't need them. I have visas but I have to get my brother out of the ten-day quarantine area. I know where there's a broken window but I need to be lifted over the fence."

In the conversation that followed, Reza learned that this man had been a resident of the camp but was released when his paperwork cleared. His brother remained inside.

The Iranian waved his hand. "Follow me." They stood off to the side and he pointed to the window with the broken lock. "They serve breakfast just after sunrise. Tell your family to wear plain, day clothes. No coats. After everyone has gone down for breakfast, they must crawl through the window and blend in with the visitors. Gather them together but walk out in twos, not a big group. This way, if you're caught, at least some of you may get out."

"I have to get everyone out. Is there anything else I can do?"

The Iranian shook his head. "No, that's your best chance." He pointed along the chain-link fence that snaked around the camp. "There's a place I know where we can get over the fence. After dark. With two of us, we can make it."

"Good. I'll meet you here after dark," Reza said.

A deep, pounding sleep enveloped Reza despite the single-digit temperatures. He awoke in his car with a start, forgetting for a moment where he was or why. A cascade of images flooded his mind and he remembered his mission. He ached with each step as he trudged through darkness to the meeting place.

"Stay low and follow me," whispered the Iranian.

After trudging across snow-covered paths and through a maze of tall, ice-laden trees, they stopped at a chain-link fence.

"What's this?" Reza asked.

"The backside," the man repeated. He looked Reza up and down. "I'm sure you can lift me over and then pull yourself over."

Although his arms trembled, Reza lifted the man over the fence. He then gripped the frozen steel and pulled himself over. He dropped into a snow drift on the other side.

"May God be with you," the man said, his white breath cutting through the air.

"You, too."

They went in separate directions and Reza followed the fence toward the quarantine area near the front of the camp. He hunched down behind a frosted bush and watched. There were several low, unmarked buildings. Judging by the rows of windows, he figured each building had four floors. Most windows were dark; some lights came from the first floor.

Reza studied the buildings once more, looking for the markings to direct him to the broken window. He crept closer and stood in the building's shadow cast by the light of the moon. Looking up toward the roof, he allowed himself a moment to admire the sparkling sky. The stars that always held his wishes, his fate.

Inside, Soraya saw him. She pressed her face against the second-floor window, her breath fogging his image. "Reza," she whispered. She tugged to open the window but it was locked. A rapid tap-tap-tap drew Reza's attention. He waved and pointed to the back of the building. After telling the guard she felt ill and needed fresh air, she met Reza just outside.

"I knew you'd come," she whispered as she hugged him tight around the neck. "I watched for you every night."

"Is everyone all right?"

"Yes. No. I don't know. Baba still coughs. They gave Pari medicine and wrapped Mariam's foot, but . . ."

"Ok, listen. There's a broken window on the second floor. Along the staircase."

"How do you—"

"Shhh, listen," Reza said. He held both her hands and looked directly into her face. "Tomorrow, go down for breakfast last. Get everyone out that window."

"Then what?"

The door opened and a deep voice said, "Girl! Come here now!"

"Go," Reza said. "I'll find you."

She hugged him and ran to the door.

Chapter Twenty-Eight

Laguna Niguel, 2010

"My sisters r coming to visit they want to meet u," Reza texts me.

"OMG! YES! When? Who?"

"Come over tomorrow."

I walk up to Reza's house with the feeling of a rock in my stomach. Before I can knock, the door flies open and I'm greeted with hugs and smiles. I'm embracing Hassan, Soraya, Pari and their beautiful families.

Soraya and Pari need to finish getting ready. They are petite, with quick movements and laughing eyes that I imagine are like their mother's. I note Pari's flawless toffee-colored skin and thick radiant hair with wonder, remembering that she was once so close to death. While they fix their make-up, I sit on the edge of the tub and they tell me stories. "We used to peek through the crack in the gym door and watch Reza wrestle," they say with a grin. "No one could beat him."

When they leave to get dressed, I go downstairs. I watch Hassan's five-year-old son through the kitchen window following his Uncle Reza about the backyard helping to garden. Hassan's son is wearing a pair of shorts and flip flops and carries a small pair of shears. Reza leans down, points to a bush and the pint-sized gardener starts snipping away. Hassan joins me and I compliment him on his son's manners. I tell Hassan how his son stuck his little hand out, introduced himself and welcomed me when I first came to the door. "He's a perfect gentleman," I say. And as I watch his son very carefully trim the next bush, I think of all Hassan suffered to bring that child into this world.

Hassan won't talk much more about his time in the Iranian or Pakistani prison, except to say the Pakistani refugee camp was "the worst place I've ever been in my life." I'm shocked to hear a refugee camp described in those terms. He prefers instead to discuss current Middle Eastern politics. "Like a lid bouncing on top of a boiling pot," he says. "The people will demand liberty. You can't clamp down a lid when the water boils over." I nod in agreement.

Soraya, Pari and I spend the rest of the afternoon chatting like girlfriends at a high school reunion. I find Soraya's eyes to be alluring as they widen with laughter and darken with tears. There is an honesty about her, an authentic spirit that gives her a strength despite her small frame.

I ask about Nimtaj and with genuine smiles they begin with the good memories. "She brought food baskets to all our gymnastics tournaments and shared with everyone," Pari says. Then a shadow crosses her face. "But when Reza and Hassan were gone, every morning she would hold their pictures in these little gold frames and she would cry."

"We didn't tell her they were not coming back, but she knew," Soraya says. "We'd say, 'maybe next week,' and she would let us think she believed us. But she knew. She knew."

When they share the memories of the night she died, the sadness is palpable. They clutch tissues and wipe falling tears, but they continue to speak. I watch as they return to that dark unfamiliar room, holding their mother, grieving again as she slips away. A beautiful silence enters our room, a peace. A stillness.

As I have found is rather common in Iranian tradition, the death of a loved one must be told in person. With Reza's family being so separated at that time, the girls were further burdened by the secret of their mother's death. "We even wrote letters as if we were our mother," they confess. "But Rasha and Mehri figured it out." Soraya reaches for Pari's hand. "It was so painful."

I see the faces of their children peering into the living room with genuine concern and so do they. It is time to change the subject. "Tell me about being rescued from the camp."

"I would look out the window every chance I got," Soraya says. "And after four or five nights, I saw Reza standing in the snow."

"Were you worried he wouldn't be able to get you out?"

They quickly shake their heads. "When Soraya said she saw Reza," Pari says, "I knew everything would be all right."

"But you were locked in a camp surrounded with snow, you were so sick, Mariam's foot was broken, your Baba was so weak and—"

"But Reza had found us."

Chapter Twenty-Nine

At the edge of the frozen river and surrounded by an ice-laden forest, the family shivered and ached in the bitter landscape. Pari's flushed body trembled and Mariam struggled with her footing on the ice-covered ground. Soraya looked at her brother. "Just take us in the car."

Reza shook his head. "We can't take a chance at the checkpoints again."

"But Mostafa gave us passports," Soraya said. "You hid them. Just show those at the checkpoints."

"You don't have a visa to enter another country," Reza said. His exhaustion crept up in his voice. "You'll get sent back to the camp and probably Iran."

"We have to cross this path." Abbas coughed and rubbed his hands. "And before anyone notices we are missing." He started down the icy trail surrounded by dark trees whose barren boughs blended into the grey sky. Although a wind continually brushed against the mountainside, it was too weak to bend the branches stiff with snow.

As Reza watched his father's body hunch over with another coughing fit, he felt an impulse to just run. Run far and run fast and run to the top of the mountain and scream into the sky.

Mariam touched his arm. "Do we follow Baba?" Reza shook his head.

"Wait, Baba," Reza said. "I must go first to look for the markings, and you go last." He turned to his sisters. "No one speaks.

Just keep your feet moving. We stop when we see the train station. Pari, can you walk?"

"*Baleh,*" she said. "I won't stop."

"Soraya, stay with Pari. Mariam, stay right in front of Baba. If I hold up my arm, that means everyone lie flat."

"In the snow?" Mariam asked.

"Yes, in the snow," Reza said. "Quickly now. No talking."

• • • • •

Two painful hours down the path and Reza turned a corner along the ridge. Although it was mid-morning, the sun stayed trapped behind clouds in the dreary sky. Except for a few birds chattering in the trees, this snow-covered trail offered no sign of life. Jagged grey rocks cut through the ice and provided neither footholds nor places to rest. Reza jogged for a few minutes up the trail until he recognized the next two markings. At least they were not lost. He blew out a slow white breath. *But at this pace, we won't make it before dark.* He went back to regroup his family. He could only see Mariam.

He watched Mariam drag her foot behind her like a club. "Come sit here, *azizam.*" He helped her to a flat rock and tried to wipe the dried blood that stuck to her nose and lips. "How many times did you fall?"

"Not too many," she said and pushed his hand away. "That makes it hurt more. Are we almost to the train station?"

"Almost. Wait here so I can get everyone else." He went back down the path.

In her weakened state, Pari had collapsed into the snow and shivered in a heap, her fever returning to ravish her body. Soraya held Pari and rocked her, singing the prayers from her childhood. Reza sprinted to his sisters.

"Why didn't you call for me?" Reza asked with a bite in his voice.

"You said to be quiet," Soraya answered, her tone equally edged.

Reza reached down but winced as he lifted Pari's baking body. With softer words, he asked, "Where's Baba?"

"Back there. Give me Pari. Maybe you need to go help him up the last ridge," Soraya said, noting Reza's look toward the path. "The last part was so steep. And Baba's not strong like he used to be."

"Baba's strong," Reza said. He carried Pari up the trail. "He'll be here."

Soraya followed him and rushed to Mariam as soon as she saw her shivering on the rock. Wrapping her arms around her baby sister, Soraya simply held her and kissed her forehead. "We're almost there," she kept whispering. "Almost there."

Reza gently laid Pari next to Mariam and the two curled up together. Pari's warmth comforted Mariam. Reza walked to the edge of the trail and Soraya stood by his side.

She looked at Reza. "How much further?"

He rubbed the back of his neck. "It can't be much. We're almost at the top and then it's downhill." He pointed to the last section. "That's going to be the worst part. The narrow ridge. The ledge follows the mountain and is only wide enough for one person. And if Mariam slips . . ." He heard a small cry from Soraya, so he didn't say more. Instead, he put his arm around her shoulder and gave her a hug. "I need to get Baba."

He started to jog back down the trail, but Pari called out. "No, stay here!"

He knelt down to comfort her, but Mariam already held her hand. "Don't cry. Reza will be right back."

Soraya looked away to hide her tears.

He kissed his sister's forehead. "I'm getting Baba and will be right back."

Reza bolted down the path after his father.

Abbas's lungs heaved in spasms from years of smoking and the altitude. Black streams of phlegm oozed down his face and splattered in the snow. He slowed to robotic steps with a haunted look. Just before Reza reached him, Abbas leaned against a tree and clenched his chest. "Just go."

Reza reached to his father. "Give me your hand."

Abbas dropped to the snow. He rolled on his side and clutched his knees, his words choked out between coughs. "Leave me."

The sun finally reached through a cloud and gave a promise of light. Ice-laden branches bent under their weight to spill grey shadows. Abbas lay still. Reza dropped to his knees and pulled his father's head into his lap. He touched the frozen, cracked skin of his face. *Help me, Naneh. Please, please help us.*

Reza took off his sweatshirt and tried to put it over Abbas. "Here, Baba. Lift your arms. Put this on. Put this . . ." Abbas barely moved. Reza grabbed his swollen, purple hand and forced it through the sleeve. "Now, give me your other . . ."

Pulling his father to his feet, he whispered, "Just one step, Baba. Look at your feet and make them move just one step."

Leaning on his son, Abbas staggered forward. When he turned the corner, Soraya ran to help Abbas.

Mariam whispered to Pari, "Reza's here."

Reza stood before his family. "The next part of the path, we have to go one at a time."

Soraya's eyes popped open and she started to speak, but then pinched her lips together and held her hands to her face. Reza continued, "Soraya, you will go first. Look for loose rocks or icy places on the path. Pari, go next, then Mariam, then Baba and me."

Icy winds blew against the mountainside, forcing branches to drop their snow. Soraya stood and with her cracked, bleeding hands lifted Pari and Mariam to their feet. No one spoke. Soraya started down the path.

It was Pari who slipped first. She stumbled forward, crashing into the cliff's face, and clung to the edge while her feet slid beneath her. Soraya spun around and grabbed her wrist to pull her to safety. Small rocks bounced down the frozen mountainside.

"What happened?" Reza called from the back.

"Pari slipped," Soraya answered. "I got her."

A spastic fit of coughing crippled Abbas. He dropped to his knees and tried to find a hold on the cliff's face. Hovering over him, Reza dangled his right foot over the edge as he tried to lift his father. "Baba, stand up. We're so close." *Keep moving.*

"Go. Take your sisters . . ." Abbas's words were barely audible.

Hoisting him to his feet, Reza steadied himself and his father. "Almost there."

Mariam could only move her good leg. Her broken foot dragged uselessly behind her. She used her hands to pull herself along the ridge; her agonizing pace made it possible for Abbas and Reza to stay close. To keep moving.

The narrow ridge ended at a tiny cave, where Soraya placed Pari inside. Soraya walked to the edge to look down over the path that should lead them to the train station. And there she spotted the two German guard towers.

Reza turned the last corner, his father in his arms. Soraya rushed to him. "Baba! Oh, God, Reza. Is he breathing?"

Reza did not answer her, but gently laid his father next to Pari and walked to the edge. "Guards in the towers?"

"Two," Soraya said as she placed her hands to her face. "What are we going to do?"

• • • • •

The fading sunlight spilled through Mehri's kitchen window and landed on her fingers as she prepared another bowl of vegetables. She moved in machine-like motion. Chopping, sorting, pickling, chopping. Dark eyes focused on each task. With the vegetables stored, she dried her hands and looked again to the phone. It mocked her with its silence.

In a trance, she moved to her main room and sat on her Persian rug. With a single finger, she retraced the pattern woven by Nimtaj. Remembering each knot and each thread lovingly pressed into the rug, she started to whisper the prayers of her mother.

The phone rang.

Mehri jumped. "Allo! Allo!"

"Have you heard from Reza?" Hassan said.

"No, we haven't, but I'm sure they're fine." She took a deep breath. "The last call we got was five days ago when Reza went to get them in Vienna."

"They've been caught at a checkpoint," Hassan said.

"That's what we think. Habbib has been making calls to the police stations in the area. Amir and Mostafa have been using their contacts, too, but no one can find them."

"It means they're safe. Reza has found a way to take them underground."

"*Inshallah.* We need to keep the phone line clear, in case."

"Of course," Hassan said.

Mehri clicked the phone back into the cradle and cried.

• • • • •

Hassan hung up and turned to Ardeshir. "*Hichi.*"

Ardeshir dropped to the floor in a plank position. His body lifted and fell in a rapid succession of push-ups. Sweat dripped from his face, and still his body rose. Hassan went into the bedroom and returned to sit next to Ardeshir. Reza's gold medal lay in his lap.

"Did you see his championship match?" Hassan asked.

Ardeshir pulled his right arm behind his back but did not stop his pace. "Yep. It was a great match."

"Did Reza win by a pin?"

"No, not a pin," Ardeshir said. He dropped his right arm, put his left behind his back and increased his pace. "He was behind by two points with twenty seconds left in the third." His breathing intensified. "The American he was wrestling was really good. Strong. Determined. But Reza, he—he just never gave up."

Hassan stood up and held Reza's gold medal straight out in front of him. He pretended to put it around an imaginary person's neck. "How did he come back in twenty seconds?"

Ardeshir collapsed to the floor and rolled onto his back. His chest heaving, his face drowning in the sweat mixed with his tears. "There were twenty, maybe eighteen seconds left. I could tell Reza's shoulder hurt, and the American figured he had Reza beat."

"But you knew he didn't, right?"

Ardeshir's breathing steadied. "The American went to score points but Reza countered and took him down. Reza scored by a gut wrench and then leg-lacing him twice." Ardeshir's huge hands wiped tears from his eyes. "He won 7-2. I'll never forget Reza's face."

"I wished I could've been there," Hassan said as he lowered his head. "But you always win by a pin right? You've never lost."

Ardeshir rolled to his side. A vacant stare washed away all expression. With deliberate rhythm, his voice echoed from another time, another place. "I did something worse than losing. I quit. And when I quit, your brother—your brother—he's—" Ardeshir took the gold medal from Hassan and wrapped his hand around it. "He's so much stronger than I am."

• • • • •

Reza looked at his family. Pari lay in Soraya's lap, her flushed face beaded with sweat. Soraya took pieces of snow and pressed them to her forehead while softly chanting her mother's prayers.

He leaned over Pari. "Can she make it?" he asked.

Pari nodded, but Soraya's lips formed "no."

Leaning against Abbas, Mariam looked like a broken doll. Reza lifted her foot and moved it side to side. "Can you walk just a little further? It's downhill now."

"I can. It's easier when I crawl. That's what I did around the ridge."

"It might be safer to crawl this time," Reza said. Then his

hands and his fears moved to his father. "Baba? You ready?"

Abbas nodded.

Reza met his eyes and also nodded. He left his family to scout the remainder of the trail.

The sun's round bottom touched the mountain's peak, sending orange fingers to stroke the landscape. The beauty of the sunset was lost to Reza. To fight the spikes of pain shooting from his feet, he stopped and leaned against a tree. He looked to the sky, whispered, "Just a little more light," and jogged back to his family.

One by one, Reza lifted them to their feet. "We're so close. I've gone down the path. It's maybe two kilometers, three at the most." Reza looked for a flash of hope. Only Mariam smiled slightly.

He continued, "And the guards barely move. We have to stay in the shadows, and that's where it's icy. So we'll crawl. That way we're low and . . ." The faces simply stared at him. "Pari, can you crawl that far for me?"

Sweat glistened against Pari's scarlet skin and her hollowed eyes blinked. "And then we go home?"

"*Baleh.*"

"Do you want me to go first again?" Soraya asked. She held Pari by the arm.

Reza surveyed his family. "Same order as before. No one speaks, no one stops."

Soraya led the family down the short drop of the ridge and moved to the shadowy part of the path. She dropped to her knees and started crawling, her bare hands leaving prints dotted with blood. The rest fell in line, inching along, too frozen and exhausted even to feel the pain.

An hour passed. Soraya alternated carrying Mariam and Pari on her back. Reza worked with Abbas. As darkness descended, Reza grew confident that they could not be seen by the guards. But he also knew the drop in temperature would take a toll on his family and make it nearly impossible to find his way back to the car parked at the camp. *If I just have enough daylight to get past the ridge, I could follow the river . . .*

"Baba," Reza whispered in a panicked cry. "Baba, get up."

Soraya spun and around and crawled to them. "What's wrong?"

Lying in the fetal position, Abbas looked at Soraya with his ashen face. He parted his cracked lips and sputtered, "Nimtaj, take the babies home."

Swinging his arms in a furious motion, Reza looked across the endless forest. *This can't be happening!*

Soraya reached for his arms that swung erratically across his body. "Reza, take Baba." She pointed to their sisters. "I'll keep them moving." He gave no response. Soraya held his wrists until his face looked into hers. She repeated slowly, "Take Baba." She waited. "Reza, can you . . ."

He closed his eyes. "Yes," he whispered.

Soraya stepped back and turned to her sisters. "Reza will help Baba. We keep moving." She reached her right arm under Pari, and Mariam leaned against her left shoulder. "We keep moving," she repeated to her sisters.

Reza watched them hobble down the darkening path. He dropped to his knees next to his father. "Baba. Baba, I'm going to lift you up."

Abbas coughed thick black blood and waved for Reza to leave.

"I'm going to reach under your arms and pull you up."

"Go. Go with your—sisters," Abbas said as he curled into a tighter ball.

"No, Baba." Reza stood and leaned over Abbas to look for a hold. "Move your arms so I can lift you."

"I rest one minute," Abbas said.

Reza paced while keeping watch on his father's rising chest and listening for the whistle of a train. When his father's breathing seemed to steady, Reza returned to his side. "We must go."

He reached down and lifted his father. He cradled him like a small child and stumbled through the dying twilight. Trembling in exhaustion, Reza looked into the pinched black and blue face. Feet slipping, arms burning, chest heaving, Reza took three more steps and fell onto the unforgiving ice. "Baba, I'm sorry. Just—I'll catch my breath—just don't—just keep . . ." Reza's words failed him.

Abbas shivered. Between coughs, he babbled the names of his children. He called for Nimtaj. He asked to die.

"No, Baba, don't say that. We're almost there. Just keep breathing. Just—here, I'm going to pick you up and we're going to meet—put your arms—Baba, lock your hands around my neck."

A very old face looked at Reza. A frozen face. A defeated face. A face with a chipped eye carved from stone. Reza reached under Abbas just as he lay limp. "Baba! You can't give up!"

Abbas called again for his wife. "Nimtaj. Nimtaj . . ."

Into the infinite cradle, the sun slipped below the mountain's ridge, leaving the sky only a ginger haze. Cold bit and crunched in the frosted trees until a perfect stillness surrounded the father and his son.

In the wind, they heard her whispers. Reza dropped to his knees and held his head in his hands. He rocked and fought for tears that would not come. *I need you Naneh. I miss you. I should have hugged you more. I want to see you one more time. I should have said "I love you" more. I will always regret that. I miss you, Naneh. I miss you so much.*

It was a distant sound, so distant Reza thought he might have imagined it. He stood up and listened again. The whistle of a train.

Reza's heart beat faster. It beat with a time of warriors, of kings and of battles won and lost. A beat that began in the womb eternal and that never yields. *Thank you, Naneh.*

He lifted his father. "I won't let you quit," Reza said. Abbas closed his eyes. He reached his frozen fingers to his son and locked them around Reza's neck.

Feeling the renewed strength from his father, Reza took in a deep, slow breath. "That's it, Baba. Just hold tight. I'm going to get you . . ." Reza rose and forced his legs to move. He willed his father to breathe and cursed the skin as it became blacker and blacker. "Almost there, just don't let go. I've got you."

In a blur, he saw the silhouette of the train station and his sisters hiding behind a cluster of bushes. Soraya turned just as Reza knelt down behind her.

"Make a place for Baba," Reza said. "He'll need you to keep him warm."

"Don't leave us again," Mariam cried.

Reza looked into his little sister's face. "I have to get the car from the camp and drive here to get you. Can you wait one more hour for me?"

Mariam nodded and Reza pulled her tight to his chest. *Please don't cry.* "I will always come back."

"You can't go," Soraya said. "It's too dark."

Reza pointed to the moon, bright and full, and smiled.

A few brave stars punctured the blue-black sky in the piece of time where each day ends before night begins. The fullness of the fresh moon brought Reza back to Kermanshah. He stopped at the ridge and searched the moon for a face. He wanted to see his mother's but he only saw the shadows.

Epilogue

I've grown to love Reza and his family. The fear and mystery dissolved away, leaving only admiration and respect. He's taught me a new word, "pahlavan," and although I still can't pronounce it, I hold it to my heart. In one of my many ah-hah moments, I realize Reza's story follows the authentic arc of the hero's journey. Fueled by the excitement of this discovery, I generate sixty-two pages of curriculum and dream that this story will be a staple in the public school system.

The ten Abedi siblings all live outside of Iran with loving families of their own. They remain very close, value their children's education and reflect genuine pride in their Iranian roots. Abbas passed away in 2003. Ardeshir also earned a college degree and barely missed an opportunity to represent America on the U.S. Olympic wrestling team. He lives with his wife in Central America. Farid stayed in Iran, where he operates a successful business.

On October 5, 1989 Reza took the oath with hundreds of others in Los Angeles to become an American citizen. On June 20, 1991 he graduated with a college degree and currently teaches Spanish to high school students. In 2000, his colleagues honored him with the prestigious "Teacher of the Year award." He is also the respected head varsity wrestling coach and in 2011 coached his oldest son in the Masters Wrestling Championship.

A note from Reza's oldest son

The first stories I can remember hearing about my dad were from the high school wrestlers who he coached when I was very young. They would tell me crazy stories about his life, like he had killed people with his bare hands. Even though I have learned that this is not true, he has done some pretty amazing things. When I heard that this book was going to be written, I was really happy because I would finally get to know everything about his past. He has been very reserved about his hard times, but I think it was his strategy of raising me. We have always had a good relationship and the life lessons he has taught me are extremely valuable. Having my dad as my wrestling coach has brought us closer together then I ever could have imagined. He has taught me more about becoming a man and an overall good person than anybody else will in my life. Lastly, I would like to thank Kristin for writing this whole story into a book because I know it has been my dad's dream.

Abedi Family Tree

Abbas (Baba): Father
Nimtaj (Naneh): Mother
Rasha: Oldest sister
Mehri: Sister
Amir: Oldest brother
Mostafa: Brother
Soraya: Sister
Reza
Hassan: Brother
Farah: Sister
Pari: Sister
Mariam: Sister
Farid: Cousin, same age as Reza
Ardeshir: Reza's friend

Discussion Questions

As established in the prologue, wresting is a theme as ancient as humankind. Discuss some of the conflicts Reza, Soraya and Ardeshir wrestled with in their lives.

When Reza is shamed by the fighter pilot, he confronts Amir and demands to be sent to the front lines to regain his honor. He says to Amir, "So, that's my choice? Die in the name of Khomeini's Islam or live like a coward? Is that what this has come to?" Is Reza correct in his assessment, or is he being unreasonable?

Today, Reza describes Hassan by saying, "He is my best friend." How is Hassan both a source of strength and conflict for Reza?

How do Reza's sisters provide interesting insights as to life in Iran for women?

Reza and Kristin chose to dedicate the book to Reza's mother, Nimtaj. Discuss her importance to her family.

At the end of his life, Abbas was able to come to America and live with Reza and his family. It was very important to Reza that Abbas see him as a successful family man and teacher. How did Reza's relationship with his father differ from that of the other important people in his life?

While working on the book, Reza said to Kristin, "You know, all my life, it seems angels have come to help me just when I needed it most." How is this true? Do you believe in angels?

Besides Hassan, Ardeshir is a close friend and loyal companion to Reza to this day. Describe their relationship and ask yourself if you have friends with whom you can trust your life.

Reza described his brother Mostafa as "two-faced." He said Mostafa had "that look" with his "soft beard" and people would believe whatever he told them and then do for him what he needed them to do. However, when "the doors closed and he was with just his family," he changed. Reza said Mostafa's chameleon nature saved their family many times. Does this make Mostafa a hypocrite or a hero?

The ambulance driver, Kahn, is a character based on Reza's statement to Kristin that he "was completely nuts." Do you find Kahn nuts? Or compelling? How did he serve to clarify the history between Iran and Iraq?

The sociopolitical climate had an increasingly dramatic effect on the Iranian families just before, during and after the Revolution. What were some of the events that had an impact on the Iranians?

Mr. Mehdian had a great deal of influence on Reza's decision to become a teacher. Reza was devastated when he learned his favorite teacher was murdered shortly after the Revolution. Discuss people in your life who have had a similar impact on your future.

Starting with the first family scene around the "mysterious box" and the neighboring families "bending antennas this way and that," how is the Abedi family similar and different from American families?

When Reza wrestled in a tournament for Cal State Fullerton, a wrestler from Stanford came up to him and said, "Do you remember me? I'm Jimmy and we wrestled when you lived in Iran." Describe how Reza's original encounter with Jimmy and the Americans added to his infatuation with all that he believes America could offer.

The concept of "pahlavan" is woven from Chapter One through to the end of the book. Discuss your understanding of pahlavan. Do you know or know of anyone you would consider a true pahlavan?

Glossary

Farsi	English
Alangoo	Gold bangle bracelets
Amou	Uncle
Agha	Sir
Ajaleh kon!	Hurry up!
Ashura holiday	Ashura is an Islamic holiday observed on the 10th of Muharram, the first month of the Islamic year. Among Shi'ites, however, Ashura is a major festival, the tazia (ta'ziyah). It commemorates the death of Husayn (also spelled Hussein), son of Imam 'Ali and grandson of Muhammad, on the 10th of Muharram, AH 61 (October 10, 680), in Karbala, Iraq. The event led to the split between the Sunni and Shia sects of Islam, and it is of central importance in Shia Islam.
Ayatollah	A religious leader in Iranian Shi'ite Islam
Azizam	Sweat heart or dear
Baba	Father
Bacheh	Child
Baleh	Yes, informal, like "ya."
Basiji	An "off-shoot" military group of the Revolutionary Guard whose primary function is to enforce Islamic Law
Baradar	Brother
Bazandeh	loser
BBC	British Broadcast Company
Bebakhshid	Sorry for a mistake
Berma'id!	Enjoy! (for meals)
Chador	A long, loose fitting cape that completely covered a woman's body.
Chai	Tea
Chashm	Yes, I will do that for you.
Deeg	A pot

Doost/ Doost-e man	Friend/ My friend
Doset daram	I love you
Enshallah	God willing
Fedayins	Largest Socialist political party in Iran
Ghahreman	Champion
Halva	A dish of flour, oil and sugar served on Thursday in remembrance of those who died.
Hichi	Nothing
Hajab	A scarf or other covering worn by Muslim woman
Hookah	A vase-like object used to smoke tobacco
Islam	Is the religion articulated by the Qur'an, a religious book considered by its adherents to be the verbatim word of the single incomparable God and by the Prophet of Islam Muhammad's demonstrations and real-life examples.
Kami	Just a little
Khaleh	Aunt
Kholma	Dessert pastry
Korsi	A small stove used for heating blankets to sit under.
Koshti	To kill
Kurds	Iranian ethnic group
Merci	Thank you
Mo'afagh bashed	Good luck!
Mojahedin	Political party of Islamic ideology based on democracy, tolerance and moderation.
Mullah	Is generally used to refer to a Muslim man, educated in Islamic theology and sacred law; Muslim clergy.
Muslim	Muslims believe that there is only one God, translated in Arabic as Allah. A believer in Islam.
Naneh	Mother
National Front	Iranian Democratic and secular political party founded by Mossadegh in the early 1950s
Nazari nadaram	I have no idea

Negahbon	Guard
Nowruz	Iranian New Year which celebrates first day of Spring
Oh, che khoob!	Oh! That's good!
Pahlavan	Warrior; hero; champion. Physically and mentally strong.
Piroozi	Victory
Pesar	Son; also boy
Ramadan	9th month of the Islamic calendar. A Muslim holiday used as a time for self-reflection and devotion to God. It is also a time of fasting.
Roosari	Headscarf
Samovar	A tea pot kept for of boiling water for afternoon tea
Salam	Hello
Savak	An acronym Shah's secret police force
Sepah	Shortened term for Revolutionary Guard
Sepahi	Shortened term for One member of the Revolutionary Guard
Sharmandeh	Ashamed, embarrassed
Shahrestani	Simple folks who live in towns, not in Tehran
Shaytoon	The devil
Shiite Muslim	One of the two sects of Islam. The other is Sunni. Shiait believe that following the prophet Muhammad's death, leadership should have passed directly to his cousin/son-in-law, Ali.
Sofreh	A spread or tablecloth placed on top of the Persian Rug for meals
Sunni Muslim	See Shiat. Sunni believe that following the prophet Muhammad's death, leadership should be passed to a leader elected among those capable of the job.
Tanoor	Brick oven
Toman	Iranian currency
Tudeh	Iranian Communist Party formed in 1941
Ulama	Muslim legal scholars

Velayat-e faqih	Ayatollah Khomeini created this document to assert religious leaders had the right to rule a Shia nation under Islamic laws.
Zood Bosh	Go faster. Hurry
Zoroastrian	The religion was founded by Zarathushtra in Persia – modern-day Iran. It may have been the world's first monotheistic faith. It was once the religion of the Persian empire, but has since been reduced in numbers to fewer than 200,000 today. Most religious historians believe the Jewish, Christian and Muslim beliefs concerning God and Satan, the soul, heaven and hell, the virgin birth of the savior, slaughter of the innocents, resurrection, the final judgment, etc. were all derived from Zoroastrianism.

Time Line

Events Relevant to the Islamic Revolution in Iran

Year	Event
1941	August-September: World War II allies Britain and Russia invade Iran. They exile Reza Shah to South Africa. His son, Muhammad Reza Pahlavi becomes the new Pahlavi Shah of Iran.
1953	August: Muhammad Reza Pahlavi approves a coup of the popular nationalist prime minister Mohammed Mossadeq. CIA and British intelligence organize "Operation Ajax" with conservative Iranians to overthrow Mossadeq.
1961	March 31: Husain Borujerdi, the prominent Marja of all Shi's dies. Khomeini emerges as one of the probable successors. His students established Society of Seminary Teachers of Qom, which played a key role during the establishment of new government after the victory of the revolution.
1962	October-November: Ruhollah Khomeini organizes opposition to Shah's Local council election bill which would have allowed women to vote and non-Muslims to run for council. Religious pressure forced government to abandon the bill. Khomeini emerges as "the regime's principal political foe" and "undisputed spiritual leader of azaar activists."

1963	January: Mohammad Reza Pahlavi proposes "White Revolution;" a six-point reform bill to be put to a nation-wide vote. Six points included woman's suffrage and other reforms. January 22nd: Khomeini issued a strongly worded declaration denouncing the Shah's plans and accused the Shah of comprehensive submission to America and Israel. Shah orders to arrest Khomeini.
1964	April 7th: Khomeini is released from custody and returns to Qom. He denounces the Shah's relationship with America's military and calls their agreement, the "Capitulation Law," as a surrender of Iranian independence and sovereignty. He is arrested and exiled. He does not return to Iran for fourteen years.
1965	January 22nd at 10am: Hassan-Ardeshir Mansur, the prime minister who passed the "Capitulation Law" is assassinated by Mohammad Bokharaii and Amir Hoveyda is appointed. September 5: Khomeini leaves Turkey for Najaf in Iraq, where he teaches in a seminary for thirteen years.
1970	January 21-February 8: Khomeini gives a series of nineteen lectures. Notes of the lecture, praising the laws of Islam, are made into a small book and smuggled into Iran.
1975	March 2: Rastakhiz (Resurrection) party as an Iranian monarchist party is founded by Mohammad Reza Pahlavi. June: For three days, students gather to recognize the anniversary of Khomeini's arrest. Shah orders military action to break-up the demonstration and causalities result. Khomeini issues a message that the disturbance to be a sign of hope that "freedom and liberation from the bonds of imperialism is at hand."
1976	Shah shows an unpopular disregard for Islamic tradition by changing from the Islamic calendar to an Imperial calendar. The Imperial calendar marked the birth of Cyrus as the first day, instead of the flight of the Prophet Muhammad from Mecca to Medina. Overnight, the year changed from 1355 to 2535.

1978 (January)	January 7: An article in the Ettel'at newspaper title 'Black and Red' Imperialism accuses Khomeini of being of Indian descent and other 'misdeeds.' January 9: 4,000 students and religious leaders in Qom demonstrate against the article. The armed police, provoked by demonstrators, fire into the crowds resulting in the death of close to 100 people. Protests credited with breaking the 'barrier of fear' of Shah's security forces.
1978 (February)	February 18: Groups, in a number of cities, march to honor the fallen and protest against the rule of the Shah. Violence erupted in Tabriz and approximately 100 demonstrators are killed.
1978 (May)	May 10: Demonstrations in varies cities. In Qom, commandos burst into the home of Ayatollah Kazem Shariatmadari, a leading cleric and quietist, and shoot dead one of his followers right in front of him
1978 (June)	June 6: Head of Savak, Nematollah Nassiri is dismissed and Nasser Moghadam, is appointed instead. This is seen as the first significant concession to the unrest.
1978 (August)	August 6: Shah pledges free elections by June 1979 in broadcast to the nation. August 12: Killing of demonstrators in Isfahan. August 16: Martial law is declared by Jamshid Amouzegar in response to vast demonstrations August 27: Jamshid Amouzegar is replaced by Jafar Sharif-Emami as prime minister. Emami reverses many of Shah's policies including closing casinos and abolishing the imperial calendar.
1978 September	September 4: Mass march at Eid al-Fitr of hundreds of thousands in Tehran by Khomeini supporters. September 8: "Black Friday". Shah declares martial in response to protests against Pahlavi dynasty. The military of Iran uses force including tanks and helicopters to break up peaceful demonstrators. 88 demonstrators are killed; however, opposition leaders spread rumors that tens of thousands are killed. September 24: Iraqi government embargoes the house of Khomeini September 25: Rastakhiz party is disbanded

1978 October	October 3: Khomeini leaves Iraq for Kuwait. He is refused entry. October 10: Khomeini takes up residence in Paris. His interviews become daily features in the world's media. October 16: To remember those killed on Black Friday, tens of thousands take to the streets. "A rapid succession of strikes cripple almost all the bazaars, universities, high schools, oil installations, banks, government ministries, newspapers, etc" and "seal the Shah's fate." October 21: Iran oil industry workers go on strike thus economically crippling the nation.
1978 November	November 4: Destructive riots. Frustrated by Shah's unsuccessful attempts at conciliation with his opponents, military hardliners decide to order troops "to stand aside and allow mobs to burn and destroy to their hearts' content." Thousands of shops, banks, restaurants and other public buildings damaged. Conciliatory Prime Minister Sharif-Emami resigns. Army raid in Tehran University, students participating in demonstrations are killed. November 5: Mohammad Reza Shah broadcasts on television a promise not to repeat past mistakes and to make amends saying, "I heard the voice of your revolution... As Shah of Iran as well as an Iranian citizen, I cannot but approve your revolution. November 6: General Gholam Reza Azhari appointed as the prime minister. Enforces martial law. November 8: Mohammad Reza Shah arrests thirteen prominent members of his own regime. November 27: Millions throughout the country celebrate "weeping" and "jumping" after seeing Khomeini's face in the moon, after rumor sweeps the land that the Imam's face will so appear on this night.

1978 December	December 10-11: 17 million people march throughout the country peacefully marching demanding the removal of the Shah and the return of Khomeini. A 17-point resolution is presented during a demonstration declaring Ayatollah Khomeini to be the leader of the Iranian people. December 29: Long-time opposition politician Shapour Bakhtiar chosen as prime minister by Shah as the Shah prepares to leave the country. Last prime minister of the Pahlavi dynasty.
1979 January	January 12: A top secret Revolutionary Council is formed by Khomeini to manage revolution. January 16: Mohammad Reza Shah and his wife leave Iran. Official reports claim he left for vacation and medical treatment. He would never return. =
1979 February	February 1: Khomeini returns to Iran from exile. According to the BBC, up to five million people line the streets of Tehran to witness his homecoming. February 9: Fighting breaks out between pro-Khomeini forces and the Iranian Air Force and Imperial Guard. February 10: Prime minister Bakhtiar announces curfew and imposes martial law. Khomeini orders followers to ignore it. Revolutionaries join rebel troops in looting arms from police and prisons. February 11: Regime collapses. Revolution victorious. Bakhtiar goes into hiding and eventually finds exile in Paris. February 18: Foundation of Islamic Republican party by revolutionary clerics.
1979 April	April 1: Iranian run media reported 98.2% of votes tallied are in favor of an Islamic Republic.

1979 June	June 5: Early indication of split between Khomeini and non-theocratic intellectuals. In a speech, Khomeini asks, "Who are they that wish to divert our Islamic movement from Islam?" June 14: Official preliminary draft of the constitution is published. It does not include Velayat-e faqih. June 15: Khomeini attacks liberal and leftwing groups as 'counter-revolutionaries.' Campaign launched to popularize the idea of the Velayat-e faqih, hitherto unknown to most Iranians.
1979 August	August 7: *Ayandegan,* the daily newspaper with the widest circulation in Iran, questioned and agitated against Velayat-e faqih, and is banned under new press laws for "counter-revolutionary policies and acts" August 10: Khomeini denounces supporters of *Ayandegan* calling them 'wild animals.' August 12: Demonstrations to protest the closing of newspapers like *Ayandegan.*
1979 October	October 14: Assembly of experts approves draft of new constitution. In it, Khomeini holds the position of velayat-e faqih, which includes "command of the armed forces." October 22: Cancer-ridden ex-Shah enters United States for medical treatment. Khomeini speaks out angrily at this "evidence of American plotting."
1979 November	November 4: Muslim student followers of Imam's Line occupied the U.S. embassy in Tehran which resulted in the Iran hostage crisis.
1980	March 21: Cultural revolution begins. In New Year's Speech, Khomeini inveighs against "imperialist universities" and declares all universities must "become Islamic." April 7: United States breaks diplomatic relations with Iran. April 25: Failed attempt to rescue hostages. June 12: Formation of the university jihad by decree of Ayatollah Khomeini. The Cultural Revolution to Isalmization of universities.

1980 (con't)	July: Approximately 20,000 teachers and nearly 8000 military officers are discharged for being un-Islamic. September 22: Iran-Iraq war begins. Massive invasion of Iran by Iraq.
1981	January 20: Ronald Reagan is inaugurated as President of United States. The hostages in the US embassy were released after 444 days. USA conceded to transfer money. June 28: Explosion of the office of Islamic Republic by MEK resulting in the death of 72 high-ranking officials. October 13: Ardeshir Khomeini, an Islamic conservative, is elected president.
2009 **June**	**June 12:** Iran's ninth presidential election. The incumbent Mahmoud Ahmadinejad ran against three challengers. The next morning the Islamic Republic News Agency, Iran's official news agency, announced that with two-thirds of the votes counted, Ahmadinejad had won the election with 62% of the votes cast and that Mir-Hossein Mousavi had received 34% of the votes cast· Several western countries expressed concern over alleged irregularities during the vote and many analysts and journalists from the United States, Europe and other western based media voiced doubts about the authenticity of the results. Millions of Iranian citizens took to the streets in protests until they were eventually beat back by the Iranian government. Many see this as a turning point the Iranian government operating as Islamic Republic to a military dictatorship.

She knew his story needed to be told. Kristin Orloff met Reza Abedi when they were colleagues at a high school in Southern California. Over a period of several years, Reza shared vignettes of life. She recognized not only his authentic hero's journey, but his steadfast loyalty to core human values. By incorporating the life changing moments in her dedication to this project, Kristin creates a universal experience for all readers.